# Durov's Pig

# Durov's Pig

## Clowns, Politics and Theatre

## Joel Schechter

**Theatre Communications Group**
New York / 1985

Durov's Pig: Clowns, Politics and Theatre is published by Theatre Communications Group, Inc., the national organization for the nonprofit professional theatre, 355 Lexington Ave., New York, NY 10017.

Permission is gratefully acknowledged for excerpts from the following sources: "Brecht: The Intellectual Tramp/An Interview with Luis Valdez" by Julia Yolanda Broyles, in *Communications of the International Brecht Society*, April 1973; "Blighters" by Siegfried Sassoon, in *The Collected Poems of Siegfried Sassoon*, New York: E.P. Dutton, Co., 1918, reprinted by permission of Viking Penguin, Inc.; *Conversations in Exile* by Bertolt Brecht, translated by Howard Brenton, copyright 1982 by Stefan Brecht; "Die Hieratz-Annonce" and "Der Vögelhandler" by Karl Valentin, in *Alles von Karl Valentin*, Munich: R. Piper and Co. Verlag, 1978; *Do It!* by Jerry Rubin, New York: Simon and Schuster, copyright 1970 by the Social Education Foundation; *For Marx* by Louis Althusser, translated by Ben Brewster, New York: Pantheon Books; *Mephisto* by Théâtre du Soleil, 1979; *Theatre and Revolution in France Since 1968* by Judith Graves Miller, Lexington: French Forum.

The illustrations in this book are reproduced with the kind permission of the following: p. 8 Leningrad Circus Museum; p. 30 Yale Repertory Theatre, photo by Bruce Siddons; p. 33 New York Public Library at Lincoln Center; p. 77 Berliner Ensemble; p. 83 Milner Library, Illinois State University; p. 115 Théâtre du Soleil; p. 122 Lotte Goslar; p. 149 (top) Chris Harris; p. 149 (bottom) Sterlazzo/Lucchese; p. 169 San Francisco Mime Troupe; p. 179 (right) El Teatro Campesino; p. 179 (left) Mark Taper Forum, photo by Jay Thompson; p. 182 Plutonium Players; p. 185 Bread and Puppet Theatre; p. 201 Erika Munk; p. 205 Green Party.

Cover: Karl Valentin and Liesl Karlstadt in concert.

Frontis: Vladimir Durov

Design: Soho Studio

Manufactured in the United States of America

First Edition


Library of Congress Cataloging-in-Publication Data

Schechter, Joel, 1947—
  Durov's pig.

  Bibliography: p.
  Includes index.
  1. Drama—20th century—History and criticism.
2. Political satire—History and criticism. 3. Theatre—
Political aspects. 4. Clowns in literature. I. Title.
PN1861.S285 1985      809.2'04      85-17369
ISBN 0-930452-51-8 (pbk.)

# Contents

# Preface

"Satire is what closes on Saturday night."

Since George S. Kaufman defined the genre in those terms, satire has become even more of a rarity in American theatre. Political satire, rarer still, can be seen occasionally in cabarets and in the plays of the San Francisco Mime Troupe and a few similar groups. However, these satires do not affect public thought as others have in the past. Barbara Garson's *MacBird* touched a nerve across the country in 1967, when it crudely compared Lyndon Johnson to Macbeth. But *MacBird* was an exception which proved the rule: American political satire does not intervene in public discourse as plays do in other cultures.

By contrast, the satires of Italian playwright-performer Dario Fo have resulted in international controversy extending from his stage in Milan to the U.S. State Department, which twice denied Fo and his wife, actress Franca Rame, permission to perform their plays in the United States. Fo's political satires have become occasions for rallies, debates and court cases in Italy. Half a million Italians watched Fo's ensemble perform *Accidental Death of an Anarchist* after its premiere in December of 1970, and the satire's exposure of state repression probed so far into the centers of power that, as Fo has pointed out, his theatre was "subjected to provocation and persecution of all kinds, sometimes more grotesque and comic in their repressive stupidity than the very farce we were performing." Harrassment and censorship are not the only measures of successful satire; production of Fo's plays around the world—and appreciative audiences—attest to his continuing popularity as clown and social critic.

When I met Fo in Italy a few years ago and said that America had no stage satirists of his caliber, I was surprised by his reply that, regrettably, Italian theatre did not have many political satirists either. Fo's preference for more rather than fewer rivals can be discerned in his conscious alignment with earlier forms of clowning. He has chosen to continue a satiric tradition which could be called that of the "political stage clown." The tradition has antecedents as old as Aristophanic satire and Atellan farce, but its modern political consciousness comes from Marx, Brecht and Mayakovsky. (Not everyone would consider Karl Marx a satirist, of course; but as the critic Walter Benjamin noted, the author of *Capital* was "a teacher of satire. And it is with Marx that Brecht has gone to school.")

These three writers influenced some of the most innovative political clowning in our century, as the works of Fo, Peter Handke, Trevor Griffiths, Lotte Goslar, the San Francisco Mime Troupe and Théâtre du Soleil attest. While these satirists differ considerably, most of them have in common yet another influence: namely, militarism, which has offered few benefits to culture other than the satire it has provoked.

This survey begins with the Russian circus clown Vladimir Durov and his satire opposing military preparations for World War I; it ends with a discussion of the German Green Party's 1983 Nuremberg tribunal, part of which satirized preparations for World War III. In between, other wars and other models of twentieth-century political clowning and satiric theatre are considered. I would like to think that all of the artists discussed here knew the story of Durov's pig and the threat that his circus act posed to the German Kaiser. (They did not all know it, but I wish that they had.) Durov's ventriloquism enabled his porcine partner to speak against Wilhelm II's militarism, and in response, the Kaiser's representatives charged Durov with treason. Clowning is not often considered this dangerous; but perhaps it should be. If a pig can mock an emperor, might not ordinary citizens watching the act also be emboldened by a satirist—Durov, Brecht, Garson or Fo—to ridicule militaristic rulers? Such is my hope.

War preparations and threats of war are still with us, and our theatres and circus rings could use more political clowns. The next war may not leave enough survivors to appreciate the satire it provokes. Rather than two, three, many more Vietnams, let there be two, three, many more Durovs.

I would like to thank a number of people who advised me during the course of my research and writing. These include Eric Bentley, Augusto Boal, Martin Bresnick, Peter Demetz, Lotte Goslar, Ron Jenkins, Pam Jordan, Stanley Kauffmann, Charles Mann, Lloyd Richards, Arthur Saxon, Laurence Senelick, Jack Zipes and the Leningrad Circus Museum.

Support for my research in Bonn, London and Gubbio, Italy was generously provided by the Whitney Griswold Fund at Yale University, and a grant to support the publication of photographs in this book was provided by the Frederick Hilles Fund. I am also grateful to the editors of *American Theatre*, *The Brecht Yearbook*, the program of the Guthrie Theater, *In These Times*, *The Partisan Review* and *Theaterwork;* sections of the book appeared previously, in different form, in these periodicals and are reprinted here with permission.

Finally, the book could not have been finished without advice and support from Laura Ross, its editor, and Diana Scott, who accompanied me to many circuses.

—J.S.

# Durov's Pig

In 1907 the Russian clown Vladimir Leonidowitch Durov was arrested, charged with treason and banished from Germany for performing a circus act with his pig. Durov's arrest on charges of *lèse majesté* initiated an important if neglected moment in the history of modern political satire. It brought to the clown's defense one of Germany's leading anti-militarists, Karl Liebknecht, who was charged with high treason himself in the same year. Durov's political satire was joined to Liebknecht's political activism, however briefly, and together the clown and the activist lawyer prepared to challenge the laws of the Empire.

This union of clowning and politics against questionable authority has been revived, in different form, by playwrights throughout the twentieth century. From Bertolt Brecht and Vladimir Mayakovsky through Dario Fo, Augusto Boal, the San Francisco Mime Troupe and Théâtre du Soleil, artists who share Durov's satiric sensibility move out of conventional theatres into circus rings, factories, public squares, sports arenas and courtrooms. They draw on popular entertainment forms—particularly circus clowning—and their plays, like carnival or holiday celebrations, suspend and mock everyday law and order. One consequence of their art is that on stage and off, clown meets activist—Durov meets Liebknecht—when both find themselves on the wrong side of the law.

While these satirists have few reasons to suppose that any government will support their activity, they may not expect the state to prosecute them either. Durov's need for a lawyer in Berlin arose from a simple, seemingly naive act of clownery. Durov placed a German officer's cap, or "helm" as he called it, in the circus ring, and his trained pig ran to retrieve it. Using ventriloquism, Durov made the pig appear to be saying "Ich will helm," meaning "I want the helmet." But the phrase could also be translated "I am Wilhelm," thereby equating Germany's Emperor, Wilhelm II, with a trained pig. "The audience understood the pun at once and applauded it. The German police understood it too," according to Russian critic Emanuel Dvinsky's account of the event.[1] Durov was arrested. The pig escaped without prosecution.

Durov himself mentions the event briefly in his 1914 pamphlet, *In a German Prison*. He reports that after he performed his "political number" with the pig and was arrested, "Liebknecht led my civil action and won it." No account of Liebknecht's defense of Durov seems to exist; in fact, it is surprising that the lawyer was free to argue on the clown's behalf at all in 1907, for he had some legal difficulties of his own that year. By October the socialist lawyer was on trial for writing *Militarism and Anti-Militarism*, a book based on lectures he delivered in 1906. The author was found guilty of high treason. His crime was the same as Durov's: opposition to militarism.

Although they employed extremely different forms of resistance to the Kaiser's militaristic planning, it was perfectly fitting that Liebknecht should defend Durov. In his book Liebknecht had already unwittingly constructed a defense for the clown when he noted that through "coercive disciplinary methods of militarism," the army generals "attempt to tame men as they tame wild beasts."[2] Durov tamed a pig much as the army tamed men; his pig wanted to wear a helmet as much as the next man, or pig or Kaiser. "Ich will helm."

At the time, Kaiser Wilhelm II was fond of wearing decorated military uniforms and being photographed in them. Both Durov and Liebknecht ridiculed a foible of the Emperor's about which he was especially sensitive. (He was sensitive about many references to himself, judging from a *New York Times* editorial of February 16, 1907, which noted that under Wilhelm II's reign, "prosecutions for *lèse majesté* have increased and multiplied . . . far beyond all precedent.")

Liebknecht's book also argued that German army uniforms have elements of carnival about them. The tailors "pander to man's love for adornment" and "trim the uniforms with tinsel like carnival costumes. All sorts of petty glittering distinctions, decorations, stripes for good shooting, etc., appeal to the same low instinct—the desire for gay apparel and for being looked up to as a distinguished soldier." Durov mocked this desire for distinction through costume, and the celebration of war as a carnival, by sharing the Kaiser's name and uniform with a pig.

Kaiser Wilhelm II reportedly followed Karl Liebknecht's trial carefully, by reading daily transcripts of the proceedings, and he congratulated the judges when they found Liebknecht guilty. It is not known whether he followed Durov's trial as closely, but once Liebknecht had sided with Durov, Wilhelm must have felt justified in prosecuting the clown.

## Of Pigs and Democracy

"The stage is one of my arms of government," the Kaiser had told actors at the Royal Theatre in Berlin. Durov's democratization of power reduced the Emperor's authority over his arms of government and his army, by sharing it with a pig. One small circus act could hardly overthrow a government, and yet it represented a freedom from state control which the Kaiser could not countenance. He needed to preserve respect for symbols, such as military medals and helmets, or risk desertion of the army by its recruits. Durov's transformation of an elite leader into one of his lesser subjects (a pig) could

*Vladimir Durov and a circus partner reading the journal* Satirikon.

even be a prelude to revolution, if it were not stopped. A hyperbolic conclusion, perhaps, but then so was the Kaiser's reaction to Durov's clown act.

Vladimir Durov and his brother Anatoly, another circus clown, were aware that their acts might not amuse Kaiser or Czar. They entered the circus ring announcing themselves as "King of Jesters, but never the King's Jester. The Jester to His Majesty the People!"³ They knew they were reversing the traditional court jester's role by jesting *against* those in power rather than for them. In this they exhibited a recurrent trait of modern political clowning, from Durov to Brecht and Mayakovsky to the present: the democratizing of situations, the temporary redistribution of power. The form that shares an Emperor's authority with a pig leads the public to feel itself equal to—or greater than—rulers of state.

This redistribution of power is achieved in several different ways, including situations in which:

—A clown representing "Everyman" or "the little man" outlives or outwits "great men" of history. Durov and pig win their defense against Kaiser Wilhelm II after ridiculing him.
—The language or image of a living politician (Kaiser Wilhelm II, for example) is "captured" through mimickry by the satirist, and put on "trial" by actors and audience, or given to a clown character in a play, or a pig in a circus ring.
—Spectators are encouraged to see themselves as judges or legislators inside the theatre and outside it. The theatre event creates a new legal or social system as a parodic or real alternative to the existing one.

## An Actor's Contract for the Kaiser

Bertolt Brecht engaged in one such effort to parody and relocate power twenty years after Durov, when he collaborated with theatre director Erwin Piscator. Piscator, too, met Wilhelm II's representatives in a Berlin court. Brecht discusses the case in his essay, "On Experimental Theatre":

> When the former German Emperor had his lawyers protest at Piscator's plan to let an actor portray him on his stage, Piscator just asked if the Emperor wouldn't be willing to appear on stage in person; he even offered him a contract.⁴

Wilhelm II declined to appear in *Rasputin*, a production on which Brecht collaborated in 1927. The court ordered Piscator to cut the portrayal of the Emperor from the play. In place of the scene, the legal writ of restraint was read aloud each night. Audiences laughed at the writ when it claimed that the scene characterized the former Kaiser as a "complete idiot" and "bigoted fool lacking any character." The court writ also insured the production a sold-out house.

In the same essay Brecht cites the *Rasputin* case as an example of Piscator's efforts to "turn the audience into a legislative body":

> Instead of a Deputy speaking about certain intolerable social conditions there was an artistic copy of these conditions. It was the stage's ambition to supply images, statistics, slogans which would enable its parliament, the audience, to reach political decisions. Piscator's stage was not indifferent to applause, but it preferred a discussion. It didn't want only to provide its spectator with an experience but also to squeeze from him a practical decision to intervene actively in life.

Brecht's own theatre experiments pursued the same goals he attributes to Piscator. He once described his concept of "epic theatre" as that in which an actor's performance "becomes a discussion (about social conditions) with the audience he is addressing. He [the actor] prompts the spectator to justify or abolish these conditions according to what class he belongs to."[5]

While Brecht did not contest the Kaiser's law in court, as Durov and Piscator did, he wanted to stage trials in the theatre. In the 1930s he told Sergei Tretyakov about a plan he had to create a new theatre devoted entirely to the staging of famous courtroom trials. This new stage would "function like a court room. Two trials an evening, each lasting an hour and a quarter. For example, the trial of Socrates, a witches' trial, the trial of Karl Marx's *Neue Rheinische Zeitung*, the trial of George Grosz on the charge of blasphemy. . . ."[6]

This plan has been carried further recently, by groups such as Germany's Berliner Kommune and Green Party. In 1983, on their own initiative, the Greens conducted a trial to deliberate the crimes of the next world war—crimes as yet only in the planning stage. There was satire implicit in the tribunal's assumption that it had to convene *before* the next war, because too few witnesses would survive to hold it afterwards.

Brecht's plan to merge theatre and the courtroom, and the Green Party's tribunal share an important feature of Durov's circus acts: their capacity to transcend the boundaries of stage and circus and "intervene actively in life." Durov's performance moved by royal command from circus arena into court of law and became a dialogue, however hostile, between clown and king. His satire and that of Brecht and the Greens crosses boundaries between art and life, art and politics, animal and man, parody and original sources. It meets a standard of success defined by Enid Welsford (in her book, *The Fool, His Social and Literary History*) wherein a buffoon "is really successful [when] he breaks down the barriers between himself and his patrons so that they too inhabit for the moment a no-man's land between the world of fact and the world of imagination. . . . He draws out the latent folly in his audience."[7] In this no-man's land, pigs represent emperors, clowns are accused of treason, and the distance between stage and courtroom disappears. The political clown moves across the boundaries separating the stage world from everyday life. As the Russian critic Mikhail Bakhtin says of carnivals, "The absence of clearly established footlights is characteristic of all popular-festive forms. The utopian truth is evident in life itself."[8]

Durov had previously been tried for riding a pig cart through the Russian city of Kharkov. He won that case, and his defense, preserved in his book *My Circus Animals*, suggests how the clown might have mocked the law at his Berlin trial. Durov recalls how, after he taught a pig named Chuska to pull him through the streets on a tiny cart, a police officer had him summoned to court for driving without a permit, obstructing public traffic and unauthorized advertising of the circus. The clown argued in court:

> There is nothing in legal regulations against using pigs for vehicular traffic; therefore I have not done anything illegal. Nor did we obstruct public traffic, as the pig has been excellently trained and we kept to the proper side of the street, going in the direction of all traffic. And not once during the whole trip did the pig give a single grunt. . . . It is unjust for human beings to hold pigs in such contempt. Strange as it may seem, it is out of a sense of cleanliness that a pig wallows in dirt; by this means he tries to scrape off the dirt which collects on his body. His short neck hinders free movement, and he cannot scratch himself like other animals. . . . There's no reason for this charge against me. I want to prove that pigs can be very useful in transporting products, just as dogs are useful in certain countries for transporting milk. I want to prove that a pig can be useful not only after his death, when his meat is to be found on the dinner-table, but also during life.[9]

Here, too, as in Germany, Durov's satire broke out of the circus arena, into the streets and courtroom. Relocating his comic act (as Brecht, Mayakovsky, Fo, Boal and others later relocated their plays, outside of legitimate theatres) first in the street and then in court, Durov intervened actively in everyday life through his clowning, challenging law and order with a pig and a cart.

Durov spoke in court at Kharkov as if the clean, quiet pig were on trial with him. When the court dared to try a pig (or a clown) for a crime, it made its own folly an extension of Durov's circus act. Within the circus ring, too, Durov pressed the boundaries of satire to the legal limit by treating his pigs' behavior as all too human, and independent of *his* behavior. He implied that pigs were no less intelligent and respectable than the average mayor or banker, when the animals performed before these officials at the circus. Mayors and bankers rarely enjoyed this insight.

Durov's ability to outwit officials by training a pig to publicly act out attitudes which a man could not safely express attracted Frank Wedekind's attention, as the writer's Paris notebooks attest. Recording a conversation he had with the clown Willi Morgenstern in December 1892, Wedekind notes:

> Duroff trains dogs, goats, pigs and rats. He earns 4,000 francs monthly [in Paris], dresses lavishly, has two servants, a carriage with two Russian ponies, drinks champagne. . . . In Russia he is loved by the people. He created a scandal in

*Poster advertising Vladimir Durov's animal railway during its first Russian appearance.*

Petersburg in dealing with a police chief named Gresser. [The name Gresser is a pun on the German word for "large."] He placed a gold ruble in the circus ring, and the pig retrieved it. He placed a silver ruble in the ring, and the pig retrieved it. He placed a paper ruble in the ring, and the pig would not retrieve it. He asked "Is this paper money so worthless even a pig won't pick it up?" He was fined 50 rubles [for this remark on devalued currency]. He did the same thing the next day, and received the same fine and a threat of expulsion. . . . The following day . . . Police Chief Gresser came to see if the pig would pick up the gold ruble again. Durov had three pigs. He told the public, "This is a small pig. This pig is somewhat larger. This [third] pig is without a doubt larger [i.e., "Grösser"]. He was ordered to leave the city. . . .[10]

As Wedekind's remarks suggest, Durov was a legend in his own lifetime, and his political satire won him admirers and enemies across the continent. A circus poster from the period, for the "Circus A. Schumann," announces: "The celebrated Russian original satirist and political clown Wladimir Duroff with his human-like animal troupe."

In his book on Wedekind, Sol Gittleman writes that the German

*Anatoly Durov and friends.*

playwright's "closest friends" in Paris were the clowns "Duroff and Morgenstern."[11] The Durov mentioned in Wedekind's diary, and by Gittleman, may be Vladimir's brother, Anatoly, who also performed with trained animals. Wedekind undoubtedly knew about the circus satire of both Durovs, in any case; he may even have inspired some of it.

## "An Onslaught on Militarism"

Wedekind too faced the charges of *lèse majesté* for an offense against Kaiser Wilhelm II, some years before Durov did. In 1898 he was convicted of publishing a satiric poem in the journal *Simplicissimus*, and he served six months in prison for the crime. His poem anticipated Durov's satire of the Kaiser, mocking the ruler's love of fancy costumes and imperial photograph sessions. The poem, "In the Holy Land" suggests that anarchists, communists and other undesirables will become calm and reverential toward the Kaiser as soon as they see photographs of his visit to Jerusalem. The portraits of him in tropical uniform, purple robes and hunting suit, will fill millions of Christians with pride. King David will rise out of the grave and play his harp in praise of the well-dressed emperor, among other miracles. The Emperor's lawyers decided Wedekind's paean was an act of treason.

In 1902 Wedekind wrote a play loosely based on his own experiences with the emperor's censors and his crime of satire. *King Nicola* concerns a king who becomes a balladeer and court jester after he is dethroned. At one point in the play, the dethroned king-turned-balladeer is told by the reigning king what Wedekind himself must have heard from the Kaiser's representatives: "You carry your jests somewhat too far there! What will the foolish multitude think when it sees royal majesty so brought to dust!"[12] Whether or not Durov's attack on "royal majesty" was inspired by Wedekind's, it is certain that Wedekind knew about Durov's clowning by 1892, some time before he wrote his poem and play.[13] It is also likely that Durov knew about Wedekind's mockery of the Kaiser's uniform years before he was arrested on similar charges.

Neither man held a monopoly on antipathy toward the Kaiser. Durov's satires of authority, fiscal policy and militarism were created at a time when Wedekind and other German artists opposed the same social developments in their own country. Karl Liebknecht notes the existence of this satirical movement, and commends it in his banned book. Observing that there are "tendencies of a scientific, artistic and ethical formation, which make an onslaught on militarism," he cites "the undermining activity of the *Simplicissimus* literature" as an example which "must in no way be underrated."[14]

Durov's clowning was part of a larger, shared comic sensibility evident in the *Simplicissimus* literature and elsewhere. Durov, Liebknecht, Wedekind, Brecht and Piscator shared the same irreverent attitude toward state militarism. A censor serving the Kaiser could have easily concluded that such artists as Durov and Brecht were conspiring with activists like Liebknecht to overthrow the Emperor; and the censor would not have been completely wrong. If these men did not meet and plot together, certainly they knew of one another's endeavors, and admired them. With immense theatricality and wit they opposed the oppressive social and political conditions in which they lived, and prompted spectators to join them in abolishing such conditions.

It is difficult to prove a direct line of influence from Durov to Brecht; Kaiser Wilhelm II and his militarism are the strongest links between them. If Brecht never knew about Durov, however, he certainly knew of the satiric, anti-militaristic impulses that Wedekind and Liebknecht had in common with the Russian clown. In 1919 Brecht attended a public protest against the murders of Liebknecht and Rosa Luxemburg. A year earlier he wrote an obituary for Frank Wedekind in which he praised the man's "brazen energy" as well as his role as the ringmaster in *Earth Spirit*. In plays such as Brecht's

*A Man's a Man*, and his poem *The Ballad of the Dead Soldier*, the same impulses to ridicule militarism and employ popular art forms (the ballad, the variety act) can be discerned.

In Russia, Vladimir Mayakovsky also carried on Durov's tradition of "democratic" clowning. He collaborated several times with Durov's disciple, Lazarenko, a clown who called himself "Jester to His Majesty the People," after Durov. Through these collaborations, which influenced such stage texts as *The Bedbug*, the theatre once more experienced Durov's comic impulses. While the innovations of Brecht and Mayakovsky owe only a small debt to Durov, his clowning anticipated a movement among satirists who were prepared to "intervene actively in life" through their art. Durov did not initiate this movement by himself, but he was at the front of the line, with Kaiser Wilhelm II's legal representatives right behind him.

Few "democratic" clowns since Durov have been as deliberate in their reversal of the better known tradition of the court jester and court writers of satire, who were retained by men of power and rarely satirized their patrons. "King of the Jesters, but never the King's jester" was a defiant claim that could only be made by a popular entertainer willing to risk arrest.

Fools and clowns have long practiced symbolic resistance to the status quo, ever since ancient Roman Saturnalia and medieval Feasts of Fools required masters and servants to change places for awhile, and elected a fool or slave as mock-king or mock-pope. But the temporary nature of these upheavals was agreed upon in advance by those at the top of the social order. Clowning like Durov's, initiated by him alone without any official sanction, is closer in spirit to insurrection than Saturnalian holiday. His humor was far more likely to be prosecuted in a court of law than welcomed in the court of a king.

## Dividing Clowns in Half

Circus clowning was a relatively new art when Durov practiced it. The first "circus" in the modern sense of the word was established in 1768, when Englishman Philip Astley began exhibiting equestrian stunts in a ring on the outskirts of London. The "circuses" and amphitheatres of Roman fame had featured chariot races and gladiatorial combats, not clowns or acrobats. Circus clowns developed as part of—and diversions from—Astley's equestrian acts. One of the most famous British clowns, John Ducrow, excelled as a stunt rider and frequently employed horses in his comedy. An engraving shows him serving tea to two ponies daintily seated at tables. Another famous nineteenth-century English clown, Joseph Grimaldi, did not perform in circuses at all, but in pantomimes on legitimate theatre stages. His whiteface makeup and style of clowning nevertheless exerted considerable influence upon his circus brethren. The acts of Grimaldi and Ducrow were devised as dramatic narratives with plots and characters; in short, they devised stage plays, some of which took place in a circus ring. The distinction between circus and stage clowns has widened considerably over the past few decades, especially in America, where circus clowns in the great three-ring establishments have been relegated to short scenes—usually sight gags—shown between other acts. Few American clowns now perform what amounts to a complete play, with plot, dialogue and repeatable gags, as Grimaldi and Lazarenko did in their pantomimes.[15]

Stage clowns existed much earlier, beginning with mimes who spoke dialogue during comic performances in ancient Greece and Rome. Since ancient times, there have been two traditions of stage clowning: one, improvisatory and popular; the other, more dependent on written texts and hired actors. Performers in the popular tradition present their own scenarios on trestle stages, at fairgrounds, public squares, in cabarets and circuses. They memorize or improvise their highly physical, slapstick routines. In general, they have not been regarded as playwrights or character actors. These clowns include Greek and Roman mimes; medieval balladeers and storytellers; circus, *commedia dell'arte*, pantomime, cabaret, and music hall performers such as Durov and Grimaldi. This tradition is politically "democratic" in a sense suggested by Arnold Hauser when he notes:

> Ancient Greek mime received no subvention from the state, in consequence did not have to take instructions from above, and so worked out its artistic principles simply and solely from its own immediate experience with audiences. It offered its public not artistically constructed dramas of tragic-heroic manners, and noble or even sublime personages, but short, sketchy, naturalistic scenes with subjects from the most trivial, everyday life. Here at last we have to do with art which has been created not merely for the people, but also in a sense by the people.[16]

Since the eighteenth century, instead of "subvention from the state," clowns in the "democratic" tradition have received funding from the public through commercial bookings—which very likely made them more responsive to their paying audiences than to their government.

Practitioners of the other comic tradition frequently received funding from the state or a court, and its "high drama" depicted "sublime personages," however comically they were portrayed. Clowns in this tradition, created by writers and acting companies, survive as characters in the dramatic texts of Aristophanes, Shakespeare, Molière, Jonson. These characters have sometimes been modeled after popular clowns; Molière learned about *commedia dell'arte* stock types from an Italian *commedia* troupe performing in Paris, for example, and Shakespeare wrote some roles for the clown and jig-dancer Will Kempe.

Brecht, Mayakovsky and other modern satirists also merged aspects of improvisational and scripted clowning by writing plays with clown roles consciously modeled on those of the popular tradition. Brecht derived some of his comic characters from Karl Valentin's cabaret persona and Charlie Chaplin's tramp. Mayakovsky wrote for the Soviet circus clown, Lazarenko. The first production of Trevor Griffiths' *Comedians* featured Jimmy Jewel, a British music hall veteran, and one scene was indebted to the Swiss clown Grock's famous circus act. France's Théâtre du Soleil recreated German cabaret satire, with some scenes based on Valentin and Tucholsky sketches, in its 1979 play *Mephisto*. Dario Fo has reconstructed and performed tales of medieval minstrels, and has based some characters in his plays on *commedia* stock figures, as do two of today's American companies, the San Francisco Mime Troupe and El Teatro Campesino.

The satires by these authors and groups require an actor to impersonate a clown, or devise a clown persona like Valentin's or Durov's. Their plays call for more than comic acting; they require a clown's attitude toward the performance space, audience and other actors. They require the senses of time and space which Bakhtin attributes to carnival clowns who always stand "on the borderline between life and art, in a peculiar midzone." For these clowns, the imaginary fourth wall exists only in order to be torn down, or stepped through. At times they may acknowledge no walls whatsoever, performing outside of conventional theatre buildings.

Before actors were placed behind an imaginary fourth wall by French director André Antoine in the nineteenth century, it was impossible to break through the fourth wall separating actors from audience; it did not exist. The actor could allude to walls around him, as Shakespeare's Pyramus does—"O wall, o swell, o lovely wall/ Show me thy chink"—but the illusion of being a character in a separate world, in a space cut off from the audience, was not actively pursued or sustained. After the advent of fourth-wall realism, breaking out of this convention to address the audience directly became rebellion against the illusions of realism, and a critique of the privacy and other-worldliness accorded characters in a play. Circus clowns have always embodied this anti-illusionist tendency; but its re-introduction into the theatre after Antoine's realism took hold was often facilitated by clowns created by Brecht and others.

## Holiday's End

*"For the rain it raineth every day."*
—Feste, *Twelfth Night*

Satire performed under the auspices of a state-sponsored festival, as Aristophanes' plays were, or a court's license, as Shakespeare's and Molière's were, or a church's approval, as some medieval plays were, generally served church and state by ridiculing deviation from the norm. If rulers of state were ridiculed by more defiant clowns and satiric playwrights during Durov's lifetime and after, the change served the new patrons of the arts—ordinary people attending mass entertainments such as the circuses and British and French pantomimes which arose in the eighteenth century. By terming himself jester to "His Majesty the People" Durov acknowledged this change in the composition of the audience which made him a spokesman for "Everyman" or "the little man."

In one sense, this was no change at all. For centuries, mimes and clowns performed for ordinary citizens at fairs and carnivals. Wandering minstrels in the Middle Ages and zannies accompanying mountebanks in the Renaissance, performed in public settings. However, while they may have sold medicines or collected coins after the show, these performers rarely sold tickets beforehand. At the same time that the clowning of Grimaldi and Durov broke from the tradition of court-patronized folly, it commercialized folk forms and holiday festivity. Such clowns were seen infrequently in a public square free of charge. Instead they became, in Bakhtin's words, "the constant accredited representatives of the carnival spirit out of carnival season."[17] They could perform during any season, in a tent or on a stage, as folk forms were divorced from the carnival season and married to a booking manager in London or Berlin.

These new, paid entertainers were not all political satirists, of course. The few who were addressed the paying public's interests, which often differed from the interests of government officials in Russia and Germany, and did not always agree with ruling interests in France or England either. Circus and the pantomime provided two of very few settings where crowds of ordinary citizens could freely, collectively and joyously applaud criticism of harsh government. In his book *Les Clowns*, Tristan Rémy observes that Durov always obtained the most enthusiastic response to his satire in popular locations, while Russia's nobility treated him with contempt and preferred the "Latin" clowns who performed in French, the language of the Russian aristocracy. When clowning in French was prohibited for a time in nineteenth-century France, silent pantomime became a popular means to evade political censorship.

In what seemed a less repressive, but economically impoverished London, the satiric clowning of Joseph Grimaldi provided nineteenth-century audiences with a needed, rare release from drudgery—a release that some members of the lower classes sought in drink. Grimaldi's most popular song was about gin; the public reacted as if his song *were* gin. The lyrics describe a woman who "to keep herself warm, she thought it no sin/ To fetch herself a quartern of - - -." To audience cries of "gin" Grimaldi would reply, with mock-morality, "Oh, for shame!" and then lead everyone in a chorus celebrating the pleasures of liquor. According to Richard Findlater, this clown "radiated great friendliness and great mischief, exuded a fine, frank, confiding jollity . . . which at once made friends, and not mere spectators, of the audience. . . . [He was] a beloved criminal free from guilt, shame, compunction or reverence for age, class or property."[18]

Grimaldi's song about gin, and his other acts, demonstrate how the stage clown became a spokesman for the "average" or "small" person, including the multitudes of gin drinkers. The performer and his audience were united by his satires of "fashionable society . . . ballerinas and boxers of the day . . . duelling and dandyism . . . the latest fashions," and his "parody of Georgian greed."[19] Grimaldi's clown marked a significant transition in clown types, from that of country bumpkin to that of highly inventive, law defying commentator on society. Findlater notes that this transformation in clowning occurred at the same time country life itself changed, as land enclosures forced citizens to move from agricultural regions into city slums and lose their own "country bumpkin" qualities.

Grimaldi anticipated Durov's crime of anti-militaristic satire. He was reprimanded for changing "a lobster into a [redcoat] soldier by boiling it."[20] And at a time when the uniform of the Hussars was admired by the Prince Regent, the clown parodied Hussar outfits by wearing black coal-scuttles (for boots), horseshoes (for heels), a muff (cap) and other odd materials. Covent Garden was threatened with withdrawal of royal patronage unless Grimaldi stopped satirizing the Horse Guards, which he did. In this instance the theatre retained its royal patronage. Later clowns and their theatres had none to lose.

Loyalty to state and court patronage can be detected behind the scenes of earlier stage clowning. In Shakespeare's plays, written for stages licensed by the court, clowns take liberties with kings and courtiers at their invitation (by their license), during agreed-upon recesses from everyday life. Thersites in *Troilus and Cressida* is urged to rail by the Greek kings whom his complaints amuse. Even in the midst of their war, the Greek kings are able to carouse and allow for holiday entertainment. Prince Hal in *Henry IV* carouses with Falstaff no longer than the Prince's obligation to the state permits such indulgence. In the plays of Aristophanes, too, mockery frequently occurs during festive occasions of sacrifice and marriage, as F.M. Cornford has noted. Characters retreat from everyday Athens to Hades or the land of the Hoopoe, or the Thesmophoriazusae, and there, removed from the normalcy of war, taxes and male-dominated government, they mock the existing social hierarchy.

If the social hierarchy is inverted in these plays, the hierarchy usually allows it. Lear's fool is appointed judge when the king and clown are in a farmhouse, far from court and power. Touchstone and Jacques in *As You Like It* jest at courtiers in the forest of Arden, similarly removed from power; exiled courtiers constitute their audience. The clowns here usually stand at the side of the main action and comment on it; they are peripheral to events. Later, stage clowns move into the center of the action and control it. The clowns in plays by Brecht, Mayakovsky and their successors attain liberty and power that have previously been denied to them; they do so despite those in power, and in the centers of oppression rather than in separate, idyllic retreats. The changes in clowning and politics reflect the changes in patronage already mentioned; representatives of "His Majesty the People" rise above ruling politicians and kings on stage, even if their constituency cannot do so in everyday life.

The concerns of these clowns, and of the ordinary citizens they represent, are summed up by Dario Fo in his remarks on "The Clown and Power": "Clowns always speak of the same thing, they speak of hunger: hunger for food, hunger for sex, but also hunger for dignity, hunger for identity, hunger for power. In fact, they introduce questions about who commands, who protests."[21] Fo's ahistorical description of hungry clowns is qualified by his stage plays, and those of other modern satirists, which favor the oppressed of specific places and times, and favor them even more strongly than Grimaldi and Durov did.

This is not to say that the new clowns are always ordinary citizens. Some become judges or referees, by imposture or appointment. (These usurpations of power recall the Saturnalia and Feasts of Fools, with differences.) Their reigns benefit the public far more than the brief judgeship of Lear's fool or other court-approved antics. The modern political clowns rule in everyday time and not holiday time, in a law court and not a king's mock-court. When Azdak becomes judge in *The Caucasian Chalk Circle*, he favors the common people so often that wealthy plaintiffs no longer know if a bribe will help their case. The clownish judge in Dario Fo's *Accidental Death of an Anarchist* makes state secrets accessible to everyone, democratizing law by exposing its hidden abuse of power. In Mayakovsky's *The Championship of the Universal Class Struggle*, when Lazarenko played the role of referee in a contest among elite statesmen, the contest placed the leaders in a popular, non-elitist forum: a circus wrestling match.

These clowns mock existing rules at the same time that they democratize the law, aggressively moving from the periphery into centers of decision-making. Important exceptions to this comic movement in modern drama can be found in the plays of Beckett and Handke, where clowns remain at the periphery of society, or leave it completely. Not all modern playwrights fit neatly into the group discussed here, but significant changes in the image and behavior of stage clowns can be seen in a group of political satires by Brecht, Mayakovsky, Griffiths, Fo, Weiss, El Teatro Campesino, Théâtre du Soleil and the San Francisco Mime Troupe. In their plays the stage clown is transformed from a lonely outcast or sidelined jester into what will be called "the political clown": a representative of ordinary people, like Vladimir Durov, Jester to His Majesty the People, whose antics favor the common man and woman. The political clown opposes militarism and undemocratic rulers in the theatre—and, when necessary, in a court of law.

In popular forms of entertainment—cabaret, music hall, circus clowning, sports events—Brecht, Mayakovsky and subsequent authors saw crowds participating—cheering, betting, watching attentively, commenting, enjoying themselves—as they did not in conventional theatre. Moreover, in the clowning of Valentin and Durov they saw popular, comic acts of resistance to authority shared by clown and audience. They observed how popular entertainment forms could provide a forum for artist and audience to share political views and collectively participate in events. Brecht notes that in sporting establishments, everyone can be an expert. "They know exactly what is going to take place." He regards the sports arena as a paradigm of pleasurable, actualized democracy, a place where spectators watch "highly trained persons developing their peculiar powers in the way most suited to them with the greatest sense of responsibility yet in such a way as to make one feel that they are doing it primarily for their own fun."[22]

Fifty years later, in 1974, Augusto Boal cited the same argument to explain his "Joker System" of stage performance. The Brazilian playwright and director, who acknowledges a large debt to Brecht and the circus, writes that his new system will "allow the spectators to know at every performance, the possibilities of the game."[23] In Boal's theatre, the "joker" on stage also suggests that everyone can be an expert; that democratic, collective decisions would be wiser than those from existing, hierarchical systems of justice.

Brecht, Boal and others adapt popular culture and clowning so that their art becomes a source of empowerment for the audience as well as the clowns on stage. Both on stage and off there is movement from voyeurism, sideline jesting and spectatorship to a more participatory and pleasurable involvement in the situation. Much as clowns destroy stage conventions and resist social conventions, the audience for its part is invited—by direct address—to consent to the rebellion, join it, celebrate its utopian goals and speak out against injustice and oppression after the play ends. To reach toward their goals of utopia and collective action, the playwrights reutilize old conventions of clowning to serve new political ends. Some of them also create artistic collectives which practice the democratic principles they would like to see in society.

The German critic Hans Mayer once noted that everywhere in modern theatre "we see the attempt to build in community, to plan against hierarchies, to tear out the apron between those acting and the observers. Democracy in all things aesthetic, it being absent in the social realm."[24] Mayer adds that "all this left Brecht cold," and he cites Brecht's decision to keep the gold-decorated proscenium arch and other accoutrements of conventional theatre at the Berliner Ensemble as evidence of resistance to democratic art. The pages that follow offer an alternative thesis: that along with other modern satirists, Brecht favored democratic and popular theatre for most of his life, even if he did not often create it. His stage clowns embody the democratic impulse to resist hierarchies and to bring actors into the world of their audience—into everyday life—and bring spectators into the politically conscious world of the actors, so that the two might become almost interchangeable. The result is an achievement of political satire and the carnival spirit as described by Bakhtin, an occasion where "the individual feels that he is an indissoluable part of this collectivity . . . the people's mass body."[25] The crowd in a theatre becomes a democratic assembly, with a clown rather than a king or president as its chief representative.

# —2

# Hanswurst in Exile

*"He who laughs has not yet heard the terrible tidings."*

—Bertolt Brecht

*"Epic theatre is lavish only in the occasions it offers for laughter."*

—Walter Benjamin

In a diary entry from 1920, long before Brecht's political and aesthetic theories were fully formed, he writes:

> Once I get my hooks on a theatre, I shall hire two clowns. They will perform in the interval and pretend to be spectators. They will bandy opinions about the play and about the members of the audience. . . . The hit of the week will be parodied. . . . The clowns will laugh about any hero as about a private individual. . . . The idea would be to bring reality back to the things on stage. For God's sake, it's the things that need to be criticized—the actions, words, gestures—not their execution.[1]

Clowning is seen as a form of social and aesthetic criticism, a means to increase disbelief in characters and attitudes, rather than suspend it. It also allows actors and spectators to become almost interchangeable, in parodic fashion, as the clowns "pretend to be spectators" during the intermission.

Later in his life, Brecht and his actors would develop "alienation" techniques that would make similar effects possible in any of his plays, with clowns or without them. The playwright knew, as he indicated in the essay "Alienation Effects in Chinese Acting," that an effort to foster disbelief in theatre, or an "effort to make incidents appear strange to the public [by alienation techniques] can be seen in a primitive form in the theatrical and pictorial displays at the old popular fairs. The way the clowns speak and the way the panoramas are painted both embody an act of alienation."[2] His youthful visits to the Augsburg fair, his idolatry of the cabaret clown Karl Valentin and his admiration for former circus employee and playwright Frank Wedekind introduced Brecht to the circus clowning which later surfaced in new form in his plays.

The origins of Brecht's politically engaged stage clown can be traced back even further, however, to eighteenth-century Germany and the banishment of Hanswurst. Hanswurst was a stage clown who represented a popular, lower-class element unwelcome by neo-classicists. The clown, also known as Jackpudding, speaks of his banishment in Ludwig Tieck's satire *Puss in Boots* (1797): "My countrymen became so wise at a certain point that they formally forbade all fun under penalty. . . . Those who laughed at me were persecuted like myself, and so I had to go into exile."[3] More than a century later, in 1926, Brecht noted the absence of "all fun" in the German theatre—a complaint remarkably similar to that of Tieck's Hanswurst. To improve the situation, Brecht called for the restoration of fun to theatre. While he did not restore Hanswurst to the stage (as Peter Weiss did later), Brecht did bring other clowns on as part of his campaign. *Spass* (fun) was his antidote to the solemnity that dominated the German stage for centuries, since Goethe forbade audiences at Weimar to disrupt performances with laughter, and since Hanswurst was banished from the stage. (Brecht once said, "We lost a great humorist in Goethe. Anyone who can represent Mephistopheles as he did ought to write all his texts humorously.")[4]

Brecht's description of the epic actor as one who prompts the spectator to justify or abolish social conditions according to his social class might be applied to Hanswurst. The persecution of this clown began early in the eighteenth century, when the neo-classicist playwright Johann Gottsched, his favorite actress Carolina Neuber, and others decided that Hanswurst's class of person had no place in their world. They called for an end to his low humor on stage since it was inimical to the French, highly literate drama they revered and the social decorum they wanted to preserve in the theatre, as well as outside it. Hanswurst's persona, made famous by the Viennese actor Josef Stranitzky, brought comic peasant manners into the theatre; he wore a multicolored costume—yellow trousers, red jacket and pointed green hat—and as a representative of the servant class he often declined to imitate or admire the heroics of his master. "So long as I can feed my face and quench my thirst, the whole world can be wretched, as far as I'm concerned," Hanswurst proclaimed in *Cicero*. He preferred wine, women and safety to honor, much like his stage ancestors in Italian *commedia* and Elizabethan drama (whose clowns had been introduced to Germany by English actors touring the continent in the seventeenth century). The neo-classicists aspired to a noble, elevated art form which could not co-exist with the sausage-eating clown.

*An engraving of
Hanswurst by Elias Baeck,
after Jacques Callot, 1716.*

As if he decided to appoint himself Hanswurst's lawyer in 1767, the critic
and playwright Gotthold Lessing entered a defense of the clown character
in his *Hamburg Dramaturgy* essays, proclaiming that "Frau Neuber is dead,
Gottsched is dead," and the fool's motley colors should be seen again on German stages. Seeing all stage fools as but one species, so that the Roman parasite
was "aught but our harlequin," Lessing suggested that Germany's version of
the fool deserved as much recognition as any other.

As Lessing notes, Frau Neuber herself had placed clowns on stage; but
instead of colorful jackets and trousers, they wore all-white costumes. The
purity of the white French Pierrots, jokes Lessing, represented "a great triumph
of good taste." His defense of Hanswurst is one fragment of Lessing's larger
critique of the aristocratic "good taste" that dominated the German stage
in his day. Opposing such taste, he called for the development of middle-
class drama and the staging of Shakespeare's plays, notorious for their mixture of kings and clowns. Clowns like Hanswurst represented everyday life
differently from the characters found in the new genre of middle-class drama;
but all were alien to the aristocratic standards dominating the stage in Lessing's age, which explains why he could advocate both dramatic forms: out
of opposition to neo-classicism's dominance.

Hanswurst was more popular than his opponents, and Carolina Neuber
eventually conceded that she could not keep the clown off Germany's stages.
He remained an exile of sorts, however—a representative of the unprivileged

classes—as he had been in all of Stranitzky's plays. Hanswurst's lack of privilege is central to what Martin Esslin calls "a genuinely common, 'plebian' kind of theatre. As the romantic plot is no longer taken seriously, the higher world of upper-class sentiments is presented from the ruthless viewpoint of the common people. The heroes are seen through the eyes of their valets and chambermaids."[5]

Hanswurst also called attention to the artificiality of theatre performances, somewhat as Brecht's actors later did through the "alienation effect." Robert Heitner notes that Hanswurst's "comic, mood-destroying antics . . . have been interpreted as a kind of necessary reassurance to naive audiences that what they were watching was just a play after all."[6]

Hanswurst, like Tieck himself, mocked romantic plots and upper-class sentiments when he returned to the stage (or at least the page, since the play was never staged until 1844) in *Puss in Boots*. But Tieck relocated Hanswurst in a fantasyland called Utopia; only in exile, it seems, could a German clown be a court jester in the late eighteenth century. The image of the German clown as exile had also been noted by Lessing in 1767. He quoted a common objection to Hanswurst: "He is a foreign creation," a reference to the clown's Viennese, English and Italian origins, to which Lessing drily replied, "What matters that? I would all fools among us were foreigners."[7] He knew that some of his countrymen, particularly those objecting to Hanswurst, were also capable of folly. Tieck's Hanswurst knew many other fools: "One can't come up with anything new at all; there are too many working in the profession," he said.[8]

Other forms of stage humor, such as political satire in cabarets and the circus, had also been suppressed in Germany prior to Brecht's arrival, as already noted in the cases of Durov and Wedekind. The persecution of clowns and satirists continued under Hitler in the 1930s, and it influenced a number of playwrights. Like Wedekind in his writing of *King Nicola*, these writers chose to portray the persecution of both artists and the ordinary people clowns represent through political clown plays. Brecht did this in *Schweyk in the Second World War* and *The Baden Learning Play*.

Other plays which portray clowns as outcasts and victims of persecution include *How Mr. Mockinpott Was Cured of His Suffering* (Peter Weiss's play, featuring Hanswurst); and *Kaspar* (the title of which, when spelled "Kasper," means "clown") and *The Unintelligent Are Dying Out* (both by Peter Handke); Théâtre du Soleil's *Mephisto*; Dario Fo's *Accidental Death of an Anarchist*; Trevor Griffiths' *Comedians*; and Lotte Goslar's *Circus Scene* (based on a scenario by Brecht). While there are thematic and stylistic continuities from Tieck and Brecht to the others, there are also significant differences in the works. The clowns become progressively more defiant of authority, finally refusing to consent to persecution.

In Trevor Griffiths' 1975 play *Comedians*, German resistance to clowns is treated quite differently from the way it had been treated earlier: A new generation's clown, Gethin Price, says "A German joke is no laughing matter." The aspiring comedian announces he will never line up to be gassed, as Jews did in Nazi Germany. His consent will be withheld—as is not always the case for clowns in Brecht's plays. These variations on the theme of Hanswurst's persecution can be regarded as a continuing satiric dialogue on freedom and utopia. The clown in exile or at the periphery of society remains unassimilated, naive and does not consent to injustice or prevalent political conditions as readily as other citizens. In this sense, the clown represents a utopian freedom from oppression. The political conditions and utopias vary from play to play, and the variations constitute a continuing discourse at the center of which is Bertolt Brecht. He transforms Hanswurst into a new, politically conscious clown whose non-consent takes the form of comic insubordination.

## Introducing Karl Valentin

Brecht's clowns, and those of the playwrights who follow him, have a more recent ancestor than Hanswurst; namely Karl Valentin. Valentin's cabaret satire was closer to proletarian and urban life than was the peasant Hanswurst. While, as Martin Esslin has noted, Valentin was "the last in a long line of great clowns and Hans Wursts stretching back to the eighteenth century,"[9] the Munich comedian parodied lower middle-class professions rather than the aristocracy and neo-classical heroism mocked by Josephy Stranitzky's clown. If Hanswurst was one of Lessing's anti-aristocratic delegates, Valentin was one of Brecht's models of proletarian resistance to middle-class complacency. Neither clown overtly articulated such political biases, but Lessing and Brecht championed the comic figures from this adversary perspective. And sometimes even Lessing and Brecht may have had simpler motives for liking the clowns; they enjoyed laughter as much as the next man (probably more, if the next man was Gottsched).

A fictionalized description of Valentin's cabaret audience is included in Lion Feuchtwanger's novel *Success*, when comedian Balthasar Hierl entertains a hall filled with "bulky, gossiping, smoking citizens stuffing themselves." Around 1920, Brecht was very much a member of this audience; in one letter he reported almost laughing himself sick at Valentin's cabaret. At the same time, he was no mere spectator. Brecht became familiar enough with the comedian's style that, according to biographer Klaus Volker, the playwright composed a new scenario for Valentin to perform in 1922, in a midnight show called *The Red Raisin*.

In the same period, Brecht played clarinet in Valentin's Oktoberfest fair booth. In 1923 he co-directed a grotesque film, *Mysteries of the Barbershop*, which features Valentin as a barber who accidentally decapitates a customer. Recalling his Munich years in *The Messingkauf Dialogues* (1942), Brecht wrote that he learned more from Valentin than from Büchner or Wedekind, the two playwrights he admired most in his early twenties.

For many years, Brecht was fond of a slogan posted in his study: "Truth is concrete." Nearby stood a toy donkey bearing around its neck the statement, "Even I must understand it." Few forms of comedy could be more concrete and more geared toward stubborn, slow-witted comprehension than Valentin's cabaret sketches.

*Karl Valentin playing military music.*

## Valentin's Axe

Karl Valentin once rushed onto the Frankfurter Hof stage in Munich with an axe and demolished everything around him. He cut up not only the scenery, but also the floorboards, much to the surprise of the audience and the other actors. Only Valentin and one actor knew that the Frankfurter Hof's management was planning to modernize the stage, and would have removed the old floorboards anyway. Valentin's wrecking party, performed at the conclusion of a cabaret sketch, pressed or even destroyed the boundaries of illusionistic theatre, along with the floorboards. While Durov had taken his satire outside the performing space and into the street and law court, Valentin pursued comparable ends by destroying the performing space itself.[10]

Brecht commended the Munich clown's battle, with and without axe, against stage illusion, when he wrote in 1922 that Valentin "shows the insufficiency of all things, including ourselves."[11] Both artists fought against the artifice and insufficiency of dramatic illusion, particularly the illusion that individual characters are unchanging and complete entities with personalities as stable and palpable as floorboards. At the time he was writing his play *A Man's a Man*, Brecht told an interviewer, "The continuity of ego is a myth," and "it's a jolly business" to see a man "forced to surrender his precious ego."[12] Valentin's cabaret sketches contained just such jolly business, as Valentin parodied the myth of ego continuity with ridiculously dogmatic, almost monotonous self-assertion. Consider the obstinate self-assurance of Valentin in the following cabaret dialogue, *The Marriage Advertisement*, performed by the Munich comedian and his partner, Liesl Karlstadt:

> *Valentin:* You may wonder, Madame, why I am here in your office. A marriage advertisement appeared in your newspaper: "Lonesome widow seeks joy in marriage for her second time, etc." I accidentally read this ad four or five weeks ago in your pages, and then I lost the newspaper. Please be so good as to find me the paper with this advertisement in it.
>
> *Karlstadt:* My goodness, if you don't know the exact date, it will be difficult.
>
> *Valentin:* The ad was about five centimeters long and three centimeters wide. "Lonesome widow seeks joy in marriage for her second time, etc."
>
> *Karlstadt:* Four or five weeks ago, you say? You're not really asking me to look through all the papers that appeared over the past five weeks.
>
> *Valentin:* If you would be so kind. Perhaps it is in the first issue.
>
> *Karlstadt:* No such luck.
>
> *Valentin:* "Lonesome widow seeks joy in marriage for her second time." The ad is about five centimeters long and three centimeters wide.
>
> *Karlstadt:* But it's impossible to find that ad among so many papers.

*Valentin:* But I know it's there, I've seen it there.

*Karlstadt:* I've seen many ads there.

*Valentin:* The rest of the ads don't interest me. I am interested only in one, which is, as I said, about five centimeters long and three centimeters wide. The text of it is: "Lonesome widow seeks joy in marriage for her second time, etc."

*Karlstadt:* Yes, as you see here, this is already the tenth newspaper. Unfortunately, I also have other work to do.

*Valentin:* Madame, if you'd be so kind. Perhaps you'll help me find my joy in life. It all depends on this ad, on this small ad, five centimeters long and three centimeters wide, "Lonesome widow seeks joy in marriage for her second time, etc."

*Karlstadt:* Yes, yes, I already know what the ad says; but as you see yourself, I can't find it.

*Valentin:* Four or five weeks ago I read this same ad: "Lonesome widow seeks. . . . "

*Karlstadt:* Please stop; let's not hear any more about the lonesome widow.

*Valentin:* Stop, madame! I intend to start something with the lonesome widow, not stop it. Therefore, I beg you, keep looking until we have it. The ad is about . . .

*Karlstadt:* Five centimeters long and three centimeters wide. In our paper announcements of that size are printed by the hundreds.

*Valentin:* Yes, yes, I believe you. But this can be recognized not only by its size, also by the message: "Lonesome widow seeks joy in marriage for her second time."

*Karlstadt:* Marriage! We don't have to find your marriage ad to find you a marriage; there are plenty of widows in Munich.

*Valentin:* No, I want only one, a lonesome widow who seeks joy in marriage her second time.

*Karlstadt:* I've had enough! Take a look! I've now looked through all the marriage ads of the past five weeks, and the one you want isn't here. Are you sure you read the ad in our newspaper?

*Valentin:* Yes, absolutely sure!

*Karlstadt:* Perhaps you read it in *The Country Herald?* This is *The City Herald* office.

*Valentin:* Yes, *The Country Herald.*

*Karlstadt:* You stupid clown.[13]

Valentin's comic persona was a variation of the Aristophanic and *commedia* stock character, the *alazon:* the impostor who claims to have greater knowledge and experience than he actually possesses. (In the case of the preceding sketch Valentin's character claims and thereby parodies a better memory than he actually has. His memory is in fact as limited here as his sexual appetite and curiosity—limited to obsession with a single, unknown widow.) At other times he mimics other forms of authority, those to which a musician or photographer's assistant might aspire in pursuit of professional respectability. Sue-Ellen Case has noted in an essay on Valentin that in his sketches, "The authority figure gives commands and tries to complete tasks, while the underling [usually Valentin himself] invents verbal strategies to escape them."[14] Liesl Karlstadt often portrayed the authority figure. These conflicts between authority figure and underling frequently take the form of a conflict between employer and employee, or parallel it. Brecht's depiction of working class discontent is anticipated in Valentin's sketches. Brecht, in fact, acknowledged as much in the *Messingkauf Dialogues*, where he recalled seeing Valentin portray "refractory employees . . . who hated their employer and made him appear ridiculous."[15]

Brecht credited Valentin's sense of artifice as the source of his own first Epic Theatre effect. When he directed *Edward II* in 1925, Brecht asked Valentin for advice on the battle scene. Walter Benjamin recounts in his *Conversations with Brecht* what happened at the rehearsal:

> Brecht . . . quoted the moment at which the idea of epic theatre first came into his head. The battle in the play is supposed to occupy the stage for three-quarters of an hour. Brecht couldn't stage manage the soldiers and neither could Asya [Lacis], his production assistant. Finally he turned in despair to Karl Valentin, at that time one of his closest friends, who was attending the rehearsal, and asked him: "Well, what is it? What's the truth about these soldiers? What about them?" Valentin: "They're pale, they're scared, that's what!" The remark settled the issue, Brecht adding: "They're tired." Whereupon the soldiers' faces were thickly made up with chalk, and that was the day the production's style was determined.[16]

Brecht had seen chalk white faces before, many times, because Valentin wore them in his clown act; so in a sense, Epic Theatre began with Valentin's clown act. In 1931, when Peter Lorre portrayed Galy Gay, the humble porter whom the army turns into a "human fighting machine" in *A Man's a Man*, he whitened his face to reveal fear—not fear of death, but "fear of life," according to Brecht's notes on the clownish army recruit.[17]

In his 1922 notes on Valentin, Brecht attributed to him a combination of "Dummheit," "Gelassenheit," and "Lebengenuss": stupidity along with self-possession and a sense of pleasure in life.[18] Valentin's "pleasure in life," visible in a cabaret atmosphere where one could smoke and drink, inspired or at least confirmed Brecht's early theories of theatre. The emphasis was on sport and fun. Valentin's farcical "Dummheit" inspired Brecht's early one-acts, such as one set during a cheap wedding where all the furniture collapses. And it led the playwright to steal at least one joke verbatim from Valentin, for use in the comic, one-act epilogue to *A Man's a Man*, entitled *The Baby Elephant*. In it, the soldier Polly says that the eyeglasses his friend Uriah loaned him have no lenses in them, and his friend replies with Valentin's punch line: "They're better than nothing."

More significantly, Valentin's foolish persona surfaces, minus the chalk white face, in some of Brecht's plays. When an "epic" actor steps out of character to show his consciousness of the character's persona, at the same time criticizing and distancing himself from the naive character, the moment is reminiscent of Valentin's behavior. Brecht observed this tendency in Valentin's persona when he told the Italian director, Giorgio Strehler, how the Munich clown had sung a song:

> Valentin always impersonated someone who was just playing for the money, with a minimum of energy, so that he barely filled his obligation. But on top of that he would suddenly have tiny amusements, not really for the public, but for himself; for instance, when he would sing a song and at the same time parody the content of the song and in any case criticize it.[19]

Valentin's double role as wage-slave artist and rebellious, critical clown reappears in the epic acting style, and in Brecht's plays when characters who want to outwit an oppressor or employer speak what Brecht called "slave language," a code of puns, understated witticisms and ironic submissions that may sound like obedience to those who make the code necessary. Much as Brecht's epic theatre style has antecedents in Lenz, Büchner and Grabbe, the comic slave language of his characters has precursors in the cabaret sketches of Valentin. The speakers of such language are familiar to a Gestapo agent, Brettschneider, in Brecht's play, *Schweyk in the Second World War*; he notes that Schweyk "sounded like an idiot who puts his seditious remarks in such a way that you can't prove anything."[20]

Schweyk is a character Brecht knew, loved, and wrote plays about, after he read Jaroslav Hasek's novel, *The Adventures of the Good Soldier Schweyk* in 1926. Hasek's sense of humor influenced Brecht as thoroughly as Valentin's, and Schweyk's "seditious remarks" provided examples of a defense mechanism similar to Valentin's. However, as a living performer, Karl Valentin showed Brecht physical humor, verbal repartée and comic timing which no novel could fully convey.

The physical grotesquerie of Valentin's comedy prominently reappeared in two stage productions Brecht supervised. The 1931 production of *A Man's a Man* featured soldiers walking on stilts and others wearing padding and the white-face already mentioned. The "scum," as these soldiers are called in the play, resembled the gallery of tall and short eccentrics visible in Valentin's cabaret sketches and films. The 1929 production of *The Baden Learning Play*, discussed later, featured a giant clown also mounted on stilts or a wooden frame and wearing white-face. The physical oddity of these figures parallels their eccentric social standing as outcasts and criminals.

Brecht's description of Valentin as a clown who portrayed refractory employees, and who (according to his 1922 notes) was a "thoroughly complicated wit out for blood," applies to many characters in his own plays. Schweyk, Gay, Matti in *Puntila* and Azdak in *The Caucasian Chalk Circle* at times display the traits for which Valentin's persona was so well-known: naiveté, hatred of employers, obstinacy, "wit out for blood" and a "minimum of energy." (Not all these qualities emerge at once, of course, even when they apply to the same character.)

In connecting Valentin's humor to Brecht's tradition, Hans Mayer notes that the comedian's dialogues frequently turned into "dialectics that wander off the track." Wandering off the track in the midst of a courtroom deliberation is a strategy the village scribe Azdak employs in *The Caucasian Chalk Circle*, as if justice can only be secured the way he himself secured his judgeship: roundabout, through an uprising or holiday from the rules.

Eric Bentley argues quite persuasively that Azdak is a modern Lord of Misrule, whose brief reign as a judge represents a utopian moment common to Saturnalian celebrations. The character finds himself appointed to the bench after a revolution—an upheaval comparable to a Feast of Fools—and Brecht might well have seen Azdak as Bentley does: "a mock king, an Abbot of Unreason, a Lord of Misrule," renewing a comic pattern depicted in earlier dramatic literature.[21] But a simpler, less literary source for such humor—Brecht's apprenticeship to Valentin—should not be forgotten.

## An Accomplished Weightlifter

Writing about epic theatre in 1931, Walter Benjamin cited Galy Gay as a representative of "the thinking man, or indeed the wise man" on Brecht's stage. He compared Gay to the sage in Plato's dialogues, and to "an empty stage on which the contradictions of our society are acted out. . . . The wise man [is] in this sense . . . the perfect empty stage."[22] Such analogies suggest that Gay is an *eiron*, a Socratic man who knows that he knows nothing, and conceals the fact by asking disingenuous questions. Benjamin's analogy is unconvincing, however, when one looks at Gay's behavior. The character is really more of an *alazon*, quite willing to pretend that he is a man of the world, an accomplished weightlifter and an entrepreneur who knows how to buy elephants. Ultimately the impostures through which Gay accepts another man's identity as his own (calling himself Jeriah Jip) are far more profitable to the social system than to him. While Gay feigns being an entrepreneur and soldier to deceive others, his deceptions are nothing compared to those perpetrated by the social system that buys, creates and controls identities en masse; whole armies of men surrender their private lives to what Brecht would later call "the false, bad collectivity." He had Hitler's army in mind at the time.[23] ("The play is not about fascism. It is a play about the relations between individual and collective," Patty Parmalee has noted, adding that *A*

*Man's a Man* is "as amoral as Brecht's earlier works." Nonetheless, she concedes that, except for the final scene, the soldiers constantly take "shameless advantage of [Gay's] simple-mindedness" by manipulating him.)[24]

Galy Gay is a fool who pretends to be wise, rather than a wise or thinking man on stage. He is, as Brecht said of Valentin, not so much a creator of jokes as a "thoroughly complicated, serious joke" himself. His seriousness, his composure and stupidity, and his working-class life make Gay another version of the Valentin persona: a "little man" who stubbornly fusses over his name and tries to keep it alive in the face of a coercive mass movement. (This brings to mind a story about one of Valentin's last sketches, before he virtually went silent in Nazi Germany: He is rumored to have executed a Nazi salute and said: "Heil . . . whatshisname." Similar stubborn individualism on the part of Galy Gay ceases about halfway through the play, after he loses his "continuity of ego," stops fussing about a name and surrenders his private identity.)

## The Canary and the Elephant

The elephant sale in *A Man's a Man* illustrates Brecht's appropriation of Valentin's comedy for his own clown, Galy Gay. Valentin often performed a sketch about the sale of a canary. Whether or not Brecht consciously borrowed from the Valentin scene, he probably knew it from his visits to the Munich beerhall where it was performed. In the sketch "Der Vogelhändler," Valentin portrays a bird-supplier who gives an empty bird cage to a customer, portrayed by Liesl Karlstadt.

> *Valentin*: Here is the canary with the cage, and here is the bill.
> *Karlstadt*: That is all correct, but wait, where is the little darling? The cage is empty. Where is the bird?
> *Valentin*: It must be in there.
> *Karlstadt*: What do you mean "must be in there?" It is not in there.
> *Valentin*: That is impossible. Why would I bring an empty bird-cage? . . . Here is the bill. I want thirteen marks to pay for everything.
> *Karlstadt*: What do you mean, everything?
> *Valentin*: The cage and the bird.
> *Karlstadt*: The bird is not in there. I can't pay for something not received.
> *Valentin*: Then I'll take the whole thing back with me.
> *Karlstadt*: "Whole thing" is good. You can only take the cage, though. The bird is not inside.
> *Valentin*: Madame, the bird must be inside. The bill says "Cage with bird." "Cage with bird," if you please. Therefore the cage must be with bird.
> *Karlstadt*: I've never heard of anything so stupid. . . . [25]

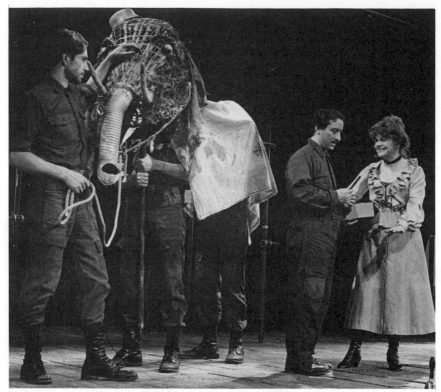

*Brecht's* A Man's a Man *at the Yale Repertory Theatre (1978), featuring, from left, John Shea, Joe Grifasi as Galy Gay and Estelle Parsons.*

Valentin stubbornly insists that the invoice proves the bird's presence. The attitude, and obvious wrongheadedness of it, reappears in *A Man's a Man*.

Galy Gay is asked if he has any doubts about the elephant for sale, which is actually two men in disguise. (A gas mask, with its long tubular filter, is sometimes used to represent the elephant's face in this scene.) "If someone's buying him, I have no doubts," says Gay. "An elephant's an elephant, especially if someone's buying him." Here, too, a written document (the check) is taken as final proof of the animal's existence. The play as a whole reveals Gay to be much like the elephant he sells—his identity is proven by the name in the paybook he carries; the name is Jeriah Jip and he accepts it as his own, after some stubborn, Valentin-like resistance to the change. Brecht was reading Marx's *Capital* while writing *A Man's a Man*, and Marx's theories about "the transformation of money into capital" might have provided another source of inspiration for this sketch concerning capital's capacity to transform men and animals; it changes identities, proves and disproves them, through paybooks and bank checks.

The elephant sale takes place in a series of variety numbers—comic sketches accompanied by songs—and it is as close as Brecht ever came to inserting cabaret sketches into one of his plays. The cabaret material takes on larger social and political meanings in the context of the whole play, as Valentin's sketches did not. And the stubborn clown Galy Gay differs from Valentin's persona in that he eventually surrenders his precious ego to the machinery of war, undergoing a transformation Valentin's clowns rarely made.

The parallel between Valentin and Gay can also be seen in *The Elephant Calf*, when Gay ends the play-within-a-play by promising to hold a boxing match between himself and a spectator; the match will supposedly resolve whether his play "was the truth . . . or whether it was theatre."[26] Instead of an axe he chooses leather gloves here; but his fight, like Valentin's, is conducted to demonstrate the "insufficiency" of all things, especially stage illusions.

# —3
# Marx, Brecht, Dialectics and Satire

*"This man Marx was the only spectator for my plays
I'd ever come across."*
—Bertolt Brecht

Valentin's influence on Brecht was second only to that of another great satirist, Karl Marx. As Walter Benjamin notes, Marx became a teacher of satire through his theory of dialectical materialism and, "it is with Marx that Brecht has gone to school."[1] Benjamin cites one example of Marxist "satire" that uses music hall rhetoric in its question and repartée:

> "When the German Kaiser sent a telegram to President Kruger, whose shares rose then and whose fell?"

> "Of course it's only the communists who ask that."

Benjamin refers to such questions as "pertinent" ones "put to imperialism," but there is also impertinence in both the question and the answer. The query, from Brecht's *The Threepenny Novel* (which he wrote after *The Threepenny Opera*), pries into men's most private affairs—their financial accounts— while the reply insults communists in order to avoid directly answering the question. (A similar mixture of impertinence, insults and evasion can be found in Valentin's beerhall comedy.)

Brecht's satire was influenced as much by Marx's materialist dialectics as by what John Willet terms the *vertrackte Dialektik* or "perverted logic" of Karl Valentin.[2] While Brecht first learned the *vertrackte Dialektik* from Valentin, he later recognized an economic and social basis for such humorous logic when he read Marx. The two traditions converge in what Hans Mayer calls Brecht's "plebian tradition" of drama, in which events are seen from the perspective of the lower classes. The resultant disclosures are "unmistakably, horribly comic," according to Mayer, because Brecht has "firmly taken sides" with one social class against another.[3] There is nothing inherently comic about misery, of course, but when misery is portrayed dialectically, as a reflection of class conflict, the *vertrackte Dialektik* can become a source of humor.

(Valentin's predecessor, Hanswurst, has also been described as a source of dialectical comedy by Peter Loeffler. In his study of Hanswurst, Loeffler notes that, "While the main action of heroic drama . . . presented the audience with the glorious deeds of heroes, with extravagant claims to honor and duty, and with solemn vows of eternal faith, Hanswurst presented the dialectical counterpart by stressing the rough, the unaffected and the down to earth. The heroic and the materialist visions of man were here juxtaposed. . . . " Not until Brecht's time, however, was this materialist dialectic consciously practiced and expounded in stage satire.)

*Karl Valentin (with tuba), Bertolt Brecht (with clarinet) and Liesl Karlstadt (with bell) at a Munich Oktoberfest, circa 1920.*

By 1931, Marxian dialectics had become so important to Brecht that he considered renaming his "epic theatre" experiments "dialectical theatre." He contemplated the same change again later in his career, although he never formally proposed it in writing published during his lifetime. Nor did he ever announce any theory as reductive as "Marx = Valentin + historical materialism," or "Satire = Valentin + Marx." But even if he did not deliberately combine the logic of Marx and Valentin in his satire, their joint impact on him can be seen in retrospect: it pervades the plays he wrote after beginning to study Marxism in 1926.

Valentin's parody of the "continuity of ego" has within it its opposite premise, that of materialist dialectics, which states that every historically developed form is in a state of change. Such continuity, defended through resistance to change and insistence on a single, fixed identity or memory, becomes the basis for comedy in Valentin's sketches and some of Brecht's plays. In *A Man's a Man*, Galy Gay agrees to change his name after lengthy hesitation, and Bloody Five shoots himself rather than surrender his name and identity; and in later plays such as *Puntila* and *The Good Person of Setzuan*, the title characters can survive only by developing a second, "schizoid" personality which neatly separates their instinct for self-preservation from their more generous natures. In these situations, the continuity of ego or a private, more permanent self, represents an unrealistic, unpreservable ideal, comparable to Hegel's ideal of the State. Marx renounces Hegel's idealism in his dialectics, and Brecht effects a similar anti-idealism in his satires.

## The Dialectic Does a Head Stand

In his second preface to *Capital*, Marx explains his departure from Hegel's idealist dialectics. The passage suggests that Hegel, too, had engaged in a *vertrackte Dialektik* by standing the dialectic on its head. Marx notes that in Hegel's dialectic, "the real world is only the external appearance of the Idea."[4] Hegel's dialectic merely transfigures and glorifies what already exists, according to Marx, who regards any ideal as "nothing but the material world reflected in the mind of man." Marx's own dialectic exists in a fluid state, containing in "its positive understanding of what exists a simultaneous recognition of its negation, its inevitable destruction." Marx gives the dialectic a rational, historically grounded form in which it "does not let itself be impressed by anything." Brecht as satirist shared Marx's anti-idealism; he, too, was rarely "impressed by anything," except, perhaps, by Marx and Valentin. But some of his comic characters come close to practicing Hegel's idealism in their own naive way. In these cases, Brecht's satire becomes an act of writing comparable to Marx's inversion of the Hegelian dialectic. Galy Gay and Puntila are "standing on their heads," glorying in their ego or individuality, blithely ignoring social discontent or war around them, until Brecht and events place them on their feet, dizzying them with change as the blood rushes out of their swelled and intoxicated heads.

Augusto Boal notes in his book *The Theatre of the Oppressed* that, "Brecht's whole poetics is basically an answer and counterproposal to the idealist poetics of Hegel."[5] Brecht's inversion of Hegel's dialectic can be seen in his ironic *Conversations in Exile*, in which an exiled intellectual named Ziffel praises Hegel excessively as one of the world's most comic philosophers. Almost anyone who has read the dry, abstract arguments in Hegel's *Logic* will recognize the irony in Ziffel's claim that the book is one of the most humorous works in world literature. Ziffel describes Hegel as a great humorist among the philosophers since Socrates. (This could simply mean that few philosophers since Socrates have been great humorists.) The discussion locates the source of Hegel's comedy in his inability to conceive of order without thinking of disorder, and his contention that the harmony of the State exists as a result of sharp conflicts among the classes. His sense of humor is dialectical, in other words.

Through anecdotes, Ziffel defines the term "dialectic" for his companion Kalle. He explains how those slippery, unstable and irresponsible entities called ideas abuse each other, fight with knives and then sit down to dinner together, as if nothing happened; how Disorder is the inseparable companion of Order and how they cannot live with or without each other. Hegel called this ongoing process the dialectic, and, Ziffel says, "Like all great humorists, he advanced the term with dead seriousness."[6] Dry wit and irony abound in Ziffel's attribution of humor to Hegel. Above all, his line that, "one needs a sense of humor to appreciate Hegel's dialectics" confirms that Ziffel is joking.

Brecht critic Darko Suvin finds more than mockery of Hegel here, however. He contends that, "In a very noteworthy passage in Brecht's *Dialogues in Exile*, the interlocutors come to agree that Hegel's dialectical method is a great humorous world principle, because it is based on switching between different levels of understanding, just like humor or wit. Thus the dialectical Brechtian vision is a new link in the classical chain of wits, the bitter or smiling debunkers going back to Lucretius and Aristophanes, Rabelais and Cervantes, Fielding and Swift. . . . "[7] Brecht's humor may well be dialectical and materialist, insofar as his later satire underscores class conflicts almost as Karl Valentin's work did, and allows common people to mock those in authority and wage class war by comic means; but such comedy is more Marxian than Hegelian. Like Marx before him, Brecht (through Ziffel) senses that Hegel stood the dialectic on its head; and he finds humor in this Hegelian headstand.

## The Dialectic at a Standstill

The materialist dialectic is revealed "at a standstill" in Brecht's plays, according to Walter Benjamin in his essay "What Is Epic Theatre?"[8] Benjamin argues that the dialectic itself is the central character on Brecht's stage. When he compares Galy Gay, the docker who becomes an obedient soldier, to "an empty stage on which the contradictions of our society are acted out," he also calls Gay "the wise man who is the perfect stage for such a dialectic." (As noted already, Gay may not be so "wise"; even Benjamin admits the character is a man "who can't say no." In Brecht's later plays characters learn to say "no" to coercion and injustice, but volunteer Gay only says "yes"—not wise in wartime.)

Benjamin suggests that Brecht's dialectic is freed from movement in time. Interruptions and gestural acting allow it to "blast open the continuum of history," as historical materialism itself does, according to Benjamin's "Theses on the Philosophy of History."[9] By stepping out of character and employing stylized gestures (which are quotations in the sense that they can be removed from their usual context, and can be repeated), the Brechtian actor isolates a historical moment in the narrative. This isolation allows spectators and those on stage to see the tensions—class conflicts, historical conjunctions leading to revolution—at their leisure, as if time has stopped.

One of these lucidly comic moments occurs in *The Threepenny Opera* when Macheath is about to be hanged. The condemned gangster mocks the suspense of the scene by breaking out of character to announce that his class, the petty bourgeoisie, is vanishing. The ironic implication is that Macheath's vanishing class includes not only gangsters, but any bourgeois person who loses out to banks and corporations—institutions which profit from the labor of others far more efficiently and legally than do petty bourgeois or proletarian professionals. "What is the burgling of a bank compared with the founding of a bank? What is the murder of a man compared to the employment of a man?" Macheath asks.[10] The historical consciousness here is Brecht's, as Macheath steps out of character and "betrays" his class by criticizing it with a dialectical analysis of the situation. The moment allows the actor to share Brecht's consciousness of the historical obsolescence of his character. Mack's speech becomes a criticism of his own role in the play, and an acknowledgement of the dialectical process at a turning point: a point where Macheath's class is still alive, but its history is about to change or end.

The presence of this consciousness allows comic figures to function as political clowns, rather than merely as comic characters. Hanswurst and Valentin could acknowledge the "insufficiency" of their roles and those of others by breaking the illusionistic frame of a scene. Brecht's clowns acknowledge the insufficiency of the theatrical framework and the social system in which they play their roles. The illusions they dispel are political as well as aesthetic.

Galy Gay, told that he is about to be shot, denies not only his name, but also the reality of the scenery around him. "I'm not going to budge. I'll hold onto this grass, yes, even if it is fake. This must all stop, I insist! But why is no one here, if a man is to be butchered?"[11] The Valentin-like reference to fake grass is not terribly humorous in a context of imminent murder, and illusions are rarely broken this crudely in Brecht's scripts. Gay lets us see that the scenery, including the grass, is as likely to be destroyed as his own fixed identity.

This interruption of the situational frame, and others which are less obvious, reveal the dialectical relationships that Walter Benjamin saw in epic theatre. He notes these relationships in his "Studies for a Theory of Epic Theatre": " . . . that of the actor to the character represented, and vice versa; that of the attitude of the actor, as determined by the authority of the text, to the critical attitude of the audience, and vice versa; that of the specific action represented to the action implied in any theatrical representation."[12] The dialectic noted here allows for changing relations inside the theatre as well as in history. The changes in relations between audience and actor, and actor and scenic illusion, their demonstration of "insufficiency" also initiates the production of a new class consciousness, a consciousness of "insufficiencies" in society and class relations outside the theatre, that parallels the spectators' consciousness of the contradictions on stage. All this Louis Althusser elaborates on in his essay on Brecht.

## Althusser and "The Dialectic-in-the-Wings"

Many other figures besides Macheath embody social contradictions that can be seen as part of a comic dialectical process in Brecht's plays. But this dialectic is not propagated exclusively by the characters themselves or at the stage's center. Louis Althusser calls it a "dialectic-in-the-wings." In his reading of Brecht, subtitled "Notes Toward a Materialist Theatre," he submits that the dialectic begins on stage but continues in the consciousness of spectators, who complete it when they become actors in real life. Althusser suggests that in Brecht's plays the dialectic is "decentered":

> . . . No character consciously contains in himself the totality of the tragedy's conditions. For him, the total, transparent consciousness of self, the mirror of the whole drama is never anything but an image of the ideological consciousness, which does include the whole world in its own tragedy, save only that this world is merely the world of morals, politics and religion, in short, of myths and drugs. In this sense these plays are decentered precisely because they have no center,

because, although the illusion-wrapped, naive consciousness is his starting-point, Brecht refuses to make it that center of the world it would like to be. . . . The critical relation, which is a real production, cannot be thematized for itself: that is why no character is in himself 'the morality of history'—except when one of them comes down to the footlights, takes off his mask and, the play over, "draws the lessons" (but then he is only a spectator reflecting on it from the outside, or rather prolonging its movement: "We have done our best, now it is up to you.")[13]

The "illusion-wrapped, naive consciousness" and "myths and drugs" of consciousness which Althusser sees as the starting point for Brechtian characters could well be those of the naive clowns in Brecht's plays, although Althusser does not say so.

He sees "consciousness of self" as part of a classical affirmation of existing ideology which conveys an image of itself in the tragic hero. He summarizes Hegel's schema for such tragedy by saying that for Hegel, the hero's "destiny was consciousness of himself as of an enemy." Brecht, departing from Hegel here as elsewhere, creates characters who are insufficiently conscious of themselves and their situation; he encourages others, especially spectators, to see the insufficiency in a context invisible or ungraspable to the characters themselves. (This recalls the demonstration of "the insufficiency of all things, including ourselves," which Brecht attributed to Valentin.)

The spectators' consciousness may change, as they cease to identify with the play's characters and begin to see more in the scenes than the limited ideology known to the characters. This change in the consciousness of others is part of the "real production" achieved by Brechtian actors, according to Althusser. It should be noted that comic figures in the plays frequently behave like Epic Theatre spectators. Like Macheath at the gallows, they "remove a mask" or break out of their situational frame for a song or an aside before the play is over, and reflect on events "from the outside," as if they too are spectators. These clown-outsiders sometimes depart from stage and social conventions as freely as the spectators whom Althusser sees becoming actors in real life.

While Althusser's arguments do not locate optimism or a comic attitude in the decentered, dialectical process he describes, Brecht hints at the possibilities of comic dialectics in his *Appendices to the Short Organon*. There, he writes about turning dialectics into a source of enjoyment:

> The unexpectedness of logical progressive or zigzag development, the instability of every circumstance, the joke of contradiction and so forth; all these are ways of enjoying the liveliness of men, things and processes, and they heighten both our capacity for life and our pleasure in it.[14]

"The joke of contradiction" is a phrase one might expect to find among Ziffel's remarks on Hegel; but Brecht employs the phrase to elaborate on an earlier reference to dialectical materialism—Marx's philosophy and not Hegel's. He does not explain his reference to the "joke of contradiction" in any detail, but Terry Eagleton explains the term, in his book *Walter Benjamin*, by arguing that dialectical theory and irony are inseparable:

> Contradictions are a joke not because they are not often intolerable, but because without the dialectic which is, so to speak, the ironic wit of history, there could be no significant life at all. History, as it were, is comic in form. . . . For Marxism, history moves under the very sign of irony. . . . The only reason for being a Marxist is to get to the point where you can stop being one . . . in that feeble piece of wit . . . much of the Marxist project is surely summarized.[15]

Eagleton's equation of irony and Marxist comedy makes both sound innocuous, "feeble" or politely amusing at best. He elsewhere suggests that comedy (not necessarily Marxist comedy) is capable of far greater force than this, when he attributes to Rabelais' carnivalesque books the "crude cackling of an ambivalently destructive and liberating laughter."[16] He might have found this comedy in some of Brecht's creations too, such as the libidinal, earthy humor of Azdak in *The Caucasian Chalk Circle.*

Hans Mayer offers another interpretation of Brecht's "joke of contradiction," when he distinguishes Brecht's interest in comedy from Hegel's.[17] Mayer notes that Hegel preferred plays with characters "comical for themselves," not for spectators, while Brecht "was concerned most with the comical effect on the spectator. Joviality and jovial recognition. Recognition of contradiction." Here, too, the comic dialectic includes the spectator, necessarily, as actor and spectator become almost interchangeable in their shared consciousness of drama and history.

Brecht's emphasis on the joke of contradiction can also be seen as a Marxian sequel to his 1922 assessment of Karl Valentin's comedy; Valentin's humor, which "demonstrates the insufficiency of all things, including ourselves," yields to a dialectical materialist "joke of contradiction" with a punch line announcing that insufficiency (like Valentin's lensless eyeglasses) is better than nothing. Brecht sees this lack of completion everywhere, especially in the life of the ruling class and its army, which could not exist without subordinate classes and the labor of men like Galy Gay, Schweyk and Matti.

Dialectics, too, may prove insufficient, as Marx suggested when he wrote that the dialectic contains within itself "a simultaneous recognition of its negation, its inevitable destruction." This insufficiency leads to another, more comic one cited by Eagleton: that the only reason for being a Marxist is to stop being one. Many of Brecht's plays promote in spectators this perspective, which Valentin's persona and Galy Gay never have: to see insufficiency of things in the play, and in their own perception of the world's conflicts, which cannot be fully resolved or explained by dialectics.

Occasionally Brecht's characters find themselves at points where dialectical history and class struggle appear to end, and property ceases to be private. It is a brief, passing illusion of utopia, a comic moment such as one in which the landowner named Puntila becomes drunk and starts to see himself from the perspective of his employees. He tells his hired man, Matti:

> If it were up to me, I'd put all the receipts of the farm in a chest, and when any of the help needed something he'd just take what he wanted, because if not for him there wouldn't be anything in the chest. Am I right?[18]

Of course it is "up to him," but Puntila never remembers his philanthropic vows when he sobers up. Matti knows about his employer's unreliability, and closes the community chest before Puntila can open it, saying "You'd go broke before you knew it and the bank would take over." Puntila drunkenly replies:

> That's your opinion. I disagree. I'm practically a communist, and if I were a hired hand, I'd make life hell for Puntila.

The hired hand, Matti, prefers to keep the master in his place. This preservation of private property is a feat, Brecht implies, that Puntila could not accomplish without hired help. The estate owner who would become a communist cannot be both; banks would not allow it, nor will his servant Matti, which amounts to a curious alliance between servant and bankers. Together they forestall the end of dialectical history.

If the cessation of history is averted, it is a comic rescue. Matti, the deadpan comedian, obeys Puntila's orders although he knows they are ridiculous. He explains that if he only carried out orders that made sense, he would be fired for twiddling his thumbs. Not all of Brecht's subversive clowns follow orders, as will be seen later. Even Matti eventually quits his job, proving the insufficiency of all things, especially reigning authority, by saying "no" to it, denying it some of its power, and guaranteeing that it will remain incomplete.

# 4

# Wedekind's Circus World

*"I want to be taken as a serious writer, and they recognize me as a clown."*

—Frank Wedekind[1]

Association with Karl Valentin brought Brecht into a world of popular entertainment—fairground sideshows and Munich cabarets—as spectator and accompanist. Marx helped him see the political and economic background of the "refractory employee" Valentin often portrayed. Watching Frank Wedekind perform, singing his ballads and following his career, Brecht learned about another, less socially acceptable side of popular culture. Wedekind's satire against the Kaiser had earned him a prison sentence, and this notoriety, along with other mordant contributions to the journal *Simplicissimus*, his performances at the "Eleven Hangmen" cabaret in Munich and his plays about the sexually uninhibited Lulu undoubtedly appealed to Brecht. The satirist's writings against German militarism also found a disciple in Brecht. As a poet and playwright who had passed the limits of the law and social decorum, Wedekind provided a model of provocative artistry.

In an obituary tribute to Wedekind, Brecht praised him for singing "songs to guitar accompaniment in a brittle voice, slightly monotonous and quite untrained. . . . No singer ever gave me such a shock, such a thrill."[2] The "hard dry metallic voice" that he attributed to Wedekind may have inspired Brecht's own vocal style. Lion Feuchtwanger describes Brecht's cabaret singing in his novel *Success*, which includes one character based on Brecht: "With open affrontery in a horribly loud shrill voice [he] began to deliver his ballads

A *comic drawing of Frank Wedekind from the German journal* Der Jugend.

to the twanging of the banjo. . . . The verses were light and malicious, spiced with impudence, carelessly full of character."[3] Brecht shared Wedekind's attitude toward balladry, as well as his intonation; to both men refinement was unnecessary in the delivery of satiric songs. Their tinny voices suited the harsh lyricism of the anti-romantic stanzas describing a world of brutal sensuality and intolerant patriotism.

More than any vocal training or lack of it, Wedekind's talent for shocking and thrilling an audience reappeared, in new forms, in Brecht's theatrical activity. Two decades after Wedekind's arrest in Munich, Brecht discovered almost the same ethos of censorship and patriotism when he sang ballads there. In 1922, soldiers disrupted Brecht's recital of "The Legend of the Dead Soldier" (a song about a corpse sent back to the battlefront because the army needs more recruits) at Trude Hesterberg's "Wild Stage" cabaret. He had begun to sing the anti-war ballad in "a shrill, aggressive monotone," accompanying himself on banjo, according to Lisa Appaignanesi in her book *Cabaret*, "and by the end of the third stanza, the audience, several *Junkers* among them, was in an uproar. . . . Hesterberg was forced to let the curtain fall on the young writer."[4] Assuming that Brecht knew patriotic soldiers were in the audience, his Munich debut may have been a calculated endeavor to "shock" and "thrill" spectators. And it would not be the last time he would do so. At the Baden Baden premiere of *The Little Mahagonny* in 1927, Brecht equipped singers with tin whistles to counter audience catcalls, and there were some; by that date he evidentally knew enough to anticipate his audience's response, and armed his singers accordingly.

If Brecht wanted to be a provocateur in the theatre, he could have found no more prominent teacher in Germany than Wedekind. Wedekind's fights against censorship and his scandalous public reputation are ample evidence of this. His plays also contain provocative scenes; one in particular impressed Brecht. In his tribute to Wedekind, Brecht vividly recalled the playwright "before the curtain as ringmaster in a red tail coat, carrying whip and revolver." The prologue delivered by Wedekind as the Ringmaster in *Earth Spirit* welcomed the audience to a circus menagerie, not a stage play, and may have helped stir Brecht's own desire for a theatre that would rival sports events in spectacle and fun.

The prologue was neither an open-armed nor an unarmed welcome, however. Halfway through it, the Ringmaster fired a pistol into the audience, an act of aggression as "brazen" as anything else done by Wedekind (whom Brecht described as "brazen" no fewer than four times in his tribute). The Ringmaster, having invited ladies and gentlemen to "step right inside to look around the zoo," where "beast and man fight in the narrow cage," suddenly declares:

> The beasts are meekly fawning round my feet,
> When (*He fires into the audience*) my revolver thunderously I pull
> The creatures tremble round me. I stay cool—
> The man stays cool!—respectfully to greet you![5]

The audience at which he shoots may not remain quite as calm as the Ringmaster. His pistol shot represents an avant-garde aesthetic summed up by Schon later in *Earth Spirit*, when he tells Lulu "The more you shock people, the greater your professional standing." Brecht uses a variant of this lesson about professionalism in *The Threepenny Opera*. Peachum, the Beggar King, announces, "Today only artists give people the right sort of shock." Brecht does not necessarily agree—Peachum is hardly an author's surrogate in other respects. But Brecht constantly pursued new techniques to estrange the audience from its hardened, habitual response to events and, at the same time, curiously, his "professional standing" increased.

## Wedekind's Clowns

Frank Wedekind pursued a circus career years before he played the role of Ringmaster in *Earth Spirit*. Some of his best friends were clowns in Paris, and he worked for several circuses himself, first as a secretary, then as an audience "plant" who conversed with clowns in the ring. The Ringmaster's speech is not motivated by love of circus alone, however. It also reflects Wedekind's cynicism toward human behavior; at the same time that he praises uninhibited creatures, he suggests that men and women can be beasts in the worst sense. They often behave as if they are caged circus animals. If Lulu, who is compared to a snake in the prologue, is not exactly the serpent in Eden, her temptation and seduction of men bears out the analogy to a degree; and death frequently follows the carnal knowledge Lulu imparts to her lovers.

One source for Wedekind's Lulu was a Parisian pantomine about a clown-dancer of the same name. French critic Jonny Ebstein suggests that Wedekind saw the pantomime during his stay in Paris.[6] The pantomime, in which Lulu falls in love with Harlequin, could have inspired the German playwright to dress Lulu as another sort of clown—the French Pierrot—as she poses for a painter in the first scene of his play. Her pastoral pose (she holds a shepherd's crook) becomes ludicrous in retrospect, once her character is more fully disclosed. The woman is hardly a traditional Pierrot; the clown's usual comic role as a lazy, calculatedly stupid male servant, or (as interpreted by Deburau) as a sullen dreamer, is usurped by a languid, calculatedly irresistible temptress. Lulu entertains men with her sensual attractions instead of *comedia lazzi*. The clown outfit's satin texture intensifies her allure, and its loose fit allows her to escape Schwarz, the painter, when he lustfully chases her around his studio. She is a seductress disguised as a clown; or perhaps it would be more appropriate to say that in Wedekind's "sex tragedy" the clown has become a source of Eros and Thanatos rather than comedy. When Lulu's elderly husband, Goll, enters the studio, he finds the clown and the painter in a compromising situation, and dies of a heart attack from the shock.

Later, the lesbian Countess Geschwitz invites Lulu to dress up as a man, and points to the Pierrot painting as proof that Lulu can look masculine. Still later, the painting is hung in the room where Lulu works as a prostitute; Schigold thinks "it will make an excellent impression on our clientele." In both instances, the clown motif serves a seductive, sexual purpose in Wedekind's play. (It should be noted that clowns in the circus and on stage haven't always been asexual characters; Harpo and Chico Marx are quite libidinal clowns, for example. But Lulu's Pierrot represents a thoroughly sexual impulse.)

Gittleman notes in his book on Wedekind that sexual mores (or the absence of them) in *Earth Spirit* can be traced back to an 1887 essay on the circus, "Zirkusgendanken," in which the playwright "developed a morality of physical perfection apart from social standards of action."[7] "The body has its own morality," Wedekind writes about circus performers. He could have said the same about Lulu, in or out of her Pierrot costume.

Wedekind's *Earth Spirit* compares human sensuality to animal behavior in a way that Brecht emulates, with variation, in his earliest full-length play, *Baal*. The poet Baal is as sexually active as Lulu. In an essay on Brecht and Wedekind, Gittleman describes Brecht as "a male counterpart to Wedekind's Lulu: a representation of primal innocence and moral irresponsibility. [In both plays] mankind is reduced to the basic animal state."[8] (The central animal metaphors differ, however. While the Ringmaster compares Lulu to a snake, teamsters compare Baal to an elephant as he becomes overweight and mentally lethargic.)

For Lulu and Baal, art and sexuality are integrally related though not interdependent. Baal's career as poet and balladeer practically disappears in the wake of his sexual career, while Lulu's fame as a dancer increases, in part because of her sexual allure. Also, Baal as a poet among teamsters, and Lulu as an *artiste* new to high society, both become sideshow attractions; the world regards artists as freaks of nature—even if the "freak" is the beautiful Lulu. They do not fit into high or low society, though they pass through both. Baal's attempt to be a poet of the people—an entertainer of teamsters—reveals Brecht's own continuing interest in proletarian art at an early stage of his career.

As the correspondences between their plays attest, Brecht's early writing is indebted to Wedekind. Even some references to the circus in *Baal* appear to be derived from Ringmaster Wedekind's description of the menagerie. Baal is called "Mr. Circus" by one of the teamsters for whom he sings ballads. The name refers not to Baal's past life as a merry-go-round operator (which policemen mention later in the play), but to his definition of "circus." After Baal encourages teamsters to kiss his upper-class, would-be lover Emily and laugh at her, he says "That was a circus! The animal has to be coaxed out."[9] His reference to Emily as part of a "circus" becomes clearer when one first reads the Ringmaster's spiel in *Earth Spirit*, which criticizes "domestic beasts [who are] well-bred in what they feel," in contrast to a "wild and lovely animal." Emily is one of the well-bred, domestic beasts, and her interest in having a private affair with Baal differs substantially from his pursuit of uninhibited sensuality. He wants the "wildness" in her to be coaxed out to the extent that a stranger's coarse kiss would not repulse her; such freedom from domestication and "well-bred feelings" is the core of a circus act, as Baal sees it. Lulu would be the perfect lover for him.

Later in the play, Baal attempts to create "a divine spectacle" by conning villagers; he asks them to bring out their prize bulls by leading them to think that he will buy the best animal. The village priest discovers this plot to create a one-species parade, and admonishes Baal: "The world isn't your circus." He rightly suspects that the amoral poet would turn the entire world into a circus ring if he could. If Baal were Ringmaster, trees and bodies, as well as farm animals, would be part of his menagerie. Like any good ringmaster or sideshow barker, Baal is a confidence man in this scene; and he is far less interested in entertaining the working class than in pleasing himself. In Brecht's later plays, characters refer to circus life less frequently than Baal's associates do; but they, too, treat fellow humans as over-domesticated beasts and coax their wildness out in combat, in a boxing ring or in that jungle of cities known as Chicago.

# —5

# The Clown Who Says Yes

## 'The Baden Learning Play'

The satiric impulses Brecht shared with Valentin, Marx and Wedekind surfaced at Baden Baden in 1929, when Brecht's oratorio *The Baden Learning Play* started a riot at the summer music festival. The primary cause of the disturbance was a scene written for three clowns. One, a giant named Schmidt (hereafter "Smith" in translation), wears a huge wooden frame for a body, and is modeled after the macabre stilt-walking clowns in Valentin's cabaret shows. Mr. Smith also wears clown's whiteface, which he comically mistakes for a sign of his own ill-health. The other, smaller clowns persuade the giant that amputation will cure his discomfort. "Help" from his fellow men (or fellow clowns) can sometimes be quite harmful, according to this didactic interlude.

The sawing-off of the giant clown's arms, legs, ears and head evidently disturbed the Baden Baden audience more than it disturbed Mr. Smith. One critic reportedly fainted during the mock-amputations. Gerhardt Hauptmann, a playwright famous for his own socially conscious writing, walked out during the scene. Theo Lingen, the actor who portrayed Smith, reports that as the other two clowns "sawed my head off . . . it started the biggest riot I've ever seen in a theatre. Everything that wasn't nailed to the walls flew to the stage. My fellow-actors fled. . . . I peered through my gauze shirt at the raging and yelling audience."[1]

The clown scene, while provocative in itself, must have been especially startling at Baden Baden. In Karl Valentin's Munich cabaret, spectators might have been amused by the giant's grotesque misfortune. Even Valentin did not usually portray such cruelty on stage, although in a 1923 film co-authored by Brecht he decapitates a barbershop customer. By revising Valentin's cabaret clowning and relocating it at a music festival, Brecht brought low comedy and *grand guignol* into a world of "art" where it was unexpected and unwelcome.

The experiment could not have been wholly unexpected; Brecht had caused a small riot two years earlier at the same festival, when he and Kurt Weill presented *The Little Mahagonny*, a cycle of six songs. The songs were derived from jazz and what Brecht once described as "cheap music"—the cabaret and operetta."[2] The staging was also untraditional; it started with a pistol shot, the same act of aggression that Ringmaster Wedekind had used to start *Earth Spirit*. Lotte Lenya's recollection of the 1927 riot suggests that Brecht might have been expecting or even asking for the audience to protest his innovations. Lenya wrote that half the public at the "snooty Baden Baden festival . . . cheered madly, the other half booed and whistled—and Brecht had provided his cast with toy whistles so that they could whistle back."[3]

In 1928 Brecht and Weill won tremendous acclaim for *The Threepenny Opera*, a musical work in which Weill again based his score on "cheap music"—street ballads, tangos, and jazz. Perhaps the 1929 audience at Baden Baden expected another musical of the same genre; that would explain why Brecht was allowed to return to the festival despite the controversy two years earlier.

Instead of returning armed with whistles again in 1929, Brecht stood onstage himself throughout the performance, a ringmaster of sorts, in the company of his composer-collaborator, Paul Hindemith. Both men intervened constantly during the show, according to Brecht, who also says he "indicated where the clown should perform, and when the public received the film depicting dead people with noisy disapproval, the playwright directed the speaker to announce at the end: 'There will be one more showing of death scenes which have been received with such antagonism.' And the film was repeated."[4]

By Brecht's account, the clown scene was not the only part of *The Baden Learning Play* which disturbed spectators; the film and the playwright's own onstage direction contributed to the overall turmoil. (It is possible that Paul Hindemith stood on stage with Brecht to restrain him. They disagreed over the work, and Hindemith subsequently withdrew his music from the collaboration. In 1930 Hindemith wanted greater control over Brecht's work when *The Measures Taken* was being prepared for its premiere at the New Music Festival in Berlin. Instead of agreeing to Hindemith's role as policeman, Brecht and composer Hanns Eisler went elsewhere with their oratorio.)

Besides Valentin's and Wedekind's influence, *The Baden Learning Play* reflects Brecht's deep immersion in Marxism; his politics, too, could have disturbed the "snooty" audience, although it was during the clown scene that they protested most. Curiously, the clown scene is almost devoid of political references; Brecht had not yet learned to integrate dialectical materialism with the *vertrackte Dialektik* of comedy.

The clowning in the oratorio is a type that Brecht once termed "purely biological humor," to distinguish it from "socially based humor." His terms clarify the playwright's attitude toward clowning in general, and help place *The Baden Learning Play* in a larger perspective.

## Dividing Clowns in Half Yet Again

Anticipating the obsolescence of his own plays, Brecht wrote in 1950 that his folk comedy *Puntila*, about an unreliable estate owner and his hired man, would be needed to portray the history of the class struggle after the struggle had been won and estates like Puntila's no longer existed. Brecht's defense of his comedy as history includes an attack on "timeless humor."[5] Analyzing the need for "socially based humor" in his notes on the Berliner Ensemble production of *Puntila*, Brecht says that the play's actors "must derive their humor from the prevailing class situation, even if that means there are one or two classes whose members will not laugh." Presumably, upper-class spectators will not laugh any more than their representative, Puntila, when Matti demolishes his master's grandfather clock and gun cabinet to build a mountain out of billiard room furniture. Brecht imagines that Puntila himself "winces and his smile becomes forced" as his alcohol-inspired orders to build the mountain are carried out by Matti.

In the same notes, Brecht observes that "even in 'timeless humor' there is a social element—the clown sets out brimming with self-confidence and falls flat on his face—but it has become overlaid to the point where the clown's fall appears like something purely biological, something that is humorous to all people under all conditions."

Brecht's use of clowns in *The Baden Learning Play* might well qualify as "timeless humor," deserving of the pejorative connotations the author of *Puntila* attributed to this category. The scene in which Smith is sawed to pieces corresponds to no special "class situation." Lee Baxandall, who translated the play into English, suggests that "Smith is the proletariat, vast in potential power but victimized again and again until it is helpless;"[6] but the scene itself offers no references to social classes. Instead the fragment answers the question, "Does man help man?" in a manner as abstract and allegorical— or as "purely biological," to use Brecht's phrase—as the question itself. In the context of the play as a whole, the scene's grotesque comedy remains a departure, an allegorical digression, lacking the class-conscious dialogue that can be found elsewhere in the script, among the choral representatives of the masses, and the air pilots and mechanics.

Brecht himself later found fault with this play, writing that it "proved at the end to be unfinished: there is too much weight given to dying in relation to its small use value."[7] One of his first *lehrstücke* (learning plays), *The Baden Learning Play* remains an interesting document of Brecht's experimental attitude toward clowning. He attempts to combine photographs of human slaughter with religious-style choral statements on self-sacrifice for collective benefit, with grotesquely violent clowning. The components are not sufficiently integrated or complementary; nor are Brecht's themes always clearly developed. Still, the play marks a transition in Brecht's writing of clown scenes. It attempts to use clowning as a commentary on an age of widespread murder and suffering—something Brecht had done earlier in *A Man's a Man* and would do again with variation in later plays.

The seemingly antithetical elements of clowning and amputation in *The Baden Learning Play* have a correlative in Brecht's own life. It may be that the clown scene was derived from Brecht's memories of his medical work in World War I. The gruesome humor of his medical service during the war is retold by the Russian writer, Sergei Tretyakov, in a memoir about Brecht:

> If a doctor had said to me: "Brecht, amputate this leg! I would have replied: "As you order, Herr Staff Doctor!" If somebody had given the order: "Brecht, trepan!" then I would have cut open the skull and poked around in the brain. In my immediate vicinity I saw how men were being rapidly patched up in order to send them to the front as soon as possible.[8]

Like one of these medical patients, Brecht's giant is reduced to helplessness by the end of the scene, after the smaller clowns violently cut him up. The physically eccentric Smith, unhappy with things in general, is literally cut down by the other clowns, who conquer him in the guise of helping him.

At the same time, Smith consents to each installment of "help" given him; his ears, arms, legs and head are removed following his consent to the amputations. One translation of the 1929 work's title is *The Baden Play for Learning Acquiescence*. The theme of acquiescence or consent—withheld or granted—recurs in a number of Brecht's later *lehrstücke*, notably *The Yes Sayer* and *The Measures Taken*. In *The Baden Learning Play*'s early, inchoate version of later themes, consent to proffered help amounts to grimly comic self-destruction. The consequences of Smith's consent are painful, and yet he lives on to consent again and again. There is grotesque biological humor inherent in Smith's deteriorating physical condition, and more in his stupid agreement to, and endurance of, further violence against him.

Despite his losses, Smith learns almost nothing, and learns too slowly, as does Karl Valentin's slow-witted persona. If there is a "social element" in the allegorical scene, it is one Brecht developed with far greater clarity in later comedies, *Puntila*, *Schweyk* and *Arturo Ui*. The scene suggests that men will consent to their own destruction, even encourage others to destroy them, if they do not learn rapidly about the debilitating consequences of "help" in contemporary society. Placed among the play's other scenes, which concern fallen air pilots asked to sacrifice themselves for the collective good, the clown allegory acquires a more specific meaning; the destruction of one clown by others parallels the Learned Chorus's refusal to help the downed pilots. The Crowd (of audience representatives) in the play advises listeners "not to count upon help" until those in power can be deprived of their power to refuse help. Otherwise, "help" may be a euphemism for the exercise of force and denial of power to others, as it is in the clown scene. The pilots in *The Baden Learning Play*, somewhat like Galy Gay—the "man who can't say no" in *A Man's a Man*—are asked to consent to their own deaths. Gay even agrees to deliver his own funeral oration, which may be the ultimate form of suicidal consent. The affinity between these clowns can be traced back to Brecht's 1920 notes for *A Man's a Man*, where he decided the play was about citizen Joseph Galgei, who "fell into the hands of bad men who maltreated him . . . and the sole problem is how long he can stand it. They lop off his feet, chuck away his arm, saw a hole in his head. . . . Is he still Galgei?"[9] This early plan anticipates aspects of both plays.

Written a few years after *A Man's a Man*, *The Baden Learning Play* also shows a clown who cannot say "no," even when it means consenting to his own destruction. The difference between Gay and Smith is that the latter suffers physically for his consent. Gay is never dismembered or wounded, only confused and frightened, as he loses his name and agrees to live the life of Jeriah Jip. He survives battle like a cartoon or silent film comedy hero, invincible.

In *The Baden Learning Play*, consent leads to torture. Submission to others is far from beneficial to Smith, whereas it strengthens Gay in the end. Smith is the last of Brecht's clowns to consent naively to self-destruction. As Brecht found himself resisting Nazi oppression in the 1930s, his comic characters followed suit. If characters in later plays, like the Young Comrade in *The Measures Taken*, also agree to sacrifice themselves, at least they do so—unlike Smith—with full knowledge of the consequences.

In later plays, Brecht's comic characters withhold their consent from those in power, in order to survive; their naiveté and humor become life-enhancing, defensive apparatuses. Matti, Schweyk and Azdak are clowns who understand all the troubling aspects of power that Smith did not want to hear. Brecht's "socially based humor" in the later plays surfaces in characters' clownish wit, the "slave language" with which they resist and circumvent oppression. Low comedy and clowning are more fully integrated in these later plays, too. Instead of placing a clown act in the middle of an oratorio, Brecht bestows clownish traits on everyday, plebian characters: a refugee, a hired laborer, a scribe, men not unlike the exiled playwright himself.

# —6——
# Heiner Müller's 'Heart Play'

In the preface to his translation of Heiner Müller's *Herzstück* (*Heart Play*), Carl Weber says that the work can't but remind the reader of Brecht's *Clownspiel* (*Clownplay*) . . . in which a Mr. Schmidt—step by step—is amputated by two other clowns, until finally his head is taken off, and they leave him dying."[1] Müller's brief, eighteen-line *Heart Play* for two actors also portrays grotesquely comic surgery; a musician consents to having his heart removed with a small knife. Weber, a stage director as well as translator, suggests that the terse dialogue in Müller's playlet "implies the broad gestures clowns employ when they perform in the circus ring."

*Heart Play* was first performed outdoors in Bochum, West Germany, during a 1981 festival of political theatre. Initially the play looks more like a musical concert than a clown show, as the violinist and pianist play a duet. The music is disrupted by a sort of comic guerrilla theatre, clowning similar to that Brecht used to interrupt his oratorio at Baden Baden. The violinist, emotionally moved by the piano music, asks to lay his heart at the feet of his partner. The pianist consents, and then helps his friend remove the heart with a pocket knife. The heart turns out to be a brick. "But it throbs only for you," says the violinist to console the disappointed pianist.

The grim, violent humor of this scenario should not surprise spectators who know Müller's other plays. (It may even amuse them.) Müller once told the German journal, *Der Spiegel*, "If you translate an idea into an image, either the image will go askew or the idea will be exploded. I prefer the explosion."[2] *Heart Play* contains a few tiny explosions of conventional imagery in its violent clowning. The work is a small *jeu* by one of East Germany's most highly regarded stage writers. Müller has been praised as the heir of Brecht in East German theatre. Some of his other plays are direct responses to, or reactions against, plays by Brecht. In *Mauser*, for example, he reconsiders the questions of revolutionary collective action which Brecht investigated in *The Measures Taken*. Its form, which requires that a chorus divide among its members the lines of a few characters, extends Brecht's own experiments with the huge Control Chorus in *The Measures Taken*, in which a workers' choir of 400 sing lyrics concerned with collective agitation.

In recent years, Müller's plays have departed substantially from Brecht's, particularly in form. He shares Brecht's interest in socialism and revolution, but he also writes about the failings of socialism, which have become more evident in Eastern Europe since Brecht's death in 1956. His writing has attempted to synthesize aspects of Artaud's ideas about Theatre of Cruelty with the Brechtian and post-Brechtian political consciousness. A turn toward surreal, visceral and highly visual imagery reflects introspection—Müller's exploration of his own dreams, and readings of history and literature, including Brecht's plays. His poetic, encoded language may also be, to a degree, an effort to evade political censors, although Müller has not admitted as much.

## Another Brick in the Wall

Little of his own past can be gleaned from a reading of *Heart Play*. Its dialogue and imagery are simple. The resonance (or explosion?) of that imagery gives it additional impact. The first musician (called "One") who wants to lay his heart at the feet of the other ("Two") is presumably moved to this homage by the Romantic music they are playing. The clichéd conceit of a heart being transported by great art is mocked—exploded if you will—by Müller, as he presents the conceit quite literally. Both men agree that One's heart should be removed. After some difficulty operating on the heart, it comes out. (Similar comic heart surgery occurs in Weiss's clown play, *Mockinpott*, discussed later.) The action here might be as comically grotesque as the amputation of Smith in Brecht's play; and yet the mutually agreed-upon cutting out of a heart with a pocket knife is so improbable that it may seem wholly comic and patently artificial in performance.

Another surprise follows, when the heart turns out to be a brick. No explanation is offered for this anatomical wonder, and it should provoke questions as well as amusement from spectators. The idea that a musician would have a heart of stone also suggests the death of Romanticism and private feelings. A man-made heart of stone replaces flesh and blood in an age of mass-produced, mass-manipulated feelings and artificial hearts.

For a German audience, and any audience familiar with Müller's life in East Berlin, the brick is especially significant. Brick walls have special meaning in Müller's imagistic landscape. He told *Der Spiegel* that his country was important to him "because all the dividing lines of our world go through this country. That's the true state of the world and it has become quite 'concrete' in the Berlin Wall." "It's better to have millions of little walls than one or two big walls," he declared in another interview, in *Semiotexte*.[3] Perhaps the transformation of a musician's heart into a brick is an optimistic sign that little walls have started to grow inside people. But the larger, external walls remain. It is questionable whether things will improve if German artists internalize the Berlin wall and the conflicts it represents. As artists grow more hardened to the world, Müller implies, they may build such walls in themselves, and develop hearts as unfeeling and strong as bricks when political contradictions threaten to tear them apart.

If one knew nothing about the author of *Heart Play*, it would be tempting to regard his scenario as a variation on an ancient ritual: playwright and audience look at the heart of a man the way priests once examined animal organs for auguries of the future. The scene shares Artaud's fascination with grotesque violence and ritual. The French theorist and director particularly admired the scene in Ford's *'Tis Pity She's a Whore* in which a brother triumphantly displays the bloody heart he has cut out of his sister. (Artaud in "The Theatre and the Plague": "You want, he [Giovanni] seems to say, my love's flesh and blood. Very well, I will throw this love in your face and shower you with its blood—for you are incapable of rising to its height! And he kills his beloved and tears out her heart as if to feast upon it in the middle of a banquet. . . . ")[4] *Heart Play* comically echoes Artaud's interest in what he called Theatre of Cruelty, as well as Brecht's experiment with violent clowns. Synthesizing these diverse attitudes with his own, Müller's play becomes an evocative, poetic commentary on art in a cold war—and cold-hearted—environment.

# 7

# The Clown Who Says No

## Brecht's 'Schweyk' and 'Conversations in Exile'

> *"I have no backbone for being exterminated. There is only one way to fight authority . . . outlive it."*
> —Bertolt Brecht[1]

In an October 1921 diary entry, Brecht describes Charlie Chaplin in terms that fit several of his own characters. Referring to Chaplin's role in the film *The Face on the Bar Room Floor*, he writes:

> Chaplin's face is always impassive, as though waxed over, a single expressive twitch rips it apart, very simple, strong, worried. A pallid clown's face complete with thick moustache, long artist's hair and a clown's tricks; he messes up his coat, sits on his palette, gives an agonized lurch, tackles a portrait by—of all things—elaborating the backside.[2]

The pallid, impassive clown's face, the face of a deadpan comedian that Brecht saw on Chaplin appears on Brecht's own characters, too. Passivity is forced upon them by political conditions. Their clown faces are socially determined—as was Chaplin's. However, one aspect of their deadpan humor differs markedly from that of the Little Tramp; Brecht's impassive clowns can talk, although they often prefer not to. The cause of their silence is best illustrated by one of Brecht's Herr Keuner anecdotes.

Herr Keuner, a stoic figure of Brecht's own invention, tells the story of a man whose impassive behavior is the prototype of the clown who says "no" to authority. In Keuner's tale, an underground resistance member is captured and forced to serve a government agent. Asked by his captor whether he will serve, the prisoner says nothing; for years he silently works as a slave. When the government agent dies, the prisoner finally answers him: "No." In the anecdote, as in some of Brecht's stage satires, refusal to serve authority occurs slowly. So much time may elapse between the question "Will you serve?" and the negative answer that silence is mistaken for consent. When the answer comes, it is as unexpected as the twitch that rips apart Chaplin's pallid face. Brecht's characters comically resist that twitch that would betray their calm exterior, until they decide to betray it. The chauffeur Matti appears to obey every order that Puntila gives him, whether the master is drunk or sober. Schweyk, the legendary "good soldier," seems to comply with Nazi regulations in occupied Czechoslovakia, even when that means marching toward his own death at Stalingrad. Ziffel and Kalle, exiles in Finland who fear the Nazis will follow them everywhere, drink beer and toast socialism quietly, so as not to attract attention.

Brecht created these comic characters during his years of flight from the Nazis and his exile; they reflect a preoccupation with resistance to fascism at a time when no form of resistance to it was succeeding. Assassination attempts on Hitler had failed, as noted in the opening lines of *Schweyk in the Second World War*. It is doubtful that Brecht expected his satires of Nazi authority to accomplish what bombs could not, but he persisted in writing anti-fascist satire throughout World War II. In *Puntila, Schweyk in the Second World War* and *Conversations in Exile* he showed pallid-faced clowns surviving oppressors by bluffing them, confusing them and refusing to serve them. (The last of these works was adapted by British playwright Howard Brenton; his version is quoted later.)

In these works, a "pallid clown's" wit places distance between him and his antagonist; humor in various deadpan or understated forms allows the comedian to separate himself from his enemy. Silences, wisecracks, innuendoes and "slave language" become distancing devices which function as the alienation effects Brecht sought in his productions; they help reduce character and audience identification with a leader or source of authority.

The distance established is both aesthetic and ideological. Without humor, the characters' assent to unjust authority would be complete. Matti, Schweyk and Kalle, "pallid clowns" all, look like cooperative citizens and do what they are told when near those who rule. But a small part of their consent is withheld. Their form of insubordination could pass for idiocy, if tested in court. Schweyk claims several times that he is a certified idiot, in order to excuse his suspicious remarks about Nazism. The traditional immunity once granted to the court jester is here adapted for use by an enemy of the state.

## "I Was Only Following Orders"

Schweyk pleads insanity to defend himself, but perhaps the best defense open to these clown characters is the claim that they are simply following orders.

The argument made famous by war criminals at Nuremberg after World War II was anticipated by Brecht, and before him by stage director Erwin Piscator; both saw that the demand for total obedience could cause the downfall of authority. After his 1928 collaboration with Brecht on an adaptation of Jaroslav Hasek's novel *The Adventures of the Good Soldier Schweyk*, Piscator wrote:

> The very existence of such a person [Schweyk] sufficed to demolish any concept of authority in Church, State, Army. Schweyk does not achieve results by attacking or rejecting existing authorities, but—on the contrary—by accepting all authority and accepting it with absolute consistency.
>
> This was Schweyk's significance: he was not just a clown whose antics ultimately affirm the state of things, but a grand skeptic whose rigid, untiring affirmation of reality reduces reality to a nullity . . . a deeply asocial element.[3]

Schweyk simultaneously affirms and undermines authority by praising it in all its contradictory and self-destructive forms, even when Hitler's orders clearly endanger Schweyk's own life and end the lives of compatriots. His "praise" could just as easily be a parody of official government statements as a tribute to them. Here the clown who said "yes" in earlier plays (*A Man's a Man*, *The Baden Learning Play*) appears to be back, consenting as usual; but government officials find his consent ambivalent, rightly suspecting it to be subversive.

In both Piscator's 1928 version of the Hasek novel and Brecht's play of 1943, Schweyk's submission to military authorities leads the cheerful, optimistic and obedient soldier to a slaughter. He himself is not killed in either version, but they imply that armies of men like him cannot survive. At the same time, Schweyk, like Matti, Kalle, Ziffel—and Brecht—is above all a survivor. The thing he does well is survive, and he knows it. "Don't ask too much of yourself," he says in Brecht's play. "It's quite a job just to be around nowadays. Keeps you so busy staying alive, you haven't time for anything else."[4] The soldier's ability to survive, not his probable death near Stalingrad, contributes most to Hitler's eventual defeat, from Brecht's satiric perspective. In his work journal (May 26, 1943) Brecht notes:

> In no event must Schweyk be made into a sly, underhanded saboteur. He is merely the opportunist of what minute opportunities are left to him. . . . His wisdom is subversive. His indestructibility makes him the inexhaustible object of abuse, and at the same time the fruitful soil of liberation.[5]

Survival as a form of subversive wisdom is discussed further in *Conversations in Exile*, when Ziffel tells Kalle, his fellow refugee from Nazi Germany, "I believe in the heroism of survival. In times like this cowardice itself can be heroic—if it keeps you alive."[6] Kalle replies, "You must give the great men a lot of trouble." Schweyk too gives the great men—Hitler and his cohorts—a lot of trouble. They depend on little men like Schweyk and Ziffel to fight their war, build their weapons and obey orders.

"How do things stand in Europe with the Little Man? Will he work hard and long when one's paying?" Brecht's Hitler asks Goring. If Schweyk is the Little Man, the answer should be "no," but Goring evades the question by suggesting that his Labor Service will force the Little Man to work.

The Little Man's cowardice, feigned idiocy and exploitation of "what minute opportunities are left" lead to comic departures from the Great Man's plan. The plan requires total order, total submission and self-sacrifice by both armies. Remnants of individuality and an instinct for survival disrupt the plan. While Brecht's earlier writings (*A Man's a Man*, for example) examine the extinction of the individual in an age of collectives and mass movements and hint that the change represents social progress, some of his later plays present individualism as a welcome—if comically eccentric—rejection of fascism. Brecht never writes what could be called paeans to individualism, but he grows less sanguine about progress through collectivity. He admits that the survival of the individual is mildly heroic at times, even as he laments that people have to be heroic.

## Brecht Reduced to Flippant Remarks

It would have been naive on Brecht's part, and on the parts of his critics, to assume that satire could defeat fascism. Even when his characters assert their individuality and gain some comic distance from their oppressors, Brecht's plays remain compensatory fantasies. And on top of that, they were not staged during the war years. Brecht acknowledged the insubstantiality of his humor on several occasions. In the midst of the comic dialogue in *Conversations in Exile*, Ziffel says that the entire world seems to be suffering convulsions which no one understands. "Discussing it you are reduced to flippant remarks."[7] A more personal admission of his own "flippancy" and other limitations surfaces in Brecht's notebook entry from September 16, 1940, during the time he was completing *Puntila* in Finland:

> *Puntila* concerns me hardly at all; the war concerns me utterly. About *Puntila* I can write almost anything, about the war nothing. And I don't mean just 'may,' I really mean 'can.' It is interesting how far literature, as a practical activity, is removed from the centers of all-decisive events.[8]

Given this belief in literature's impracticality, why did he persist in writing satire? One could say (as Brecht did in his *Short Organon*), "It is the superfluous for which we live," and which we find in the pleasures of art.

The plays also reflect Brecht's sense of removal "from the centers of all-decisive events" as they focus on the removal of other "little men" from centers of power; the characters, like their creator, find themselves failing in individual efforts to influence or avert the course of history. "Little men" acknowledge their distance from the policies conducted by "great men" like Hitler. This distance is desirable, in that it separates oppressors from oppressed. Brecht was delineating this separation through public political statements in the 1940s, during the same period he wrote the plays. In August 1943, he met with Thomas and Heinrich Mann, Lion Feuchtwanger and other exiled German writers to compose a statement about the German people and their relationship to Hitler. The statement was disputed, and repudiated by Thomas Mann, but at least a fragment of it repeats the argument of Brecht's theatre writings:

> [We welcome] the manifesto of the German prisoners of war and emigrants in the Soviet Union calling upon the German People to force its oppressors to unconditional surrender and fight for a strong democracy in Germany. We also consider it necessary to make a sharp distinction between the Hitler regime and its allied elements on the one hand, and the German people on the other.[9]

The distinction between Hitler's regime and the German people was not one that everyone made at the time. The American FBI, for example, followed Brecht around the United States during these years, assuming that he might be an agent, either for the German government or the Soviets. The fact that Brecht allied himself with "the German people" against Hitler was reiterated by him at the House Un-American Activities Committee hearings, when he admitted he had advocated the overthrow of a government—Hitler's, not America's. Brecht was rarely this explicit an advocate in his playwriting, though some direct opposition to Hitler surfaces in *Arturo Ui*.

## Schweyk as Saboteur

It is curious that Brecht's notes deny that Schweyk is a saboteur; the good soldier commits industrial sabotage of Nazi operations at least once. When Schweyk confuses a guard about the number on a boxcar containing machine guns so that the guns will end up in Bavaria instead of Stalingrad, his comic distraction tactics are conscious sabotage, whatever Brecht says in his notes. It is only after Schweyk says, "It's lucky for us that we're here with a heavy armed guard watching us to keep us from committing sabotage and getting shot," admitting the danger of the situation, that he commits the sabotage.[10]

"It's not the way you think, he doesn't commit sabotage and curse Hitler," says Schweyk when describing someone else as a "genuine Czech."[11] He, too, is a "genuine Czech," not a daring, death-defying member of the resistance, but an ordinary (if slightly idiotic) person who tries to survive Nazi occupation of his homeland without completely losing his freedom and sense of self. Schweyk's tenure as a saboteur is short-lived in the play; a later scene reveals that he has been fired from the freight station position on the grounds (again) that he is a certified idiot. Brecht makes the time Schweyk spends there short because he is not writing a play about industrial sabotage or its perpetrators. He is not so much a fantasist as to suggest that Schweyk's comic sabotage, accomplished with the verbal adeptness of a con artist or vaudevillian, would fool armed guards for long. "Flippant remarks" and idiocy (real or feigned), are not enough to stop an army's shipment of guns. By demonstrating this limit to Schweyk's "subversive" wisdom, Brecht also acknowledges the limits of his own, would-be subversive humor. A clown or playwright can say "no" to authority, but the refusal of totalitarian rule through irony and humor is more realistic as a strategy to help one outlive authority than to destroy it.

## Meanwhile at a Finnish Train Station

After a train brought Lenin to the Finland Station in 1917, he was able to lead the Russian Revolution in person, in Petrograd, his forced exile at an end. The men who wait at a Finnish train station in Brecht's *Conversations in Exile* are far less likely to start a revolution. The two refugees fleeing Hitler's army converse, between drinks, about political issues. Their discussion is filled with hesitations and ironic statements which camouflage the arguments. Neither Kalle the proletarian Communist, nor Ziffel the intellectual and physicist, asserts much more than the fact that he is alive; Brecht underscores this by using a line from a P.G. Wodehouse novel to preface the dialogues:

> He knew that he was still alive.
> More he could not say.

Kalle has survived life in a concentration camp, and his speech is particularly guarded. Both men know that their opposition to fascism and their advocacy of socialism could result in their arrest if they were to be overheard by the wrong eavesdropper, or if they themselves were to converse with a government agent. As they talk, two German army divisions are driving across the country, and the exiles have not yet obtained visas with which to exit. If the dialogue (not originally intended for production) were to be staged, it would be most effective if spoken in stage whispers at times, to dramatize the men's need for secrecy.

Much of Brecht's *Schweyk* play is set in a bar, the Flagon. One of the Czech citizens' last refuges from militarized society, even the Flagon is visited by Nazis, however. The customers have to guard their words, and they cannot "have fun," as one of the regulars complains early in the play. In staging *Conversations in Exile* a similar setting of beer tables will allow the dialogue between Kalle and Ziffel to seem as casual as their beer drinking—except that their libations are accompanied by serious, comically subversive discussions of the state, militarism and resistance to fascism. Fun becomes synonymous with subversion. The same situation occurs briefly in *Schweyk*, when customers dance to drive the S.S. men out of the Flagon and regain some privacy from the occupying forces.

"You can have any opinion you want . . it's true everywhere," says Kalle before adding, "You can have any opinion you want in Germany: the Gestapo will call, but you're free to have the opinion. What you can't do with an opinion, anywhere, is express it."[12] Even in a neutral country like Switzerland, advocacy of resistance to Nazism would be suppressed, Kalle claims; the Swiss would say that anti-Nazi statements endanger their freedom by provoking the Nazis to counter-attack. (Today this freedom can be obtained in a democratic country like America by anyone rich enough to buy a newspaper company; that is true freedom of the press, as the press critic A.J. Liebling once remarked.)

The exiles in Brecht's dialogue toast socialism with caution. They speak for posterity; they are conscious that someone else (a theatre audience or police officer) might overhear their words and repeat them later. One curious exchange between Kalle and Ziffel reveals just how far their subtle, private jokes against the German army are removed from the public circus satire of Durov. In a discussion of humor, the two men agree that jokes failed to stop the advance of the Nazis into Denmark. The Danes had been neutral in World War I and prospered by selling pig meat to both sides. They thought that Germany would not invade them in the Second World War, because war would interfere with Denmark's sale of pigs to Europe. The Danes must have been joking about the importance of their pigs, but they "were democrats and insisted everyone had the right to make a joke"—as if the democracy inherent in universal access to humor would protect them against fascism. "Unfortunately," says Kalle, "their jokes are largely puns about pigs and lost on the Germans. Now the Danes get only paper receipts [no laughter or cash] for their pigs." Durov and his pig had at least won a court case against the Kaiser, even if they had not succeeded in ending military respect for the helmeted emperor.

Humor may not be the best defense against Nazism; but Kalle and Ziffel agree that survival is a form of heroism, and they keep their senses of humor alive with their other senses. Ziffel observes that, "To live in a country without humor is unbearable. But it is also unbearable to live in a country where one needs humor." In *Galileo*, Brecht's physicist speaks a variant of these lines when he calls the country that needs a hero an "unhappy nation." Heroism, like humor, is most necessary in bad times. The humor of such wits as Kalle, Ziffel and Brecht will not defeat fascism by itself, but its survival, like that of the exiles, appears to trouble the fascist state. The democratic impulse behind their insistence on "the right to make a joke" preserves at least a token of what the barbarians would destroy, even if it does not defeat them.

# —8—
# Waiting for Puntila
## Brecht Against Beckett

*"[In Poland] we do [Brecht] when we want Fantasy.
When we want Realism, we do* Waiting for Godot.*"*
—Jan Kott[1]

Hans Mayer once noted that *Conversations in Exile* and *Puntila* represent Brecht's counter-argument to *Waiting for Godot*.[2] Since Brecht wrote the plays before Beckett wrote *Godot*, the earlier works cannot be a conscious response to Beckett. Brecht was in fact contemplating such a response in 1953, when he prepared preliminary notes for a counterplay to *Godot*. The substance of his response, and the nature of the project itself, can only be guessed; it was never completed. But it is possible that Brecht wanted to defend his own innovative concept of clowning against Beckett's.

After his various efforts to redefine the stage clown in political terms and to invest comic characters with a capacity to resist illegitimate authority, Brecht saw Beckett's play as a step back; the clowns in *Waiting for Godot* were once again representative of ineptitude and inaction. The play's innovative form located clowning in an abstract setting, "a country road" removed from all recognizable society, and employed abstract dialogue. It might be called metaphysical vaudeville. This *Umfunktionierung*, or reutilization, of comic tradition was far different from Brecht's; where Brecht had endeavored to politicize clowning by setting it in the midst of social struggles, Beckett removed it almost entirely from society.

Beckett's abstraction is precisely what Brecht wanted to challenge in his counterplay, if his 1953 notes are any indication. In Brecht's adaptation, he intended to give Beckett's characters specific social backgrounds, transforming the history-less tramps into men with a past. According to Hans Mayer's essay "Dogs, Beckett, Brecht," the adaptation would have moved toward greater "social concreteness. The sham abstraction of the clowns in Beckett's play displeased the Marxist dramaturg Brecht."[3] Brecht's annotations indicate that he would have turned Vladimir into an intellectual; Estragon into a proletarian; Lucky, a fool or policeman; and Pozzo, an estate owner.

Mayer further suggests that if Brecht had written the new work, its "reutilization (Umfunktionierung) of Beckett would not have produced anything new for Brecht, merely a repetition of Herr Puntila and Conversations of Refugees [Exiles]." Mayer does not belabor his speculation, and it can stand elaboration.

Puntila and His Servant Matti can be read as Brecht's counterplay to Waiting for Godot, even though he wrote it a decade before he read Beckett. The form of Beckett's play is more daring than Brecht's; the episodic structure of Puntila seems old-fashioned when compared to the virtually plotless comic dialogue Beckett sets on stage. And Beckett's rich Irish wit allows for more subtle humor than Brecht's almost mathematical plotting of ironies. Still, in purely schematic terms, Puntila does foreshadow Waiting for Godot. The play depicts a chauffeur, Matti, constantly awaiting the arrival and sobering up of his employer, Puntila. Puntila, unlike Godot, does arrive occasionally, but his drunken promises are no more reliable than those attributed to Godot by Beckett's tramps.

Few playwrights in our century have differed more in their politics than Brecht and Beckett. They share some common sources however. Both were influenced by Chaplin's films. The tramps in Godot resemble clowns in their slapstick pratfalls, hat tricks and use of the Swiss clown Grock's famous question "Why?" ("Pourquoi?" in the French of Beckett and Grock). They also walk with the stiff, short steps of Chaplin's Little Tramp as they await Godot on a nondescript country road. The two tramps seem resigned to their static situation; they sometimes respond to the boredom of waiting with gallows humor, as if expecting to meet death instead of Monsieur Godot. Instead of stasis and grim humor, on the other hand, Brecht's Puntila emphasizes comic possibilities for change and improvement. Matti is subjected to the drunken whims of a millionaire, much as the Little Tramp in Chaplin's City Lights (1931) is; but Matti knows Puntila's habits well enough to anticipate when his employer's mood will change for the better, however briefly. The chauffeur is able to predict the future in that sense, and act accordingly. A pallid-faced clown, Matti plays straight-man to his master's drunken antics. He is a subversive clown, his deadpan behavior encouraging the landowner to make a fool of himself. In this play and others by Brecht, a deadpan clown in working-class clothes undermines authority while seeming to cooperate with it, or, on other occasions, pretending not to comprehend it.

Beckett's characters have been described as "stoic" comedians by Hugh Kenner. The phrase suggests they share the fatalism of Greek philosophers, although Kenner initially defines the phrase without reference to the Greeks. For him, the stoic is "one who considers, with neither panic nor indifference, that the field of possibilities available to him is . . . closed."[4] For Brecht's clowns, the field remains open, even if they have to keep it open themselves. Matti is never far from walking out on Puntila, and for this reason, among others, he cannot be called stoic. Still, he conceals his feelings from Puntila (and from the master's daughter, too), and for this he might be called a stolid comedian if not a stoic.

While Matti conceals emotions and thoughts in conversations with his employer, the tramps in *Waiting for Godot* have no need to feign ignorance. They really *don't* know much about their situation, and cannot foresee any change with certainty; their ignorance and impotence become sources of self-deprecating humor.

The two types of clowns here represent more than different forms of comedy; they reflect distinct contemporary attitudes toward historical consciousness and social change as well.

## Nothing Immoral or Blasphemous

In her book *The Fool: His Social and Literary History*, Enid Welsford argues for an ahistorical function on the part of fools and clowns:

> There is nothing essentially immoral or blasphemous or rebellious about clownage. On the contrary, it may easily act as a social preservative by providing a corrective to the pretentious vanity of officialdom, a safety-valve for unruliness, a wholesome nourishment to the sense of secret spiritual independence of that which would otherwise be the intolerable tyranny of circumstance. In the Middle Ages professional and amateur fools frequently served all these purposes. . . . Clowns serve some of the same purposes today. It cannot, of course, be denied that fools and clowns have at times been made to serve political ends, but that in no way affects the essential nature of clownage.[5]

On the contrary, the essential nature of clownage is affected in a major way by writers who consciously alter its purpose and make it serve "political" ends, as have Brecht, Mayakovsky, Weiss, Boal, Fo, Griffiths and others.

Welsford's history of clowning ends with references to Chaplin. Brecht and Beckett's different responses to Chaplin's comedy is one place to begin a revised history of the subject. As evinced by the short, stiff strides and bowler hats of the tramps in *Godot*, Beckett borrows primarily from Chaplin's physical, slapstick style of behavior.* Brecht, in the scenes he wrote for Matti

*See Appendix, p. 69.

and Puntila, elaborates the social relationship that Chaplin developed between the tramp and a wealthy drunkard in his film *City Lights*. Both the
film and Brecht's play satirize a man of wealth who has within him a generous
social conscience inhibited by sobriety and property.

While Beckett derives aspects of ahistorical, biological humor from
Chaplin's comedy, Brecht explores the historical and class-related aspects of
one Chaplin plot. The clowns in *Waiting for Godot*, who agree that they
are "incapable of keeping silent," speak, as French playwright Jacques
Audiberti noted in 1953, "like Charlie Chaplin would have spoken, not as
the Count of Limelight [a "talky" film], but when he had nothing to say."[6]
Their inexhaustible banter is a verbal equivalent of the Little Tramp's
resilience, his ability to bounce back after a pratfall. But if this is so, the speech
of the tramps in *Godot* serves primarily to affirm its own possibility. The
tramps have, to paraphrase their creator's own *Three Dialogues*, nothing to
express, only the obligation to express it.

Matti offers a counter-example to the verbosity of Beckett's clowns; while
they know nothing for certain and say a great deal, Matti knows more about
his situation than he is free to say, if he wants to keep his job. The boss's
daughter Eva suspects as much when she tells Matti, "I never know when
you're making fun of me and laughing behind my back. With you I can never
be sure."[7] Matti's temperament is the most unpredictable one at Puntila
Farms, also the one freest from the ties of property and fealty. His sudden
departure, like Godot's arrival, is the event pending throughout the play. The
chauffeur is a clown who has nothing to lose but his reference letter, and
this freedom makes him potentially more subversive than Puntila ever dreams,
more of a stolid comedian than Eva ever realizes.

## The Idle Class

In the first scene of Brecht's play, Matti informs his master, "I've been sitting
in the car for two days, waiting for you." The chauffeur knows exactly whom
he awaits, unlike Vladimir and Estragon; and yet Matti, too, must bide his
time, or waste it, conversing with Puntila and his daughter, unable to leave
them until given permission—or until he is fired or quits his job. While he
seems prepared to quit in the opening scene, like many of Beckett's characters,
it takes him a long time (eleven more scenes) to do so. (Beckett's Pozzo could
be speaking for the chauffeur when he says, "I don't seem to be able to
depart.")

Before he finally departs, Matti agrees to help Puntila destroy the furniture in the family library. This disregard for private property is as close
as Matti comes to vandalism, and then it is only at his master's request. Yet
the master's repeated references to Matti as a subversive are not without foun-

dation. When Puntila vows to give up liquor, he celebrates the vow with a few last drinks. Without being asked, Matti brings in an empty glass and eases the landlord into his drunken spree. This over-efficiency on Matti's part could be loyal anticipation of his master's every need; but it is also a temptation the boss cannot resist. It is no accident that Brecht has Puntila accuse his hired man of subversion just as Matti arrives with the empty glass.

Matti has no need to mock Puntila behind his back; he can mock him to his face simply by serving the employer without question. At one point he confides to another worker that Puntila is "too familiar . . . he's got me in the car, and before I know it he's acting human. I won't be able to take it much longer." With greater restraint, Matti speaks to Puntila and Eva about the limits of familiarity beyond which they should not pass. (He refuses to see sex as a great leveler, and declines Eva's advances due to her class background.) A deadpan comedian in a driver's cap, Matti stolidly obeys an unwritten social code, maintains decorum and keeps a straight face in the most ludicrous circumstances. The hired man reveals his consciousness of this comic role when he tells Puntila, "If I only carried out orders that made sense, you'd fire me for twiddling my thumbs."

Like the tramps in *Godot*, Matti bides his time with idle talk; but it is idle talk initiated by members of an idle class. "I'm not driving at anything, just talking to pass the time and keep you company," Matti tells Eva. He adds, "When I'm talking to my employers, I never have any opinions. They don't like the help to have opinions." This is a socially based, less abstract version of Estragon's advice to Vladimir: "Don't let's do anything. It's safer."

Estragon claims he has been beaten overnight by malefactors whose motives remain unknown to him. The lives of Beckett's tramps are dominated by the unknown, the uncertain (whose non-objective correlative is Godot), rather than any social hierarchy. For the most part they serve themselves— not others—by playing verbal games that resemble music hall patter and afford them a sense of companionship in the face of isolation.

Entertaining each other, Vladimir and Estragon create a small society for themselves which parodies the conventions of our own society but is not ours in any conventional way, being devoid of history, wealth and labor. Their artificially induced society alleviates the tramps' sense of homelessness, and permits them to feign nostalgia for a past they can only recall enough to sense that their memories, manners and traditions are sliding toward dessication or extinction. Why these characters are threatened, and what threatens them besides death and their own imaginations, is never certain. George Lukacs comments (in *Realism in Our Time*) on modernism in terms applicable to Beckett's play. In such works, he notes, man appears to be, "by nature solitary, asocial, unable to enter into relationships with other human beings . . . Man, thus conceived, is an ahistorical being. . . . The hero has no pre-existent reality beyond his own self, no reality acting upon him or being acted upon him. . . .

And he is without personal history. He is thrown-into-the-world, meaningless-ly, unfathomably."[8]

Puntila, too, loses his memory. When sober he forgets his generous, drunken promises to the poor and his curses against capitalists like himself. When he drinks he forgets his threats against the poor and his promises to the wealthy and powerful. His drinking eradicates ideas faster than do self-doubt and time in *Godot*. Godot's tramps share Puntila's disaffection for lasting memory: "What is terrible is to have thought," says Vladimir, to which Estragon replies, "When did that ever happen to us?" The difference in Brecht's play is that Matti remembers everything said by his employer; his cumulative memories lead him to leave Puntila Farms. Knowing that things have changed, remembering events, Matti also sees that they will change in the future. He concludes with a prophecy of a workers' democracy, foresee-ing that hired hands will "quickly find good masters when/ The masters are working men."

The allegorical, ahistorical relation of master to servant in *Godot* parodies that of a fairy tale. Unlike Jack, taking the family cow to market, Pozzo is bringing Lucky to the fair, where he hopes "to get a good price for him." At the hiring market in Brecht's play, men sell their labor instead of being sold as slaves. The situations are similar, but by no means the same. Beckett's depiction of the labor market is more grotesque and metaphoric; by the play's end, the scenes with Lucky and Pozzo have become metaphors for the un-predictability (which is not to say the changeability) of events. Pozzo is blind and nearly helpless in Act II but the change is attributed to chance and uncer-tainty (one moment born, the next dead), and not to any social upheaval or to a rational, measured passage of time and encroaching old age. In Brecht's play, the labor market scene is an occasion for analysis and predictions of Puntila's behavior by Matti; it allows Matti and spectators to sense the calculability of human behavior under market conditions. "Marx is the only spectator for my plays," Brecht once said, but others might also appreciate the scene.

"When our theatres perform plays of other periods they like to annihilate the distance, fill in the gap, gloss over the differences. But what then becomes of our delight in comparisons, in distance, in dissimilarity?" Brecht queries in his appendix to the *Short Organon*. His plans for rewriting *Waiting for Godot* never went beyond preliminary notes, but he was constantly rewriting clown scenes in the course of his career: Chaplin's, Hasek's, Wedekind's, Valen-tin's. More important, Brecht changed and refined his own image of the clown in succeeding plays, creating characters progressively more militant in their refusal and mimicry of abusive authority. The series of clowns in his work, as well as the political clowns developed by subsequent playwrights, repre-sent the practice of *Umfunktionierung*, which Brecht employed for most of his life. Through this practice he was able to criticize society, his own past work, and the work of other writers (including Beckett). The method stressed comparison, distance, dissimilarity, all aspects of the historical sense in which he delighted as a dialectician and a satirist.

## APPENDIX: How the Little Tramp Arrived in Paris

Charlie Chaplin was not the first comedian to portray a tramp, but the origins of his Little Tramp persona are particularly relevant to Beckett's tramps. The baggy trousers and stiff, short strides common to Chaplin's character and the tramps in *Waiting for Godot* are exterior manifestations of their resemblance, but the history of their characters—or anti-history, if you will—shares more than physical traits.

In his autobiography Chaplin notes that one of his earliest ambitions was to play the role of a "millionaire tramp." The music halls in England featured comic tramps circa 1905 (when Chaplin was fifteen years old). The comic type developed late in the nineteenth century in England and America, as the industrial revolution created forms of unemployment new to urban society. Men wandered the country in search of work; unable to afford permanent housing or a new suit, they took on an appearance that was not meant to be amusing. But music hall and vaudeville entertainers began to imitate the appearance of hobos. In *Clowns* John Towsen notes that the figure's trademarks were "an unshaven face, red nose, battered top hat and garments even a real tramp would discard. . . . These tramps came in several varieties, such as sad or happy, philosophical or larcenous."

Chaplin never portrayed one of these men until his arrival at Mack Sennett's Keystone Studio in 1914. But he knew the comic tramp type long before that. In his autobiography he recalls:

> My first impulse to do something other than dance was to be funny. My ideal was a double act, two boys dressed as comedy tramps. . . . We would call ourselves "Bristol and Chaplin, the Millionaire Tramps," and we would wear tramp whiskers and big diamond rings. It embraced every aspect of what we thought funny and profitable, but, alas, it never materialized.[9]

He also recalls that around his mid-teens one of the performers who impressed him most was "Zarmo, the comedy tramp juggler," whom he saw rehearsing backstage, "balancing a billiard cue on his chin, and throwing a billiard ball up and catching it on the tip of the cue, then throwing up another and catching that on top of the first ball. . . ."

Chaplin's own early theatrical endeavors required him to portray comic drunks, not tramps. But it may have been his early childhood ambition, and his admiration for agile tramps like Zarmo, that led him suddenly, spontaneously to create the Little Tramp for Mack Sennett. If Chaplin's own account of the Little Tramp's creation can be believed, he had almost no idea about the character until he was costumed in a tramp outfit. Sennett told him, "We need some gags here. . . . Put on a comedy make-up. Anything will do." Chaplin writes:

> I had no idea what make-up to put on. I did not like my getup as the press reporter. However, on the way to the wardrobe I thought I would dress in baggy pants, big shoes, a cane and a derby hat. I wanted everything a contradiction: the pants baggy, the coat tight, the hat small and the shoes large. I was undecided

*Charlie Chaplin as the Little Tramp.*

whether to look old or young, but . . . I added a small moustache. . . . I had no idea of the character. But the moment I was dressed, the clothes and the make-up made me feel the person he was. I began to know him, and by the time I walked onto the stage he was fully born. When I confronted Sennett I assumed the character and strutted about, swinging my cane and parading past him. Gags and comedy ideas went racing through my mind.[10]

The genesis reported here is remarkable if it is accurate. We know that Chaplin later spent enormous amounts of money and time improvising whole scenes for his own films, then discarding them, so his improvisational tendency may well be reported with accuracy here.

The same kind of spontaneously generated tramp characters can be seen in Beckett's playwriting. Vladimir and Estragon lack a history even when they are on stage— they attempt to create personal histories or recall them throughout the performance—and their entire existence on stage resembles the moment Chaplin describes by saying, "By the time I walked on stage he was fully born." Beckett's tramps live only on stage, in the present tense, creating identities and losing them from moment to moment. It is almost as if they had donned their tramp outfits moments before walking on stage—as Chaplin did for Sennett—and then had to try and invent a past and present for their characters. Of course, neither Chaplin's tramp nor Beckett's bums were born wholly *in vacuo*; their creators were familiar with the tradition of tramp comedy and borrowed at least its outward trappings. But the trappings were then taken out of context, into the semi-realism of a film studio set in Chaplin's case, and the nearly bare stage representing a country road in Beckett's case.

Vladimir and Estragon are homeless in an aesthetic sense: deprived of the film set Chaplin gave his tramp, deprived of the billiard cues that comic tramps like Zarmo and W.C. Fields juggled, deprived of any chance to acknowledge the audience as music hall tramps could. They have even less than Chaplin's improvised tramp, who at least knew who he was once he was on stage, swinging his cane and strutting about. Chaplin was able to tell himself, "I was just a tramp wanting a little shelter," before he entered the set of a hotel and stumbled over a woman's foot, turned and raised his hat to apologize, then stumbled over a cuspidor and turned and raised his hat to the cuspidor, in the Little Tramp's first film. Beckett's tramps cannot say they simply want shelter; they have to say they're "waiting for Godot," a figure they do not know, have never met, may never meet. Comedy is not born from such abstractions, which deprive them of the reality Chaplin's tramp knew. Their homelessness extends beyond the Absurdity defined by Camus in *The Myth of Sisyphus* (and quoted by Martin Esslin for the title of his book *The Theatre of the Absurd*). Camus describes the absurd man as "an irremediable exile . . . deprived of memories of a lost homeland as much as [lacking] the hope of a promised land to come. This divorce between man and his life, the actor and his setting, truly constitutes the feeling of Absurdity." Beckett's tramps are doubly divorced from their setting, as they are comic types from a past era (Zarmo's and Chaplin's) thrust onto a modern stage; and they cannot even see that they are on stage at all.

# 9

# 'Arturo Uï' and the Politics of Spectacle

### Brecht and the Naive

Manfred Wekwerth, Brecht's colleague at the Berliner Ensemble and currently that theatre's artistic director, has suggested that Brecht's interest in clowns culminated in the rediscovery of an aesthetic category—the "naive":

> During the last months of his life, while he was working on the "Dialectic in the Theatre," Brecht astonished us with the declaration that the key to his work was naiveté. . . . Like good comedians who insist on getting attention, we [on stage] entered into a naive compact with the audience, making it clear that it was we ourselves who rehearsed this particular story, which we present without keeping our opinions about it to ourselves.[1]

The new naiveté became possible for the same reason that Schiller sensed an older naiveté had been destroyed: scientific advancement. "The surest road to artistic naiveté led through the lecture halls of the materialists," especially Marx, writes Wekwerth. Marx composed "naive philosophical questions" such as, "How can man enjoy the fruits of his work? Why does enormous overproduction exist side by side with hunger?" These naive questions find artistic expression in Brecht's plays.

Wekwerth concludes that Brecht's experiments had always been moving toward this new naiveté, "Beginning . . . back in the '20s when the young man from Augsburg rammed his head against and through the fourth wall":

> The wall screened all the events onstage from the crudity of the real world, so that the stage turned a deaf ear to whatever came from below, even hissing and booing. Old Sophocles would have been astounded to see what went on, at all the things that were invented to obscure the fact that the audience was sitting together in a theatre and not in front of a peep hole. Naiveté was banned, together with the jester, who had permitted himself the inelegance of addressing the audience directly.[2]

As discussed earlier, Brecht sought to restore this "inelegance" and naiveté by returning the jester to the stage in a variety of costumes and situations, and employing his new epic acting style. Wekwerth, who understood this development in Brecht's work, emphasized naiveté through clowning in his production of *The Resistible Rise of Arturo Ui* at the Berliner Ensemble in 1959. The director's rendering of the anti-Hitler satire offers one more perspective on the political clowns in Brecht's work.

## History as Farce, Farce as History

*"Power is getting to be more and more spectacular*
*and unreal. It becomes a power-play. Its theatrical*
*elements are increasingly clear."*
>                                       —Heiner Müller[3]

*The Resistible Rise of Arturo Ui* has been regarded as one of Brecht's least successful satires. Written in 1941 with a wartime American production in mind, the play was not staged in Brecht's lifetime. The topical parable conceived as an anti-fascist primer portrays the rise of a Chicago gangster in episodes which correspond to Hitler's career. Arturo Ui wins control of a cauliflower business through murder, threats, shady business deals and mastery of an ersatz classical acting style. His triumphs are hardly as complex or dire as Hitler's, and Brecht himself acknowledged the difference in notes on the play.

Brecht explains that he wrote the play with "the aim of destroying the dangerous respect commonly felt for great killers. . . . The great political criminals must be thoroughly stripped bare and exposed to ridicule. Because they are not great political criminals at all, but the perpetrators of great political crimes, which is something very different."[4] Critic Frederick Ewen saw Brecht's satire as a miscalculation because "gangsterism is scarcely a phenomenon that could adequately describe Nazism and its atrocities. Nor does control of the 'cauliflower trust' adequately parallel the economic manipulations that made Nazism possible."[5] Ewen's objections are difficult to refute, if one assumes that Brecht meant to describe the Nazi phenomenon adequately, and not merely to trivialize it.

If Brecht's intention was to intervene socially in life by ridiculing respect for Hitler out of existence during the 1940s, he was naive, or at least overambitious. Only in retrospect, after Hitler's defeat, has the Nazi leader become truly vulnerable to ridicule. In a sense, Brecht's satire exemplifies the failings of satire and clowning as instruments for social change.

There is a basis for another reading of the play that neither Brecht nor his critics have acknowledged. *Arturo Ui* confirms Marx's observation that history repeats itself as farce. In the opening passages of his *Eighteenth Brumaire of Louis Bonaparte*, Marx provides the premises for a theory of stage farce; his reading of history, like Brecht's satiric parable, sees clowning and farce as forms through which to analyze the past century's political events. If history can display the attributes of farce, farce can display those of history, and so it does in *Arturo Ui*. From this perspective, Brecht's play is useful as a comic history lesson rather than topical satire.

Marx notes in the *Eighteenth Brumaire* that, "Hegel remarks somewhere that all facts and personages of great importance in world history occur, as it were, twice. He forgot to add: the first time as tragedy, the second time as farce." The reason for the recurrence, Marx suggests, is that "men make their own history, but they do not make it just as they please. . . . [In] periods of revolutionary crisis, they anxiously conjure up the spirits of the past to their service and borrow from them names, battle cries and costumes in order to present the new scene of world history in time-honored disguise and in borrowed language." Arturo Ui, Brecht's would-be tyrant, conjures up spirits of the past and borrows their language. He learns archaic Shakespearean acting gestures and fragments of Shakespeare's Roman speeches midway through the play. Ui continues to refine and practice his oratory until the play's end, as he echoes Shakespeare's Mark Antony, appealing to "Friends, countrymen! Chicagoans and Ciceronians." He even borrows from Christ, announcing, "If anyone's/ Not for me he's against me and has only/ Himself to blame for anything that happens." Through this parody, Brecht intimates that modern statesmen such as Hitler have become actors; they practice a politics of spectacle in "time-honored disguise and in borrowed language."

Brecht ridicules Arturo Ui's thespian skills less overtly than he parodies economic manipulation as practiced by the Nazi party. But the manipulations of Ui and his associates, their behavior at the trial and at public assemblies are also forms of theatre—spectacles staged to advance their programs, much as the Nazis staged massive rallies. While *Arturo Ui* does not exactly achieve the goals of the theatre of trials about which Brecht spoke a decade earlier, it does attempt a comparable feat: Brecht includes the trial and other historical events in a larger framework, making the play a spectacle about spectacle.[6] He attempts to use the Nazis' own means (organized spectacle, theatre for the masses) against them; if he fails in this attempt, it may be due to the limits of theatre itself. The Nazis had a national network of radio and film media to advance their politics; Brecht had only the stage—and not even that, when denied a production—upon which to respond. His play was far less successful in resisting the politics of media than the Nazis were in promoting it.

Several years before he wrote *Arturo Ui*, Brecht ridiculed the Nazis for their theatrical bent, in a poem entitled "Prohibition of Theatre Criticism":

> The regime
> Dearly loves the theatre. Its accomplishments
> Are mainly on the theatrical plane.
> Its brilliant manipulation of the spotlight
> Has done no less than has its
> Brilliant manipulation of the rubber truncheon.
> Its gala performances
> Are broadcast by radio across the entire Reich.
> In three supercolossal films.
> Of which the last was 26,000 feet long
> The leading actor played the Führer.[7]

The poem, published in 1937, preceded Charlie Chaplin's portrait of Hitler as a buffoon in *The Great Dictator*; it shows that Brecht, too, saw in Hitler's oratory a theatrical style worthy of ridicule. The poem, along with *Arturo Ui*, suggests that Brecht shared Walter Benjamin's awareness of the Nazis' dependence on mass media. In 1936, in his essay on "The Work of Art in the Age of Mechanical Reproduction," Benjamin wrote:

> Radio and film not only affect the function of the professional actor but likewise the function of those who also exhibit themselves before this mechanical equipment, those who govern. . . . This results in a new selection, a selection before the equipment from which the star and the dictator emerge victorious.[8]

The Nazi leaders exploited mass media successfully in their political campaigns, as Brecht and Benjamin both witnessed with great regret. More recently, the rise of a film actor to the presidency of the United States again showed how stage and screen presence can be a crucial factor in a political campaign.


## Chaplin as Hitler, Hitler as Chaplin

*Arturo Ui* is, in part, a satire of men who "exhibit themselves" in order to govern the public. Ui learns performance techniques from a professional actor, for the purpose of dignifying his public image. The physical gestures he masters may be more ridiculous, or more visibly so, than the blustery words of his speeches, but Ui never knows it. He performs ersatz versions of scenes from *Faust, Julius Caesar* and *Richard II* with confidence after his acting lessons. Earlier, he had bellowed and cried to his listeners, seeming incapable of more refined (if old-fashioned and inappropriate) oratory. Ui's solemn adaptation of archaic acting tricks makes him a comic figure, and it offers actors portraying him an opportunity to develop extraordinary comic gestures. Kenneth Tynan praised Ekkehard Schall's portrait of Ui at the Berliner Ensemble for infusing the role "with all the deadpan gymnastic ability of the young Chaplin," and for swerving "from pure knockabout to sudden glooms of fearful intensity."[9] Schall's tyrant—according to English director Keith Hack, who objected to the interpretation—was something of a superman. At the same time, a dictator who turns backflips off the top of a chair, as Schall did in Berlin, is also a showman; a circus performer, if you will.

The 1959 Berliner Ensemble production of the play, directed by Manfred Wekwerth and Peter Palitzsch, stressed the showmanship of its characters by evoking the worlds of the circus tent and fairbooth. Wekwerth knew that Brecht had initially conceived the play as a Broadway spectacle with overtones of musical comedy and vaudeville.[10] The actors wore colored masks inspired by clown make-up; dark red lips and eyes outlined in violet stood out against green complexions. Their non-naturalistic faces contrasted with their realistic, 1930s American gentlemen's clothes, and encouraged spectators to see the gangsters as entertainers—as were the actors in the Hollywood gangster films that inspired the play's Chicago setting.

The Berliner Ensemble's revolving stage was turned into the gangsters' own showroom—a space for spectacle and salesmanship. On it, Arturo Ui and his gang could produce their equivalent of the Nazis' "gala performances," about which Brecht wrote his poem in 1937. Tynan's review of the production noted, "The revolve whizzes around . . squalling Dixieland jazz interlaces the scenes . . . [of] macabre farce."[11] According to notes by Wekwerth and

*Ekkehard Schall and Ruth Drexel in the Berliner Ensemble production of Brecht's* The Resistible Rise of Arturo Ui, *1959.*

dramaturg Joachim Tenschart, the stage displayed the veneer and sham, gravestones and flowers, machine guns and riotous music of a spectacular show. Circus and fairground elements were adapted in order to provoke audience laughter, and thereby foster in spectators an irreverent, critical attitude toward the rise of the gangsters.[12] In short, the clowning and circus atmosphere were employed as distancing effects.

A 1963 production of *Arturo Ui* in Warsaw varied the Berlin interpretation of the play slightly, by presenting Hitler as a clown who is not funny. Jan Kott, commenting on the Polish production which was most probably influenced by the earlier one in Berlin, notes that the actor Lomnicki, in the title role, "was never funny," but became quite terrifying during the course of the evening. "From the first to the last scene he is a clown; but not once does he make the audience laugh. And this is [Lomnicki's] greatest achievement."[13] A clown who is not funny appears in some other plays (by Goslar and Griffiths) discussed later; and in these cases, too, the horrors of Nazism give rise to a stage clown incapable of a comic performance.

Brecht's text does not specifically call for the clown masks or circus spectacle that the Berlin and Warsaw directors employed. But the playwright's own exploration of politicians as showmen was amplified in these productions. Both Ui and his creator are aware that modern politicians have to create a respected public image for themselves when they cannot create popular policy. In 1967 in Glasgow, director Keith Hack chose Scene Six (in which Ui takes acting lessons) as "the conceptual pivot" of a production he devised with Michael Blakemore. Hack regards this scene as "a demonstration in concrete terms of what the demagogue can learn from public relations technique";[14] but he neglects to note how archaic, ludicrous and clownish the techniques studied by Ui are.

Scene Six of *Ui* is grotesquely comic in concept as well as specifics. Brecht, who speaks of the learning process so favorably in other works and was rarely averse to didacticism, here parodies education. Hitler himself learned speech skills from a Munich actor, so the scene has a historical basis in fact; but the implications of the scene apply to the politics of spectacle on a much broader scale. Politicians who perform before the public are liable to employ an acting style as naive in quality, and as susceptible to parody, as the ideas they propound. The naive, clown-like form of delivery and the content are inseparable in such cases as Ui's, if not in those of Hitler and Ronald Reagan.

A down-and-out actor named Mahonney teaches Arturo Ui how to walk; the footsteps, not described with specificity in the script, might resemble Nazi goosesteps or those of Chaplin's Little Tramp; in any case, Ui's aide, Givola, senses that the instructions are ludicrous. "I think you've got the wrong guy, boss," he says of Mahonney. "He's out of date. . . . You can't walk like that in front of cauliflower men. It ain't natural." To this Ui replies, "What do you mean it ain't natural? Nobody's natural in this day and age. When I walk I want people to know I'm walking."[15]

In an age of industrial manufacturing and mass-media advertising, politicians fabricate even themselves. Brecht's Ui wants to reshape himself in a distinct image that will attract the public's attention, and if archaic gestures—"time-honored disguise" and "borrowed language," in Marx's words—will make him distinctive, those are fine with Ui. (His preference for non-naturalistic acting is not wholly different from Brecht's. Brecht, too, wanted the public to perceive his characters in all their strangeness.)

From Mahonney, Ui learns some odd, unnatural gestures. His pronounced gait requires that his head be held back and his feet touch the ground toe first, with arms joined in front of his private parts or folded "in such a way that the backs of his hands remain visible. His palms are resting on his arms not far from the shoulder." The gestures are above all awkward and unintentionally comic, not unlike Chaplin's parody of Hitler (or Hitler's own unintentional self-parody.) Ui's arms and hands are not poised so much as they are guarded, hiding privates; the leader looks as if he had been caught with his pants down, or with dainty breasts exposed, in these positions. The style is derived from nineteenth-century melodrama, but the gestures are more suitable to a women in distress than to a Führer. No wonder Givola objects. The emperor holds his arms as if he has no clothes on.

In the same scene, Ui is asked by the skeptical Givola why he is learning to act in this new style, and Ui replies, "It's for the little people." He wants to impress them with a show of grandeur, and his "object is the little man's image of his master." Presumably the masses—raised to respect the grandeur of classical acting—will respond with similar enthusiasm to these political posturings.[16] It turns out that Ui's style of acting wins him no respect: it is his coercive and violent tactics that triumph. The gangster, not the classical actor, dominates, and his rhetoric reveals as much. Speeches graciously calling for cooperation end with blunt threats that mar whatever delicacy the verse had to begin with. Contradictions between modern gangster jargon and its conveyance through classical blank verse recur throughout the play.

Such contrasts between artful entreaty and crude threat form a dialectic comparable to that between a politician and a "grade B" actor, or between a clown and a gangster, or, to return to Karl Valentin's model, between the unlearned, petty bourgeois and the person who aspires to professional knowledge and respectability. Ui sums up these contradictions when he tells Roma how he plans to take over businesses in other cities:

Through
The front door, through the back door, through the windows.
Resisted, sent away, called back again:
Booed and acclaimed. With threats and supplications,
Appeals and insults, gentle force and steel
Embrace. . . .
I have in mind a kind of dress rehearsal
In a small town. . . . In Cicero.[17]

Here again Ui resorts to show business procedure—a dress rehearsal—to implement his coercive policies.

There can be no synthesis of the contradictions in Ui's character except through his tyrannical replacement of all contradictions with absolutism; this is Ui's final solution. "What I demand," he says to Chicagoans and Ciceronians, "is one unanimous and joyful 'Yes'. . . . I want this and everything else I want to be complete. . . ."

## Dictators and Acrobats

In his portrait of the dictator as naive actor, Brecht realizes one of his most important theatre concepts: *Gestus*—the expression of social attitudes and circumstances through a stage performance. The play's text, as well as the Berliner Ensemble production's emphasis on clownery, underscore the gestural nature of political oration by focusing on the learned and repeatable forms through which Ui expresses his attitudes toward society.

Moreover, there is a leveling and democratizing effect inherent in an epic actor's impersonation of a tyrant learning to act; the actor's talents become as important as the politician's. More important, witnessing the actor perform this scene, contemporary audiences in a sense triumph over the dictator: they see him reduced to the status of being *their* performer. This diminution of a "great man" to the stature of a great entertainer implements Brecht's idea that an actor should not conceal the fact that he has rehearsed his gestures "any more than an acrobat conceals his training."[18] Brecht's satire discloses and mocks Ui's training and suggests that other politicians' gestures—their social attitudes and the means of their expression—should also be regarded as products of training for public exhibition: training common to actors, acrobats, clowns and other showpeople.

# —10

# Brecht, Mayakovsky, Lazarenko

W hile Brecht was bringing clowns into the theatre, Vladimir Mayakovsky was taking playwriting into the circus. Mayakovsky left the proscenium arch and all that went with it, at least temporarily, while he ran away to the circus and wrote scenarios for clowns.

The Russian Revolution altered practically everything in the U.S.S.R., including the circus. After 1917, Charlie Chaplin impersonations could be seen throughout Russia in cabarets and circus rings. Performers expected that his irrepressible, lower-class persona would win approval from the new regime, while most of their old routines were likely to be condemned as remnants of bourgeois entertainment. The large-scale condemnations these clowns anticipated never occurred. But when the Soviet state nationalized the circus, it did encourage new pro-Revolutionary forms of entertainment.[1]

## Elephants and Statesmen

Among the new, state-sponsored circus acts were several developed by Mayakovsky and the clown Vitaly Lazarenko. The two had known each other before the Revolution. As a Futurist in 1914, Mayakovsky had recited poetry in locations as unexpected as the sequences of words he arranged. He and three other Futurist poets had walked down a busy Moscow street at noon, reciting new poems and wearing wooden spoons in their buttonholes. Ordinary citizens, taken aback by this behavior, whispered in awe when Mayakovsky began to eat an orange in public—he made even that simple gesture seem extraordinary. His interest in the creation of public spectacle was manifest in his plays as well. He acted the role of "Simply Man" in *Mystery Bouffe* by reciting lines from a trapeze suspended over the audience. He planned to recite poetry while riding an elephant. The poet enchanted by elephants, trapezes and other spectacles befriended Lazarenko in 1914. The clown was famous for a Pathe film in which he leaped over three elephants, and had appeared in the Futurist film *I want to Be a Futurist*. According to V. Kamensky (quoted by Frantisek Deak):

> At the circus, Lazarenko once wore the costume of an equestrienne with a huge red hat, rhinestones in his ears, an enormous black radish on his chest. "Why the black radish?" asked Volodia (Mayakovsky). Lazarenko explains: "I'm incarnating an equestrienne who is madly in love with Mayakovsky. You are usually wearing radishes in your buttonhole, and she is trying to please you and seduce you by also wearing a radish. Hopelessly in love, she recites your poetry riding in the arena of the circus and, constantly falling off the horse, she presses the radish to her heart and exclaims: 'Oh! Mayakovsky, Mayakovsky, why did you make me lose my head?'"[2]

This parody of Mayakovsky's Futurist, elephant-riding fantasy is said to have occasioned the first meeting of the two men. Their friendship led them from a common interest in Futurism to collaboration on political circus clowning after the Revolution. Both had a pre-Revolutionary interest in radical politics. Mayakovsky spent six months in prison for allegedly aiding Bolsheviks in Tzarist Russia. Early in his career, Lazarenko had met and learned from Durov. Like Durov, Lazarenko called himself "Jester to His Majesty the People," the title suggesting their shared preference for popular art:[3] They would jest *at* nobility, rather than *for* it. For Durov, the choice necessitated the use of pigs and rats as symbols of greed, disguised as harmless animal acts. Lazarenko was already staging his own political satires when Mayakovsky began to visit the circus and suggest new themes for his routines.

The first of their notable collaborative creations was Lazarenko's 1919 performance based on Mayakovsky's "Soviet Alphabet." For each letter of the alphabet, the poet wrote a satiric verse. Lazarenko recited or sang the verses, according to Deak, while "he carried huge painted letters into the arena . . . showing them to the public." The form of Mayakovsky's poem was not entirely new; soldiers had been known to sing obscene lyrics for each letter of the alphabet. Besides altering the lyrics to make them satiric rather than obscene, Mayakovsky and Lazarenko increased the educational function of the verse by allowing the public to read the alphabet from the blocks while it was recited by Lazarenko. (The public was not wholly literate at this point in Russian history, and the circus performance helped audiences to learn the alphabet in an entertaining manner.)

The "Soviet Alphabet" act was a rudimentary combination of poetry and clowning; but then its creators were experiencing a new, perhaps unprecedented, state of affairs. Previously they had been avant-garde artists, Futurists who saw themselves as an advanced minority; now the State itself was an avant-garde advocate of revolutionary change—in art as well as government. John Berger and Anna Bostock note the significance of this historical moment in their essay "Mayakovsky: Language and Death of a Revolutionary Poet":

> After the Revolution, as a result of the extensive government literary campaign, every Soviety writer was more or less aware that a vast new reading public was being created. Industrialization was to enlarge the proletariat and the new pro-

*A painting of Vitaly Lazarenko in the circus ring, wearing multicolored overalls.*

letarians would be 'virgin' readers, in the sense that they had not previously been corrupted by purely commercial reading. It was possible to think, without unnecessary rhetoric, of the revolutionary class claiming and using the written word as a revolutionary right. Thus the advent of a literate proletariat might enrich and extend written language in the U.S.S.R. instead of impoverishing it as had happened under capitalism in the West. For Mayakovsky after 1917 this was a fundamental article of faith. Consequently he could believe that the formal innovations of his poetry were a form of political action. . . . When he toured the Soviet Union giving unprecedented public poetry readings to large audiences of workers he believed that by way of his words he would actually introduce new turns of phrase, and thus new concepts, into the workers' language.[4]

Berger and Bostock go on to suggest that after Lenin's death, Soviet bureaucracy began to corrupt language, turning the promise of slogans into clichés and evasions; Mayakovsky saw the change and shared his perception of it in later satires.

He may have taught illiterate workers the alphabet through his first collaboration with Lazarenko, but Mayakovsky could not teach the literate; he could only ridicule them and turn them into clowns, while they turned the Revolution into a bureaucratic farce. His initial optimism about prospects for a new language and culture faded, and he never returned to the cheerful perspective of his first post-Revolutionary play, *Mystery Bouffe*. That allegory of proletarian revolution embraces everyday speech and the circus in its performance as well as in its dialogue. The preface announces:

> The verses of *Mystery Bouffe* are the slogans of meetings, street cries, the language of newspapers. The action of *Mystery Bouffe* is the movement of the crowd, the struggle of classes, the combat of ideas; it is a world miniaturized to the size of a circus.[5]

The slogans and situations in which he had first seen poetry later become sources of parody. In *The Bedbug* Mayakovsky ridicules the *petit-bourgeois* who refuses to join the Revolution and abuses the opportunity it offers. In *The Bathhouse* he ridicules government bureaucrats, converting official government slogans and rhetoric into clown conversations as a defense of language against its abuses. As Claudine Amiard-Chevrel suggests in her excellent essay on Mayakovsky's major satires, he turns the betrayers of the Revolution's promise into clowns. She notes that Mayakovsky was "wounded in the massacre of the Russian language" that occured in newspapers and official discourse. His response was "to carry their system to the point of the absurd, to create the verbal make-up of a new clown. . . . The process was that of parody already practiced in the cabaret theatre, but not previously so visibly political."[6]

The actor who originally portrayed the *petit-bourgeois* oaf in *The Bedbug* resorted to clown techniques under Meyerhold's direction, and "created the character of a dull-witted buffoon, consumed by rudeness and pride . . .

[and displaying] a melancholy and a disorder recalling those of Chaplin," according to Ripellino.[7] The actor Igor Illinsky had previously shown these traits in other roles, deriving them from the circus, the operetta and the cabaret.

## Crying in the Aisles

One result of his experiment in circus arts is that Mayakovsky subsequently "opened up" the stage in his dramatic satires. Amiard-Chevrel calls this innovation "circusization" of the theatre. *The Bedbug*'s opening scene demonstrates the anti-illusionist tendency embodied by circus clowns when they serve (as Lazarenko did) as master of ceremonies, directly addressing the audience and performing in a ring surrounded by noisy crowds. The play begins as if the theatre auditorium were one huge street fair, with vendors parading through the aisles crying their wares. Later the entire audience is treated as part of an assembly touring a museum, where a rare creature from the twentieth century, Prisypkin, has become a curiosity because of his longevity. (According to the scenario, he was frozen in the 1920s and thawed out sixty years later.) When the buffoonish de-thaw-ee "discovers" the audience watching him, he cries out, "Citizens! My own people! Dear ones! How did you get here?"[8] The scene is not exactly the same as Durov's equation of his trained pig with Kaiser Wilhelm II, but it brings the audience into the life of the play in a comparably satiric manner. The imprisoned man who equates himself with spectators is a virtually extinct type at that moment. The recognition scene implies that his disapproved-of, idle behavior is not as rare as the scientists in the play claim; in fact, the audience may share Prisypkin's allegedly archaic, *petit-bourgeois* vices—love of song, drink and celebration.

While his captors do not call Prisypkin a clown, they note that he has the skill to "lure his victim with monstrous mimetic powers, sometimes in the guise of a chirruping rhymster, sometimes a crooning songbird." He is the last minstrel in Stalin's Russia, a stand-in for the playwright himself, perhaps, although Mayakovsky ridicules the guitar-player's *petit-bourgeois* nostalgia at the same time that he celebrates the vanishing artistic freedom he represents.

## Diplomats and Wrestling Mats

Before Mayakovsky became disillusioned with the Revolution, he realized the potential for new art forms and a new audience at the circus. Following collaboration on "The Soviet Alphabet," he wrote a small play for Lazarenko in 1920. The play, entitled *The Championship of the Universal Class Strug-*

*gle*, is hardly as complex or subtle as Mayakovsky's full-length satires. Its significance is now primarily historical and documentary. But it represents another direction in which Mayakovsky's political satire turned with the encouragement of the Soviet state and his friend Lazarenko. The play parodies a circus wrestling match. The wrestlers are clowns who mimic international statesmen. All of them lack the strength to wrestle with a character called The World Champion, Revolution. Lazarenko first played the role of Uncle Referee, a character who introduces the international contestants and ridicules them in the process. The contestants, Prime Minister Lloyd George of England, President Wilson of America, Premier Millerand of France, White Russian Army Commander Wrangel and others, lay hands on one another; but all of them withdraw when Revolution challenges them, asking "How many of you, dried, will make a pound?"

All the statesmen, as represented by clowns in the circus arena, must have looked like living political cartoons. Their wrestling match was a parody of an actual circus event and of international diplomacy, which even today continues to reflect a philosophy of "negotiating from strength." The strength of the diplomats in the scene is reduced to brute comic wrestling; all pretense of gentility and intelligence disappears in the fight.

The play was created at a time when Great Britain, France, Japan and the United States had troops in Russia supporting the White Army and opposing the Reds. The military invasion amounted to a counterrevolutionary expedition and, in Mayakovsky's clown fantasy, the invaders were repulsed; the play was prophetic, but it was also an immediate, timely attack on the dignity of the invading states, meant to weaken the foreigners' image while the Red Army was weakening the enemy's military force.

The play is quite chauvinistic in its glorification of Revolution and ends on a note of exhortation. If the spectators want the Reds to win after the intermission, says Uncle Referee, they should "go home and tomorrow go to the front as volunteers" to fight the White Russians. Approximately one month after the play was performed, on November 15, 1920, the Red Army won its fight against the Whites. No great credit is due to the circus for this victory, but considering that the Soviets were at war at the time of the playlet's performance, the chauvinism is understandable.

## Brecht as a Sporting Man

Mayakovsky's clown wrestling match has a few counterparts in the plays of Brecht. Brecht, too, saw a source for theatre in sports such as wrestling and boxing. In his prologue to *In the Jungle of the Cities*, spectators are urged to watch the contest on stage as if it were a wrestling match. In the song cycle of *Little Mahagonny*, as well as in *Mahagonny* and the premiere of

*The Measures Taken,* roped rings were set up on stage so that events would be viewed as if taking place in a boxing ring. Despite his use of these devices, Brecht's plays differ considerably in concept from the Lazarenko/Mayakovsky scenario for *The Championship.* . . . The Soviet artists located their parody of circus wrestling in a setting where such matches were actually held; they brought their satire to the same audience that would see the original, non-satirical matches. Brecht set up his roped rings in conventional theatre houses, as if he could turn a middle-class theatre audience into a proletarian mass simply by emphasizing sports. (There is one notable exception: *The Measures Taken,* which had virtually no audience at all since the Control Chorus role was played by a 400-member Workers' Chorus; the chorus members constituted many of the people at the performance, and may have appreciated the boxing ring on stage more than the bourgeois spectators who had booed *The Little Mahagonny* in its rope ring at Baden Baden. Walter Benjamin writes that with *The Measures Taken,* Brecht and composer Hanns Eisler transformed "a concert into a political meeting.")[9]

Brecht might have preferred audiences like those at the Soviet circus, but he never sought them in comparable Berlin locations. John McGrath suggests the significance of this difference between Brecht and Mayakovsky when he observes that Brecht and fellow German Erwin Piscator, "in spite of professions to the contrary and occasional unsuccessful attempts to change things, were committed to working within the Berlin smart-bourgeois theatre, albeit as 'oppositional' forces. . . . [Neither made] a decisive break with his intellectual and artistic formation. . . . Brecht's Berliner Ensemble retained many of the forms and structures of bourgeois theatre."[10]

## Collapsible Aesthetics

"Besides being popular, there is such a thing as becoming popular," Brecht wrote in his essay "The Popular and the Realistic." Brecht attempted to incorporate popular forms such as wrestling and beer hall comedy into his plays, and he no doubt hoped to become as popular with proletarian audiences as boxing or cabaret. However, it is curious that in the same essay, Brecht defines "popular" art as that which is "intelligible to the broad masses, taking over their forms of expression and enriching them, adopting and consolidating their standpoint, representing the most progressive section of the people in such a way that it can take over the leadership . . . linking the tradition and carrying it further. . . ."[11] This definition contains a slightly disturbing hint that Brecht would expropriate culture from the lower classes, not those in power, by "taking over their forms of expression," and not simply enriching those forms. But one can hardly accuse Brecht of plotting to start a "dictatorship of the proletariat" or its art, given his acceptance of a Berlin worker's aesthetic criticism, recounted in the same essay. "I shall never forget," he writes, "how one worker [commenting on *The Measures Taken*] looked at me when I answered his request to include something extra in a song about the U.S.S.R. . . . by saying it would wreck the artistic form; he put his head on one side and smiled. At this polite smile a whole section of aesthetics collapsed." Who else but a proponent of clowning and popular humor could so agreeably concede that his own folly had been revealed by a worker's smile?

According to Kathe Rulicke-Weiler, in *Brecht As They Knew Him*, Brecht knew Mayakovsky's early play *Mystery Bouffe* "at any early date."[12] Rulicke-Weiler specifies no exact date and it is difficult to establish exactly how well Brecht knew the Soviet satirist's work. She also claims that Brecht was aware of "the proletarian partisanship," the "gestic content" and the "scenes of action for the class struggle" in Mayakovsky's writing, but these assertions are presented without further details. If Brecht knew that Meyerhold had staged *Mystery Bouffe* with acrobatics and *commedia lazzi* in 1921, the knowledge could have informed his own satiric writing. After he saw a Moscow production of *The Bathhouse* in 1955, Brecht said that the socialist classics had taught him a most important lesson: "That a future for mankind could only be envisioned from below, from the viewpoint of the oppressed and the exploited." The statement could serve as a summary of the rebellion in *Mystery Bouffe*. But it is more likely that Brecht was thinking of Marx, Lenin and even Stalin when he spoke about the "socialist classics" in 1955. He was accepting the Stalin Prize at the time, in recognition of his own achievements—a prize Stalin never would have offered Mayakovsky.

## Moscow Circus Fire

After Stalin came to power Mayakovsky wrote one more circus play, which was staged a week before the poet's suicide in 1930. While it is doubtful that the production of *Moscow Is Burning* drove Mayakovsky to his death, it was less successful than his collaborations with Lazarenko. It required extensive recital of verse in a setting—the circus—not conducive to careful listening. One Moscow newspaper commented that "the public failed to hear all of the spoken words . . . due to faulty acoustics and to the lack of training of the majority of the performers. Indeed, circus performers were taking part for the first time in a show where the spoken word was so widely used, and it is well-known how difficult it is for the public to hear in the circus."[13]

The most impressive aspect of *Moscow Is Burning* is its stage directions, which call for Kerensky to jump through a hoop into the Tzarina's bedroom, as well as for a human pyramid thirty-three feet high to represent Tzarist social structure—complete with a dwarfish clown in a huge crown at the top. The text of *Moscow Is Burning*, commemorating the twenty-fifth an-

*The Phosphorescent Woman (Zinaida Raikh) and the bureaucrat Pobedonosikov (Maxim Shtraukh) in a 1930 production of Mayakovsky's* The Bathhouse, *directed by Meyerhold.*

niversary of the 1905 Revolution, is immersed in slogans and historical references, making it a far cry from the simple, highly accessible farce of Mayakovsky's 1920 clown play.

Mayakovsky may have had some reservations about his collaboration on the 1930 circus scenario. In his play *The Bathhouse*, staged a month before *Moscow Is Burning*, he parodies the same acrobatic stunts he used in the circus play. The Director in Act III of *The Bathhouse* asks his performers to "build a pyramid with your would-be powerful bodies, personifying in plastic form a symbol of communism."[14] A moment later *The Bathhouse* suggests why the author parodied his own circus scenario, when the bureaucrat Pobedonosikov applauds the pyramid "symbol of communism" as "real art" which makes sense to him and the masses. The buffoonish bureaucrat had earlier warned the Director against art that alarms or agitates spectators: "Think it over, you alarm clock! Instead of arousing me, you should create pleasant sights and sounds." The official is asking for positive statements that glorify the state and soothe the masses. A journalist in the room chimes in "Our appetite is small./ Just give us bread and circuses—/ We'll cheer anything at all." The satire here suggests that the state wants its art to appease the masses and amuse them, rather than alert them to problems. The Roman concept of bread and circuses has arrived in Stalinist Moscow. This state of affairs could be part of the reason Mayakovsky shot himself a week before the premiere of *Moscow Is Burning*.

The subtitle of *The Bathhouse*—"A Drama in Six Acts, with a Circus and Fireworks"—indicates that the play contains "a circus" within it. The parody just described, with its silly acrobatics and juggling, is as close as any scene in the play comes to being a circus. Perhaps this was the playwright's way of saying that by 1930 the Soviet circus, like the Revolution itself, was no longer the large and promising arena for artistic innovation that he had once thought it.

## Meyerhold the Melancholy Pierrot

As Mayakovsky's attitude toward the circus of the Revolution turned cynical, Meyerhold's did too. The director who collaborated on the 1930 production of *The Bathhouse* had been intrigued by the circus world even longer than Mayakovsky, and the two worked together on several circus-influenced productions.

Years before he met Mayakovsky, Meyerhold had shown a fascination with the circus, and the relation between its performers and its audience, in a 1903 production of Franz von Schönthan's *The Acrobats*. According to Marjorie Hoover, the director translated the play, directed it and played the central role in it—that of a Pierrot named Landowski:

> He went beyond the recreation of a milieu [the circus] . . . to add some touches of his own. First Meyerhold, as the old clown beyond his successful years, was seen between the two audiences, the audience in the play and the actual theatre audience. Then, as he listened for applause which did not come, he stood forward, almost directly addressing the real audience, like the melancholy Pierrot.[15]

Meyerhold wanted to free his actors from the proscenium stage frame; he would stage productions so that, "Like a circus arena, ringed on all sides by spectators, the stage apron comes close to the audience."[16] In directing Mayakovsky's plays he pursued this aim repeatedly. According to Edward Braun, his first collaboration with the playwright, on two productions of *Mystery Bouffe* (1919, 1921), included some broad comic acting "in the manner of the popular travelling shows"—a direct application of the skills explored at Meyerhold's studio—and circus acrobatics.[17] The 1921 production featured Lazarenko as a devil in Hell (Act III). Stage directions indicate that the devils leap "clear across the stage" with pitchforks; it is likely that these actions were conceived especially for the clown who could leap over three elephants. Lazarenko entered "by sliding down a wire and performing acrobatic tricks." At the end of the play, action spilled over into boxes next to the stage, and the audience was invited to mix with actors in the promised future land of paradise.[18] According to the stage directions, "All the spectators mount the stage," after they are told the following:

Today,
these are only stage-prop doors
but tomorrow, reality will replace
this theatrical trash.
We know this.
We believe in it.
Up here, spectator![19]

The optimism inherent in Mayakovsky and Meyerhold's invitation to create a communal, celebratory space on stage faded, finally, into the small parodic circus scene of *The Bathhouse* in 1930, as both playwright and director saw Soviet bureaucracy stifling the Revolution.

Mayakovsky wrote not only for circus audiences, of course. Besides his best known plays and poems, he created posters bearing political cartoons and slogans when he worked for ROSTA, the Soviet telegraph agency. For Moscow's Theatre of Satire he wrote a series of short agitprop plays, one of which was staged on a military school's firing range. All of this evinces his ability to "rethink the notions of literary forms or genres . . . to find forms appropriate to the literary energy of our time," as Benjamin said of another innovative Soviet writer Tretyakov, and of Brecht.[20] There can be no doubt that some of the "literary energy" of Mayakovsky's time was to be found in the circus. Its spectacles, humor and daring feats offered a variety of metaphors for the achievements of the Revolution, as well as a means to celebrate them.


## Clowns After Mayakovsky

Mayakovsky's writing influenced a number of later satirists, notably Yuri Lyubimov, Heiner Müller and Dario Fo. Lyubimov, director of Moscow's Taganka Theatre from 1964 to 1984, staged many political satires at what he called his "theatre of buffoonery." One production that Lyubimov titled *Listen* was a tribute to Mayakovsky, based on his poems and biography. In 1983 Heiner Müller translated Mayakovsky's earliest play (*Vladimir Mayakovsky, A Tragedy*) into German; and, according to Carl Weber, the Russian playwright is one of the three authors Müller "seems to have admired and who most clearly influenced him," the other two being Brecht and Büchner.[21] The Italian playwright and performer Dario Fo has acknowledged a debt to Mayakovsky by titling his one-man show *Mistero Buffo*, a variant on the title of Mayakovsky's *Mystery Bouffe*. The circus acrobatics and *commedia dell'arte lazzi* which Meyerhold employed for *Mystery Bouffe* might also be appropriate for staging some of Dario Fo's plays. Fo, like Lyubimov and Müller, has often been harrassed by censors, and he once quoted Mayakovsky as saying, "The end of satire is the first alarm bell signalling the end of real democracy." Fo added that Mayakovsky knew what he was talking about, having been "censured to begin with, then . . . banned, and then . . . driven to suicide."[22] Perhaps it is a measure of the lack of "real democracy" in the United States that Dario Fo has not yet been permitted to perform his satires in our country. The U.S. State Department denied him entry in 1980 and 1983, finally allowing him in briefly in 1984, but not to perform. It seems that Mayakovsky's experience as a persecuted writer lives on, along with his satires.

# —II————

# **Weiss and Handke**
## Clowns After Brecht

### Mockinpott or Kaspar?

Six days before Peter Weiss' clown, Herr Mockinpott, stepped onto a Hannover stage in 1968, a different clown appeared in Frankfurt, in a play by Peter Handke. (The title of Handke's play, *Kaspar*, means "clown" in German when spelled *kasper*.) The coincidence of the nearly simultaneous openings of clown plays by two of Germany's leading playwrights was noted by Henning Rischbieter in the journal *Theater Heute*.[1] He asked whether the emergence of the two texts was not "a fortunate event for the theatre" and a movement toward a new "sensual, gestural and clownish" type of theatre, "a theatrical theatre." Answering his own question in the negative, Rischbieter noted that the two approaches represented quite different attitudes toward the theatre and society. He saw Weiss consciously going back to older fairbooth and circus clown forms—as Weiss himself had once said he planned to do—while Handke's play took an extremely contemporary form and did not merely draw on theatre antiquity. It could be argued that Weiss' clown play was not wholly derivative or regressive either, but Rischbieter was certainly correct in seeing Handke's play as the more innovative of the two.

In their different ways, both playwrights extend Brecht's experiments in political clowning. The gestures and speech of their characters, expressed in comic styles which obviously require training and rehearsal, serve as indicators of learned behavior. The practiced pratfalls and stunts in these plays are analogous to the processes of conformity and socialization which Weiss and Handke examine.

## How Mockinpott the Clown
## Became Marat the Revolutionary

Although he began work on his clown play *How Mr. Mockinpott Was Cured of His Suffering* some time before he wrote *Marat/Sade*, Weiss did not complete the earlier project until 1968, four years after his successful play about the French Revolution. *Mockinpott* probably would have received little attention if it had opened before *Marat/Sade*. Its doggerel verse is tedious; its scenes are underdeveloped. But the play reveals an early impulse in Weiss' writing to explore issues of justice and equality in experimental dramatic forms. Like Brecht, Weiss chose to explore these issues at least once in a clown play. The clowning in *Mockinpott* anticipated, and in retrospect illuminates, the elements of buffoonery in Weiss' more popular play *Marat/Sade*.

*Mockinpott* is more allegorical and far less historical or biographical than Weiss' later plays. Like Brecht, who proceeded to situate his clownish personae in specific social situations and offer "socially based humor" in his comedies after *The Baden Learning Play*, Weiss developed comic forms of insubordination which come to acquire specificity in later works. As in Brecht's case, the specificity followed a study of Marxism and an encounter with Nazism.

Like Brecht's *Baden Learning Play*, Weiss' *Mockinpott* portrays in allegorical form the persecution of a naive, maladroit clown. The play begins with Mockinpott's Kafkaesque imprisonment. Following release for his unexplained arrest, he loses his money, then his job, then his wife's fidelity. A modern, clownish Job, Mockinpott meets another clown, Hanswurst, and then God; neither of them can satisfactorily tell him why he has suffered. But while Brecht's disfigured Smith is left helpless in *The Baden Learning Play*, Mockinpott begins to question the causes of injustice and betrayal during his journey. He learns to walk without a walking stick and with his shoes on the correct feet, tasks his persecutors had previously made difficult. His new knowledge is hardly profound, but it is cause for optimism. As the character overcomes his physical clumsiness, his intellectual naiveté also diminishes. From pratfalls and false steps early in the play, he progresses to dancer-like grace; from incomprehension he progresses to anger at injustice. The clown's control over his motor coordination becomes emblematic of his increased resistance to persecution; the sequence is an inversion of the events in Brecht's clown play, where loss of limbs results from acceptance of persecution euphemistically termed "help." Mockinpott's progression from incomprehension to anger at injustice is repeated in other political clown plays, by other playwrights also influenced by Brecht; the pattern has become almost standard in political satire since Brecht first politicized naiveté in modern theatre.

In his naiveté, Mockinpott initially sees himself as an outcast; he cannot understand the causes of discrimination against him, or the fact that his own passivity and acceptance of injustice sustain that injustice:

> Why is it always I who is undone
> though I never fight with anyone
> or get involved in argument
> or say anything anyone might resent? . . .[2]

By the end of the play, if Mockinpott has not learned to argue, at least he is capable of saying something that others will resent.

As Weiss' clown figure acquires an education, he frees himself from the authority of those figures whose answers do not alleviate his incomprehension of injustice. Throughout the learning process, Mockinpott is guided by Hanswurst (alias Jackpudding), the traditional German clown. Weiss portrays him as a fat, lazy, mischievous man who eats and drinks heartily and perpetrates pranks on nurses and on Mockinpott. Hanswurst assumes the role of surgeon and operates on Mockinpott's brain as if cooking a stew. The grotesque operation could be seen as brainwashing or lobotomy, meant to reduce Mockinpott's curiosity, but it could simply be an act of mischief on Jackpudding's part. The clown-doctor discovers Mockinpott's heart during the operation, which allows Weiss a crude visual pun; the clown's heart is located in his posterior—he is soft-hearted, "close to an ass" in matters of the heart. Doctor Jackpudding moves the heart to its proper location in his parody of surgery. In the unorthodox operation, as elsewhere, Hanswurst shows he has no respect for authority. Later he mimics government spokesmen as they blather bureaucratic nonsense, and he asks rather personal, embarrassing questions of God when they meet.

In his 1968 review of the Hannover premiere of *Mockinpott*, Rischbieter notes that neither Weiss' text nor the staging define Hanswurst's role very clearly; Rischbieter suggests that the role could be clarified if an actor portrayed him as a cynic, a whip or a cunning agitator for enlightenment. Hanswurst could then struggle intellectually with Mockinpott, giving the play a strong line of dramatic tension. One can see this tension developed with far greater skill and complexity in *Marat/Sade*. In the later work the Marquis de Sade embodies Hanswurst's hedonism and mischievous tendencies in an extreme, massive exercise of personal liberty, while Jean-Paul Marat goes beyond Mockinpott's innocent search for justice, to make plans for revolution.

If not exactly an agitator, Weiss' Hanswurst is a mischief-maker, and his irreverence infects Mockinpott by the play's end. Yet Mockinpott appears to reject Hanswurst's cynicism. He moves toward constructive improvement of his own condition and to anger at injustice. His journey and sufferings could be compared to those of the Biblical Job, until he rejects God.[3] Besides its Biblical parallel, the play includes a choral commentary by angels and a meeting with God which echo scenes from medieval morality plays. But Weiss' play comes closer to blasphemy than to Christian testimony in its depiction of God. Wearing a fur coat, puffing a cigar and speaking of the world as his business firm, God is a caricature of a capitalist. Mockinpott becomes defiant when he hears God say that injustice is an inevitable, uncorrectable part of His business firm; such a world is a "swindle," in Mockinpott's view. His irreverence anticipates Marat's denial of the idea that "it is the will of God" that oppressed people should suffer. Mockinpott is on his way to becoming another Marat, albeit a clownish one, at the play's end.

In *Marat/Sade* the Herald, dressed in a coxcomb and harlequin's motley, also functions as a clown—a master of ceremonies ironically commenting from the sidelines—as Hanswurst did in traditional eighteenth-century plays. However, the Herald's clown act serves Sade's larger goal of rebellion against societal limits forced on him by institutional confinement. As Michel Foucault notes in his book *Madness and Civilization*, confinement in asylums was a "police" matter in eighteenth-century Europe; such measures were directed against nonconformists with a philosophical basis for their alleged "sickness," and not only against the sick. If the asylum in *Marat/Sade* is part of a police state, then the rebellion directed by Sade, and abetted by the Herald, is not simply a whimsical act of disobedience or illness; it constitutes a conscious resistance to unjust law: resistance enacted in the guise of playacting and clowning.


## Madmen from Brecht to Artaud

Mr. Mockinpott's softspoken, innocent inquiries about justice become wild shouts in the Charenton asylum of Sade and Marat. The imprisonment and brain surgery suffered by Mockinpott also have a counterpart in *Marat/Sade*, where a whole ward of mental patients demands:

> Who keeps us prisoner
> Who locks us in
> We're normal and we want our freedom.[4]

While a number of critics have detected the influence of Artaud's Theatre of Cruelty in Weiss's mental asylum scenes, it could be argued that Brecht, too, created a "theatre of cruelty" which influenced Weiss' *Mockinpott* and *Marat/Sade*, and Heiner Müller's *Heart Play*. The surgery that Hanswurst performs on Mr. Mockinpott is comparable to the amputation of Smith's wooden limbs by clowns in *The Baden Learning Play*. It may be that in their pursuit of shock tactics, Brecht and Artaud have more in common than is generally acknowledged. Peter Weiss managed to synthesize their theories in *Marat/Sade* in a way that illuminates his predecessors as well as history. Weiss undoubtedly shared Artaud's fascination with the Marquis de Sade's libertine philosophy. The grotesque violence in *Marat/Sade* also owes something to the playwright's interest in fairground spectacle, evident in his earlier "Hanswurstian" work.

Weiss overtly acknowledged a debt to Brecht's sense of humor and his social concern in a 1964 interview with *The London Times*:

> Brecht influenced me as a dramatist. I learnt most from Brecht. I learnt clarity from him; the necessity of making clear the social questions in the play. I learnt from his lightness. He is never heavy in the psychological German way.[5]

At the same time, Weiss departed from Brecht both thematically and stylistically, in his dramatization of madness (*Mockinpott, Marat/Sade* and *Holderlin*) and genocide (*The Investigation, Discourse on Vietnam*). He visited North Vietnam during American raids there, and attended the Auschwitz trials in 1964; his plays based on these events and similar ones are closer to journalism or documentary drama than were Brecht's histories and parables. (Even *Marat/Sade* reiterates with irony that the madness and cruelty of 1793 are no longer with us—meaning that they are with us, but are not always publicly acknowledged.)

Weiss' post-Auschwitz consciousness led him beyond Brecht as he addressed postwar issues of complicity in mass murder and genocidal warfare which Brecht had never overtly dramatized. Brecht's ironic, coolly distant analyses of society through parables such as *Arturo Ui* yields in Weiss' work to fervently topical forms of social debate, using forms of sadistic grand guignol and fairground spectacle.

Interviewed by A. Alvarez in *Encore*, Weiss spoke of his departure from Brecht's concerns and style when asked whether it was "to shock the audience into attention" that he used a lunatic asylum as the setting for *Marat/Sade*. He replied:

> In a surrounding like that it is possible to say almost everything; in the surrounding of insane people you have an absolute freedom. You can say things which are very dangerous and mad, whatever you want, and at the same time you can mix them with the political agitation, which I want to get through too. If I should do this play in a pedagogic way, as Brecht perhaps might have done it, I couldn't get the strong emotional effects which I wanted . . . because those people are mad everything gets so much stronger when they express it.[6]

From Weiss' perspective, individual and nationwide madness in modern states required more disturbing and visceral forms of drama than those Brecht developed. In the same interview, Alvarez asked if Weiss meant that "politics itself is a form of madness" and whether it follows that Weiss was not a political writer—despite his intentions. Weiss responded:

> No, perhaps not, because as soon as I get involved with political conflicts, I get in touch with the mad world we are living in. When I read the speeches of the politicians they are very close to madness to me.

The persecution of innocent Mockinpott anticipates scenes of far greater violence and injustice in later plays, where the violence is either prelude or sequel to revolution. Violence comes to pervade the later plays, as Marat, Trotsky and others suffer government persecution. Their persecutor is no longer a mysterious or omnipotent divinity, but the state, and they can resist it or see it destroy them. Even in *Mockinpott* we see the beginnings of a revolutionary impulse. As Michael Roloff notes in his introduction to the English translation of the play, "Mockinpott does not lack revolutionary potential. What if he should ever decide to make the world conform to his disappointed illusion of it? There would be no end to his outrage."[7]

### Wittgenstein or Frankenstein?

Peter Handke's clown play portrays a learning process comparable to those in *Mockinpott* and *The Baden Learning Play*. A naive clown, Kaspar learns to move and speak through the prompting of voices hidden in the prompter's box on stage. It is tempting to say that a disciple of Ludwig Wittgenstein hides inside the box; Handke's investigation of language and its relationship to action recalls that of his countryman at times, as it presses speech habits to the limits of logic—or past those limits. Kaspar hears "model" sentences from his prompters, and their instructions and examples of sentence construction lead him to speak with eloquence. Initially Kaspar is both physically clumsy and nearly speechless. He trips, he accidentally knocks over furniture, his hand gets caught in a table drawer.

Kaspar's inability to walk around objects is linked by Handke to ignorance of language; once the clown can name objects and distinguish them, he can separate himself from them. As Kaspar's verbal fluency increases, so does his physical coordination. Handke suggests that the acquisition of language not only enables us to order our perceptions, but it may order our actual experience, determining movement and thought in a tyrannical way. As Kaspar says late in the play, "Already with my first sentence I was trapped." In the course of the action he becomes a model speaker, totally assimilating language—or being assimilated by it. Then Kaspar struggles and fails to regain a sense of private identity. He has no language of his own; even his anger is expressed in someone else's words. It is the rage of Othello—"goats and monkeys"—Kaspar repeats as the curtain falls.

Kaspar's first sentence, the one that "traps" him into submission to language, is, "I want to be a person like somebody else was once." The clown has this wish fulfilled, as June Schlueter notes in her essay on the play, when "Handke directs that five other clownlike figures roam about . . . populating the stage with duplicates of Kaspar."[8] The presence of six clowns on stage could lead to some farcical antics, but Handke uses the clowns in a manner far removed from conventional farce and satire. Kaspar is dressed like a Hanswurstian clown, in a wide-brimmed hat, colorful jacket, wide pants, clumsy shoes; however, the author notes at the start that he "does not resemble any other clown. Rather, when he comes on stage he resembles Frankenstein's monster (or King Kong)." Handke's disclaimer about no resemblance between Kaspar and other clowns leads Schlueter to compare the figure to several versions of Frankenstein's monster; but in doing so she misses the point of the disclaimer. While Kaspar may physically resemble a monster, he *is* a clown.

These two aspects of Kaspar—comedian and monster—are contained in the play's title as well as its action. Besides the linguistic affinity between *Kaspar* and *Kasperl*, the German name for a Hanswurstian clown, "Kaspar" was the name of an autistic Nuremberg youth who lived his first sixteen years alone in a room, without any education. When he left his isolation in 1828, Kaspar Hauser was suddenly exposed to a process of socialization that most people experience in infancy. Physically mature but lacking knowledge of language, himself and society, Hauser was something like Frankenstein's monster.

Handke explained his interest in Hauser's case history to Arthur Joseph, in a 1969 interview:

In Kaspar Hauser I discovered the model of a sort of linguistic myth. The character made me curious. A human being lives in a closet for sixteen or seventeen years, [then] suddenly encounters the outside world, although he is unable to speak. . . . He sees the green trees and thinks they're shutters, because he can't distinguish between planes and space. He can't tell two-dimensionality from three-dimensionality. Can't separate space from time. He can't speak; he's virtually incapable of any correct perception. . . . To me, this Kaspar Hauser seemed a mythical figure, interesting not only as such, but as a model of men at odds with themselves and their environment, men who feel isolated. . . . For me this was a model of conduct, building a person into society's course of conduct by language, by giving him words to repeat . . . he is reconstructed by voices, by language models. . . .[9]

Handke goes on to note that *Kaspar* shows "the idiocy of language. In constantly pretending to express something it expresses nothing but its own stupidity." In this "idiocy," the clown-like and monstrous qualities of Handke's Kaspar meet. Frankenstein's monster and circus clowns are usually associated with non-verbal idiocy: lack of social graces; impulsive, crude or violent

*Wolf Redl as Kaspar in the 1968 Frankfurt production of Peter Handke's play by the same name, directed by Claus Peymann.*

assaults against others; mechanical or clumsy motor coordination. But the idiocy of clowns can also be verbal, as Hanswurst, Valentin and Brecht's comic characters prove. Handke's Kaspar displays both types of stupidity. He is, indeed, a hybrid.

Kaspar manifests his idiocy physically at the start of the play. He has trouble entering through the curtain and more trouble handling stage furniture; these moments might easily turn into comic routines in another play. Handke counteracts the potential humor of the routines with the voices of the prompters and Kaspar's own voice; their words jar and distract instead of matching the physical action. Many comic gags, stifled in performance by the voices and other production elements, can be discovered in the stage directions:

> He opens the drawer wide, with one hand. He puts the matches in the drawer, pushing the drawer shut with the other hand, whereupon the first hand gets caught in the drawer. He pulls on the caught hand while pushing in with the other hand, exerting himself more and more in both endeavors. Finally he is able to free his hand with one violent pull, while the other hand, with one violent push, pushes in the drawer.[10]

While Kaspar performs this routine, invisible voices tell him about the

room, the table, about how "the furnishings should complement you" and how "there is a place for everything and everything in its place." His physical maladroitness contradicts the platitudes praising the rightness of everything. The contradiction here between words and action might be comic, but the voices are relentless and the words function less as punchlines than as filibusters, wearing away Kaspar's resistance to authority.

Frequently the words spoken by the prompters and Kaspar parody conventional forms of speech; they offer half-complete sentences or jumbled thoughts which distort the persuasive power and control inherent in rhetoric. Here, too, Handke subverts the comic potential. The mechanical pace of the prompter's delivery does not allow for comic timing of the sort a regular comedian might employ; no pauses are allowed for laughter. Like the Dadaist stage dialogues of Tristan Tzara, passages in Handke's play function as assaults on logic, and on language's power to command obedience and convey information credibly. The author creates exaggerated examples of "the idiocy of language . . . constantly pretending to express something," by having Kaspar speak such homilies as "Every split straw is a vote for the progressive forces. No country fair means security for all. Each dripping faucet is an example of a healthy life."

Handke's militant assault on language is about as comic as Ludwig Wittgenstein's notebooks. While the playwright populates his stage with six clownlike characters, Kaspar could be regarded as an anti-clown play, a performance in which the comic naiveté of a clown is aggressively destroyed by his educators (the prompters), and by language itself. Nicholas Hern has speculated that "Handke's denial of [Kaspar's] clownishness presumably stems from a Brechtian fear that recognition of a funny and lovable stereotype (rather than a sinister monster) will prevent the audience from seeing the serious implications of Kaspar's fate and its application to their society."[11] (Whether this fear is "Brechtian" or "Handkean" is a matter for debate, since Brecht frequently created comic characters, though not necessarily stereotypes.)

In earlier clown plays and Brecht's comedies, the questioning of authority by a Mockinpott or a Schweyk constituted utopian freedom, a way of resisting unjust authority through language. Handke's anti-utopian play portrays loss of freedom through language, or to it. As the author pointed out to Arthur Joseph:

> Kaspar is a purely anarchic play: it conveys no social utopia; it merely negates everything it comes across. I don't care whether it yields a positive utopia. The only thing that preoccupies me as a writer . . . is nausea at stupid speechification and the resulting brutalization of people.[12]

Handke's anarchist critique of language in Kaspar is closer to Orwell's satire of totalitarian doublespeak than to Brecht's use of language to satirize and resist illegitimate authority. Kaspar and later Handke plays reveal language as permitting the abuses of authority—the "brutalization of people." (There is a note of optimism toward the end of Kaspar, when the phrase "If only" is repeated; but the slightly utopian wish for improvement of things is more of a minority report than a major counter-statement.)

In his interview with Joseph, Handke offers a specific example of a group deprived of its own language; the German Leftists of the '60s. Much as Weiss' aesthetics were formed by his witnessing of the Auschwitz trials and the American bombings of Vietnam, Handke's approach to playwriting was also influenced by—or at least a response to—the political events of that decade.

Handke's fear that the German Left had no language of its own reflects his own political position to a degree: that of a Leftist critical of the Left. He has called himself a Marxist on several occasions, and his focus on language and the cultural superstructure as sources of exploitation is not wholly a departure from traditional Marxist theories which see economic motives behind abuse of authority. Handke links these two perspectives in The Unintelligent Are Dying Out. The play, about a group of corporate executives, suggests that consciousness itself is subject to industrial commodification, as advertising uses language to control the public's behavior in the marketplace. Alienation from language coincides with the alienation from labor about which Marx wrote voluminously, when, for example, industrialist Von Wullnow in The Unintelligent Are Dying Out notes that his employees don't sing on the job as workers once did: "They get the work over and done with, mutely and indifferently. . . . Their thoughts are elsewhere." At other points in the play Handke suggests that the industrial magnates, too, are alienated from language, since they have also sacrificed individuality to corporate consciousness. They become victims of their own advertising campaigns. Quitt, the magnate who, by corporate standards, goes mad (the standards are relatively low), claims to hear voices: "But not the kind of voices that madmen hear: no religious phrases, or poetry regurgitated from schooldays . . . none of the traditional formulas—but movie titles, pop tunes, advertising slogans." In short, he suffers from an experience the general public encounters whenever it turns on the radio or TV.

## The Clown in the Board Room

*The Unintelligent Are Dying Out* and *The Ride Across Lake Constance*, both written after *Kaspar*, dramatize language's brutalization of people, but with an important difference: language is no longer a disembodied phenomenon, a series of sentences delivered by invisible prompters. Instead, the speakers appear onstage as characters (a radical departure from Handke's earlier refusal to use plot and character conventions). In *The Ride Across Lake Constance* the speakers represent film actors; in *The Unintelligent Are Dying Out* they are corporate executives, plus one servant, one executive wife and one clown. These later plays suggest that speech, however virulent, is a malleable, humanly controllable material which actors can use to play roles and businessmen can use to manipulate the public for profit.

Handke's dramatization of the malleable, artificial aspects of language and the consciousness that language creates owes a debt to Brecht, which the Austrian acknowledged in his 1968 essay, "Brecht, Play, Theatre, Agitation." He objects to aspects of Brecht's theatre in the essay, but first he credits his predecessor:

> [Brecht has helped me see] the state of the world, which had hitherto been taken as intrinsic and natural . . . to be manufactured—and precisely therefore manufacturable and alterable. Not natural, not non-historical, but artificial, capable of alteration, possible of alteration, and understandably needful of alteration. [In this] Brecht has helped to educate me.[13]

In all of his plays, Handke stresses the artifice of the situation to insure that actors are seen as actors on a stage. If the world is manufactured, so are the stage and its language. Handke's opposition to the illusions of realism in theatre recalls Brecht's, but his battle against the imaginary fourth wall and other fictions has been far more aggressive.

An early Handke one-act, *Offending the Audience*, openly denies its audience any opportunity for empathy or voyeurism behind the imaginary fourth wall; instead the artifice of the event is discussed by the actors, and spectators are insulted and called names, making them the subject of the play. Brecht's performers occasionally offered their listeners a direct address, but nothing like the harangue in Handke's play.

In *Kaspar*, too, Handke strips away plot, character and other conventions of drama, creating something closer to non-representational, abstract art. His title character has even less of a personal history than the real Kaspar Hauser; Kaspar the clown is simply there on stage, born when he emerges from behind the curtain. It is not his past but the language given to him by the playwright that determines his behavior. The stage, Handke specifies, should not be seen "as a representation of a room that exists somewhere, but as a representation of a stage." The anti-illusionism that Handke seeks here is also achieved by circus clowns, as the playwright suggested to Arthur Joseph:

> The objects [in my plays] are deprived of their normal function in reality. They have an artificial function in the game I force them to play. They are like the objects a circus clown makes factually unreal.[14]

Language, like the clown, denies the reality of objects, giving them "artificial functions" and changing their reality in *The Unintelligent Are Dying Out* as in earlier Handke plays.

Handke's satire of social control and linguistic alienation, *The Unintelligent Are Dying Out*, focuses on Hermann Quitt, an industrialist who attempts to rescue a sense of private identity from his corporate way of life. Quitt finds himself imprisoned by the laws and commodified consciousness of the business world—somewhat as Kaspar is trapped by the language his prompters give him. The industrial magnate attempts to escape his confining world and eventually commits suicide, which may be the only escape open to him.

Throughout the play Quitt and his business associates tolerate the presence of a clown named Franz Kilb. They solicit and mimic Kilb's opposition to their business practices. Franz Kilb calls himself "the terror of the board of directors, the clown of the stockholders' meetings, the tick in the navel of the economy with the nuisance value of 100;"[15] and he is accurate in claiming to be a clown. A modern Hanswurst, Kilb resorts to Harpo Marx's raised thigh trick and other slapstick routines, and gets out some one-line insults at corporate board meetings. He is permitted to watch Quitt and other industrialists plan price-fixing, and he also sees Quitt break the monopolistic agreement and undersell his associates.

Kilb is welcomed by the executives, especially Quitt; Quitt's Lear-like rantings are complemented by Kilb's role as court jester. Before he kills himself, Quitt kills Kilb, as if their lives are inseparable. The dual murder is hardly a lovers' suicide pact, however. The two men are linked by their nonconformity, their different forms of opposition to the majority of businessmen around them; and also by their symbiotic dependency on each other. Each allows the other to play his respective role: that of rich, autocratic capitalist and that of protester.

Critic June Schlueter has suggested that Quitt's servant Hans is the magnate's *doppelganger* and alter ego.[16] She is quite correct to note that Hans wants to be like Quitt; Hans, the proletarian, may eventually find the self-expressive freedom his master sought. Kilb has no such ambition. He does not want to be Quitt. Despite this, he resembles Hermann Quitt in his inability to speak as an individual free from corporate control.

Kilb's activity constitutes a rather trivial form of free speech. Because he owns "one share of every major corporation in the country," he is entitled by law to be heard at stockholders' meetings. This permits him to interject words of protest and ridicule at the capitalists' conferences, and to affirm their significance. As he notes, "Stockholders' meetings where the board ignores someone who asks for the floor are null and void." Kilb's role as professional gadfly has some basis in fact; critics of corporate capitalism have purchased stock in General Electric and Dow Chemical, for example, to argue against production of military weapons at annual shareholders' meetings. But Handke makes a caricature of his protester, a cartoon of the Leftists whom he had criticized at the time he wrote *Kaspar* for not having a language of their own. The gadfly's words are innocuous and subservient to those who permit him to speak. To compensate for his verbal inadequacy, Kilb nonverbally disrupts the proceedings with farting noises, punches, crude physical gestures.

Once they have searched the intruder so they know he cannot tape-record their speeches and use their own words against them, Quitt and associates let Kilb hear their price-fixing plans, confident that the buffoon is incapable of saying anything, during their meeting or after it, that would spoil their monopoly. The businessmen know their plan is safe from Kilb's assaults, and drink to their success, soon after Quitt asks the gadfly to "repeat what I've just said." Instead of repeating their plan to fix prices, reduce wages, etc., Kilb "moves his lips, falters, tries again, shakes his head," then says, "Anyway it sounded logical." He makes a disrespectful facial gesture, with tongue extended, to demonstrate how logical it sounded. The fact that he has no words with which to frighten the magnates testifies to Kilb's harmlessness. His interjections merely provide them with a sense of their own superiority and safety, as well as with diverting entertainment—just what royalty has always expected from a court jester.

Kilb and the businessmen are conscious of their respective roles, and they acknowledge these roles during the course of the play. Their behavior resembles a game with rather clearcut rules, until Quitt decides to break the rules and proceed on his own. Such anarchic individualism undercuts the price agreements, and even the very premises of monopoly capital; but Quitt's breakaway is destined to fail in the highly structured society of the play. Hermann Quitt commits suicide shortly after he vows, "I want to speak about myself without using categories. I don't want to mean anything anymore, please, not to be a character in a story anymore." He can only depart from role-playing through death. Quitt, like Handke in some of his essays, calls for the elimination of fiction. "I'm playing at something that doesn't even exist, and that's the despair of it," says Quitt when he resolves to end the game.

## Fear of Satire

But even his death is suitable only for a character in a story. He falls into the category mentioned in the play's title—and in the play itself—when Paula Tax tells Quitt, "Your time has finally come. Actually, your time as Quitt who suffers his life in exemplary bourgeois fashion has long since passed." The rest of the play more or less confirms her analysis, as it shows Quitt incapable of Romantic, exemplary suffering. Quitt offers his servant Hans a rebuke which might be addressed to Handke, as well:

> You're making fun of my language. I would much prefer to express myself inarticulately like the little people in the play recently, do you remember? This way I suffer my articulateness as part of my suffering. The only ones that you and your kind pity are those who can't speak about their suffering.

Quitt would feel more comfortable in a play by Franz Xaver Kroetz, it seems; but he is too articulate to suffer like Kroetz's lower-class farmers and factory workers do. Instead he suffers from a fear of satire. He accuses Hans of mocking him and senses that, "Everything that is meant to be serious immediately becomes a joke with me."

Even his death is preceded by a joke. Kilb enters, knife in hand, and recites an assassination speech, warning Quitt, "You have to die now. It's no use. . . . It's our last way out. Don't contradict me." Then Kilb notices that his prospective victim isn't in the room. Hans encourages Kilb to find and kill his master: the disenfranchised appear for a moment to be conspiring against the ruling class. Quitt enters before Kilb is psychologically ready for the kill, and, proficient man that he is, Quitt murders the clown and kills himself. In the failed assassination attempt, as elsewhere, Kilb is a foil to Quitt, a jester who insures that everything will end as a joke.

At one point in the first act Kilb becomes extremely conscious of his own role, and angry over it: "Is it my job to take care of the entertainment?" he asks the assembled businessmen. He then proceeds to answer his own question in the affirmative, and to caricature his role as entertainer, slapping his thighs and shoe soles like a folk dancer. He mocks the others: "Let's swing a little. . . . A little circus atmosphere! Not just words against which the brain is defenseless anyway." But, for the most part, he gets only words from men playing at something that may soon cease to exist—an economic and philosophical system that is dying out—or that has already died. Against such imaginary constructs the clown is defenseless; he is a contemporary, articulate version of Brecht's Mr. Smith.

Peter Handke himself could be regarded as a kind of Kilb if one were in an ungenerous mood. Writing about the end of late capitalism and Romantic individualism for high bourgeois spectators (who else could comprehend his work?) seems somewhat futile. Handke holds a cracked mirror up to an audience which, if his mirror is accurate, will have little concern about what it sees; in this sense he is like Kilb, writing satires of people who merely find diversion in his comic art.

# –12
# Théâtre du Soleil's 'Mephisto'
## Hitler in the Cabaret

Since its creation of *The Clowns* in 1969, Théâtre du Soleil has returned several times to such popular theatre forms as circus clowning. In a work called *1789*, its first play about the French Revolution, the company created a fairground, complete with acrobats, puppets and jugglers; it turned to *commedia dell'arte* for comic characters in *L'Age d'Or (The Golden Age)*, the story of a North African living in contemporary France; and it re-used some of Valentin's cabaret satires in its *Mephisto*, based on Klaus Mann's novel about theatre and politics in Nazi Germany. The collective has not concentrated exclusively on popular forms, but its use of puppetry and cabaret humor is indicative of more than a comic sensibility. Théâtre du Soleil reinvents past theatre forms to find analogies for present day situations in art and society. Brecht's idea of prompting spectators to "intervene actively in life" is adapted by the company as it attempts to intervene in history: to recreate the past, to write and tell history anew—and to discover metaphors for present-day events—through its fairground clowning and cabaret satire.

Théâtre du Soleil has used these festive comic forms to celebrate some important moments in history, and parody others. Two plays about the French Revolution, *1789* and *1793*, were also indirect commentaries on the events of May 1968, when expectations for another revolution briefly arose in France after nationwide strikes and demonstrations. The failures of the historic French

Revolution were implicitly compared to the failures of May 1968. Michael Kustow, the British critic and director, reports that when the actor playing the "liberal" aristocrat LaFayette stepped into the carnival arena that constituted the performance space in *1789*, and told the crowd that the Revolution was over and all public celebrations were forbidden, audience members booed the character and began chanting a slogan from May '68: "This is only the beginning, the struggle continues."[1] For Théâtre du Soleil, the struggle continued beyond 1968, at least through its 1979 production of *Mephisto*.

Its contemporary use of popular theatre techniques began when Théâtre du Soleil actors created their own comic personae for a collaborative work, *The Clowns*. The group's exploration of clowning is partially indebted to Jacques Lecoq, the French mime with whom Théâtre du Soleil director Ariane Mnouchkine once studied. Lecoq encourages each of his students to discover his "own clown," to find a mask, a walk and eccentricities peculiar to him. When the Théâtre du Soleil actors created a play out of these individual exercises, they began to develop a language for future collective creation. Not only did the company members contribute characters (their own) to the play, they invented scenes together, through improvisation and clown rehearsal. In subsequent productions, as they turned their attention to themes of revolution, unemployment and fascism, the company continued to develop these themes as they developed the clowning itself: collectively, creating roles through improvisations based on studies of history, theatre history and literature.

## From Clowns to Revolutionaries

While the study of clowning is not necessarily preparation for the creation of revolutionary plays, it has served that purpose for Théâtre du Soleil. Judith Graves Miller describes the importance of *The Clowns* in her book, *Revolution and Theater in France Since 1968*:

> To overcome its discouragement over the outcome of the May events, the Théâtre du Soleil in its next production [after *A Midsummer Night's Dream*, staged, incidentally, at the Parisian circus space, Cirque de Montmartre], examined one of the most difficult problems raised in May: the relationship of the artist to society. The actors adopted the clothing, gestures and techniques of clowns in order to free their own personalities for analysis. Starting from *le degré zero*, each actor improvised a series of autobiographical sketches in order to find a personal "clown," or an incarnation of his own attitude as an artist toward society. Once these individual characters were created two or three actors worked together to develop the basic skits which make up the work. Mnouchkine assumed the position of objective observer. Her criticism modified and refined the dialogues and actions and perfected the final version. . . . In creating *Les Clowns*, the

members of the Théâtre du Soleil clarified their political position, for despite the title of the work, the play repudiated the political impotence of artists.[2]

This self-reflexive tendency to consider the relationship between their art and society recurs in later work by the ensemble, notably its film about Molière and the play *Mephisto*.

The freeing of the actors' own personalities through the assumption of clown masks reflects a continuing practice on the part of Théâtre du Soleil: to immerse itself in popular theatre forms, particularly comic ones, as a means of avoiding or reducing the degree of psychological realism in performance. Instead of presenting individual personalities or psychologies, the company's plays tend to depict the broad canvas of society, with emphasis on breadth and the interrelations of the whole, rather than in-depth focus on specific characters. This lack of depth was evident in *Mephisto*, as critic Jack Zipes noted: "Mnouchkine's dramatic adaptation does not deeply probe the characters or their motives. The dramatic rendition is more like an epic canvas with one-dimensional figures illustrating general themes."[3] Mnouchkine might regard that assessment as a compliment; she herself once said that she did not want to present "a type of mystifying spectacle where history becomes a succession of psychological conflicts between 'great' men."[4] Rather than portray famous historical figures realistically, Théâtre du Soleil generally presents these men as puppets or clowns whose psychology is simple, almost nonexistent. What interests Mnouchkine and her ensemble is not the greatness of these men, but their images and their relation to history as it is perceived by lesser men: actors, acrobats, ordinary and oppressed citizens.

## Why Should a Leading French Troupe Adapt a German Novel?

After *The Clowns*, Théâtre du Soleil turned to the French Revolution to examine its failures—and its successes—from the perspective of "popular" historians, fairground entertainers who might well see history unconventionally. "We try and show the Revolution played all the time on the level of people, but from a critical distance," declares Mnouchkine. "Acrobats, strolling players, town criers or agitators show that they experience, they know, how 'historic' events and major characters belong to them. We never show Louis XVI. The spectator sees Louis XVI through the eyes of a strolling player."[5] Of course this "strolling player" is a contemporary actor playing the role of an eighteenth-century entertainer; some distance from both the political events of 1789 and later events is built into the situation. Still, the notion that a public performer can possess history, can know that it belongs to him by virtue of recreating it, suggests that history is not owned or controlled exclusively by those who own publishing companies or estates, or rule nations. History is accessible even to lowly strolling actors and their *1789* audience. The concept of democratic or collective creation and ownership of history was to recur again in the Théâtre du Soleil's staging of *Mephisto*, and it may have been a factor in the company's decision to adapt the German novel in the first place.

Klaus Mann's novel about actors in Nazi Germany was banned in West Germany until 1981, due to the threat of a libel suit from the son of one of the *roman à clef's* central characters. The character, Hendrik Höfgen in the novel, is based on the German actor Gustaf Gründgens, who married Klaus Mann's sister Erika in 1926. Mann wrote the novel primarily as a study of Gründgens' suspiciously successful acting career. Gründgens, who married into the Mann family to advance his career, was not only famous as Thomas Mann's son-in-law. Hitler appointed him director of the State Theatre in Berlin after he had endeared himself to Nazi Minister Goering—and all of Nazi Germany—by playing the role of Mephisto in Goethe's *Faust*. This actor achieved fame and admiration by portraying a devil on stage—an act of collaboration with Hitler's regime which seems more plausible as a metaphor than as historical fact, though it did happen.

Théâtre du Soleil began to adapt the novel for its stage several years before a Hungarian film, directed by István Szabó and based on the same novel, was released. The fact that both the play and the film were created in the past decade suggests that the issues in Klaus Mann's novel are far from dated. The theatre company may have chosen to adapt the novel because, as Jack Zipes has noted, they realized that "political amnesia" about collaboration with the Nazis "is not peculiar to Germany." While the novel about an actor's collaboration with Hitler was long-banned in West Germany, in France, too, writes Zipes, "the fascist past and its continuation in the present is a taboo subject. . . . French collaboration with the Nazis is a topic that is carefully avoided."[6] Théâtre du Soleil avoided this topic by focusing entirely on German events, as the novel does. But the themes of *Mephisto* clearly offer an "exemplary parable" of the problems faced by artists and intellectuals today, as Mnouchkine notes:

> "Hendrik Höfgen chooses Nazism and Otto Ulrich [another actor in the book, based on the German actor and underground resistance member Hans Otto] the party of the revolution. One [Höfgen] receives all the honors, the other is murdered by the Gestapo. Ever since this time we have realized that the slightest choice, the slightest tendency, which at first glance appears to be minor, has in fact extreme importance."[7]

To further emphasize the choices available in the situation, Théâtre du Soleil created a number of scenes not included in Klaus Mann's novel or in the Hungarian film. These include three scenes in the Stormbird Cabaret, the revolutionary theatre to which Otto Ulrich devotes his energies while Hendrik Höfgen advances his career in Berlin by pleasing Nazi generals. The cabaret scenes, developed by company actors through improvisation and study of German cabaret material by Karl Valentin and Kurt Tucholsky, allow spectators to see more of the alternative, anti-authoritarian career of Ulrich, and heighten the contrast between the life he chooses and Höfgen's. Initially, Höfgen, too, talks of joining the Stormbird's revolutionary working-class theatre; but he later conveniently forgets these vows along with the communist political leanings that went with them.

## Hitler in the Cabaret

The Stormbird scenes all involve clown acts, satire and masks, for which Théâtre du Soleil's actors had been prepared by earlier productions. To some extent, Ulrich's theatre is theirs; his preference for nonrealistic acting and political commentary is shared by Mnouchkine and her company. But all of the cabaret scenes end with characters debating the efficacy of their theatre. In their debates the self-doubts of Théâtre du Soleil are also reflected.

In the first Stormbird rehearsal scene a pregnant woman enters a German welfare office seeking assistance. She has been there six times already and is confronted with bureaucratic evasions each time she visits. The dialogue of evasion and nonsense resembles some of Karl Valentin's cabaret humor, only it is far more overtly political. (As an aside, it might be noted that the leftwing theatre scene rehearsed in Szabó's film of *Mephisto* is derived from Brecht's didactic play *The Breadshop*. Théâtre du Soleil seems more indebted to Valentin, to Brecht's *Arturo Ui* and to the Bread and Puppet Theatre for its antiauthoritarian cabaret scenes—as will be evident shortly.) Here is an excerpt from the first cabaret scene:

> *Woman:* I'm expecting twins, my husband is a war invalid. I can't find any work and I don't have any housing anymore.
> *Employee* [played by Otto]: Oh well . . . let's start from the beginning— your address?
> *Woman:* But I just told you that I'm out in the street.
> *Employee:* Have you got a certificate?
> *Woman:* A certificate?
> *Employee:* Certifying that you're out in the street.
> *Woman:* Why no!
> *Employee:* Well then, where do you expect me to send the reply to your application for assistance?
> *Woman:* To my sister's, number 14, on the street—on the street all fared better in the time of the Emperor.
> *Employee:* When did you lose your housing?
> *Woman:* The 20th of November.
> *Employee:* That's too bad.

*Woman:* Of course it's too bad.

*Employee:* Because if you'd lost it on the 21st you would have been eligible for special assistance, thanks to the decree of the 30th which takes effect on the 21st but not on the 17th.[8]

This *badinage* continues until the Employee takes off his cap and announces, "I've been listening to the three of you [you and your unborn twins] for an hour now. I've got other things to do. . . . This was my last day. From now on, I'm unemployed. So I'm standing in line at the assistance bureau." When even the welfare clerks are unemployed and stand behind their clients in line, we know the country is in trouble.

Myriam Horowitz, who performs the skit with Otto, has doubts about it after they finish rehearsing. Otto rhetorically asks the actress whether she thinks that theatre is powerless in its depiction of society. He himself does not: at least he finds such powerlessness unacceptable. He wants to dramatize the problems of inflation, for example, and "why, how, because of whom, for whom" such problems exist. When pressed by another actress (Carola, modeled on Brecht's friend Carola Neher), however, Otto claims he is "not interested in theatre. . . . I'm a communist. That's my only profession, my only vocation in this world. The theatre is only a roof over my head and the butter on my bread." Later in the play, when he loses his job as an actor, Otto has a chance to practice his true and only vocation by other means, passing on information about Nazi prisoners and prison camps for the underground. The political cabaret clown becomes a full-time activist and Otto leaves the world of theatre satire for anti-fascist activities, much as he wanted his spectators to do when they left the theatre.

The second Stormbird rehearsal scene, also set in 1923, features an actor wearing prison stripes and a huge *papier mâché* head of Hitler. The scene involves Hitler in prison, visited by a munitions manufacturer who berates him for failing to stem the tide of Bolshevism. The manufacturer then attempts to introduce the Führer to a clownish army general who keeps vowing to annex various countries and thereby reunite the German people. In this scene the Hitler figure says nothing. He furiously gestures as if addressing a mass rally but the soldier and the arms manufacturer do the talking; the imprisoned Nazi is their puppet, a means to their ends, the scene implies. The acting style is far from realistic, with characters wearing large false heads and all three resembling awkward, stupid clowns. One other actor disrupts the rehearsal and starts a debate by announcing that he wants to keep Hitler's visitors in prison permanently. The actor, Alex, then improvises a speech to be addressed directly to the cabaret audience, warning against Hitler's cohorts:

Comrades! The game's up. Do you know what's in there? Capitalists! Down with the bourgeoisie. Down with International Capitalism. . . . Long live the international revolution! Greetings to the Soviet Union! There you are. . . . Clear. Straightforward. Optimistic. Positive.

Alex creates a positive proletarian hero unintentionally funnier than he imagines. His social realist aesthetic is ridiculously inappropriate to the grotesque cartoon style of the rest of the sketch, and it makes him look as silly or even sillier than the Hitler puppet. Another actor on the scene informs Alex that he is no actor, "he's a vulgar propagandist." Alex replies that his colleagues are only "using patterns of bourgeois entertainment . . . not doing revolutionary theatre." and he wants their plays "to be as effective as [their] tracts." (Later, Alex has a chance to focus more directly on effective tracts, along with Otto and the underground resistance movement, after the Stormbird is closed.)

The last words in this debate come not from an actor, but from an act of vandalism, discovered when the actors lower their new backdrop. On it someone has painted the words, "Jews, communists, social democrats . . . Patience . . . we'll get you." The sketch has been effective even before it has opened, perhaps; already the Stormbird has enemies. It is an embattled theatre, and the vandalism testifies to its value as an outspoken representative of several endangered species.

Conversations critical of political rhetoric recur throughout *Mephisto* and prevent the play from becoming the sort of effective tract Alex might have in mind. After Otto Ulrich attempts to comfort an actress by telling her, "When one's afraid, the struggle is the only remedy," she replies, "I don't like you when you talk like a pamphlet." The dangers of rhetoric become fully evident to Otto later, when a new Nazi Intendant at the state theatre in Hamburg informs the actors that they must stage great classical German work and modern German plays which serve the national interest. The Intendant adds, "An art can only be good if it is at the service of the people and their revolution." Otto recognizes the cliché as one he himself might have used at another time; and he observes, "Some phrases are like belladonna. Sometimes a remedy, it becomes poison in the hands of an assassin."

The only character whose susceptibility to rhetoric remains unchecked is the careerist, Hendrik Höfgen. He lives as if his entire life is a play. His emotions all seem derived from scripts. When he professes love to Erika Mann, he sounds like a man in a sentimental melodrama. The literate woman might have known better than to fall for his cheap theatrics, but she marries him only to be abandoned when her famous name no longer serves his career. When Höfgen departs Hamburg for success in Berlin, Erika decides to join the Stormbird Cabaret troupe as a writer and actress. The schism between husband and wife underlines the division of the theatrical and political worlds between which these characters must choose.

In the third and final cabaret scene Erika Mann offers a virtuoso clown performance as Mrs. Moanalot. She parodies Nazi anti-semitism by deliver-

ing a sermon which attributes all the problems of German society to the
telephone. She accuses the phone of daring to ring in her own German home;
she defames it as a swine, a foreigner, an accursed race, and in the midst
of her curses she concedes, "Ah, I'm having a great time." The performance,
featuring Mann in bulbous red rubber nose and rag doll clothing (innocence
itself, but for a swastika-decked apron), is quite a funny parody of Nazi logic.
It is also the last Stormbird scene. After they rehearse it, we learn that the
actors need worry about censorship no longer. Nazi stormtroopers will simply disrupt any show that disturbs them. Moreover, news arrives that Hitler
has become Chancellor of Germany. The date is January 30, 1933. After this,
the Stormbird actors and their friends will have to flee Germany or commit
suicide or go underground, if they cannot face collaboration or prison.

*Josephine Derenne as Mrs.*
*Moanalot in the Stormbird*
*Cabaret sequence of Théâtre du*
*Soleil's* Mephisto, *1979.*

## What Do You Say When the General Strike Fails?
## "Farewell to the Working Class"

The last Stormbird rehearsal ends with a brief, quiet discussion of alternative political strategies now that Hitler is in power. While not obviously related to the comic act that precedes it, it constitutes a rather interesting commentary on the Stormbird Cabaret and its failure to prevent the rise of Hitler through satire.

Otto Ulrich asks his friends whether there can be a General Strike by workers to resist Hitler's new power. The General Strike, a work stoppage through which all the unions of a city, country or continent exercise their collective strength for a period of time, has become more of a legend than an achievable goal in many nations. (France experienced something akin to it in May 1968, as Théâtre du Soleil audiences watching *Mephisto* would have known.) In whispers Otto asks his question, and the painfully comic, understated reply is that there can be no hope for a General Strike when seven million Germans are unemployed. This is a ghastly joke, not delivered as one, to hear in the Stormbird Cabaret, a stage dedicated to the working class and its revolution. The working class has been decimated through unemployment so it is no wonder that a working class theatre should terminate before it has really begun. The scene ends as Otto starts to vomit.

The absence of a strategy to organize the working class in a General Strike parallels or underscores the failure of Otto's cabaret to organize a working class audience around his satires. Théâtre du Soleil intimates that old strategies to organize for revolution, and to satirize fascism out of existence (or even adequately resist fascism) through cabaret theatre have outlived their usefulness. The social analysis implicit in the scene might be described as a "Farewell to the Working Class," a phrase used as the title of a recent book by French social analyst André Gorz. His theory about the obsolescence of working-class organizing strategies, articulated a year after *Mephisto* opened, reveals an important resonance between the company's play and contemporary social developments. Gorz writes:

> Loss of the ability to identify with one's work is tantamount to the disappearance of any sense of belonging to a class. Just as the work remains external to the individual, so, too, does class being. Just as work has become a nondescript task carried out without any personal involvement . . . so, too, has class membership come to be lived as a contingent and meaningless fact. . . . For workers, it is no longer a question of freeing themselves within work, putting themselves in control of work or seizing power within the framework of work. The point now is to free oneself from work by rejecting its nature, content, necessity and modalities. But to reject work is also to reject the traditional strategy and organizational forms of the working class movement.[9]

While Gorz's reasons for saying farewell to the working class are not quite the same as Théâtre du Soleil's, both point to an exhaustion of traditional leftist strategies derived from Marxist theories about working class politics. The events of January 1933, and those of May 1968 and beyond, all point to the need for new strategies, and rejection of past ones revered only because they come from the man Gorz wryly calls Saint Marx. The debate over this issue is not central to *Mephisto*, but it is present, in understated form, throughout the play.

## Two Theatres, One Audience

Spectators attending performances of *Mephisto* actually visited two theatres for the price of one. The performance space was designed so that the grand, ornately decorated state theatre of Höfgen's triumphs was located at one end and the brightly muraled wall of the Stormbird Cabaret was situated at the opposite end. As scenes alternated, audience members, seated on reversible benches, had to move around to view the two settings. The arrangement allowed less mobility than the multiple stages and walk-around fairground setting of *1789*, but then its purpose was different. In *Mephisto* the opposition between two ways of life—and two ways of art—was emphasized. Only one could be seen at a time, as only one choice could be made by a character.

There were some curious crossovers during the performance—moments when the world of the state theatre seemed overrun by grotesque cabaret imagery—moments when the vision of the satirists came alive in those satirized, without their knowing it. These moments were among the most acute and subtle ones in the production. When, for example, the new Nazi Intendant appointed to run the Hamburg theatre questions one of his older employees, he asks the man to tell a joke. The employee, a longtime Nazi, is suspected of having once told an anti-Nazi story. After some reluctance, he hesitantly recites the joke backstage at the Hamburg theatre for the benefit of the censorial Intendant. It seems that an Englishman once praised Germans for having three qualities: "They are polite, intelligent, and they are National Socialists." "But," said the Englishman, "they are never all three at once. If they are polite, they are not intelligent. If they are intelligent they are not polite. And if they are polite and intelligent, they are not National Socialists!" The joke does not amuse the Intendant, but its delivery, in halting phrases on the now Nazi-controlled stage, is quite ironic, something only a Stormbird writer or an "unintelligent" National Socialist might have instigated.

## Why Is Mephisto in Whiteface? He's Scared.

Another curious blend of the grotesque and the realistic occurs near the end of *Mephisto*, after Hendrik Höfgen's greatest triumph. Still in his greasepaint after a performance (not shown) as Mephisto, he is informed that Hitler has appointed him director of the State Theatre in Berlin. Höfgen, surprisingly, is not happy about the news. He lingers around the stage after everyone else has gone, his white face becoming that of a frightened, lonely man. The allegedly fearless agent of the devil, the darling of the Nazis, is scared. The situation is reminiscent of the story Brecht used to tell about how cabaret satirist Karl Valentin advised him to paint the faces of soldiers white: "They're scared," said Valentin, when Brecht asked him how the soldiers should look.

Moreover, Höfgen has cause to be frightened when Otto's friend Alex appears in the shadows, having escaped from a Gestapo van, and tells Höfgen about Otto's murder. While Höfgen is frightened and less than happy in his present life, it seems Otto was triumphant and heroic in death. He had refused to reveal the names of any underground resistance colleagues to his Gestapo torturers. And when word of Otto's death reached prisoners in Dachau, 6,000 of them began to sing in his honor. No one will ever sing like that for Hendrik Höfgen, Alex tells him.

Höfgen ends the conversation by asking his mistress, an actress, why his former Stormbird friends pursue him. "I haven't done anything," he says. "What can I do? I'm only an ordinary actor." In these lines he denies what has been the whole aim of his career: to become extraordinary and powerful. And perhaps he has failed completely; he is no more than Hitler's servant, Mephistopheles serving the Führer of a German hell.

After these words, the lights go down and a film of names is projected on a screen. The names are those of German artists and intellectuals who lost their lives in concentration camps or committed suicide as a result of their experiences with Nazism. A song (perhaps the same one sung in Otto's honor at Dachau) is heard. It is a Russian funeral march that had been sung in 1905 to honor Russian revolutionaries, and later illegally sung by resistance groups in Nazi prisons. It praises those who were ready to sacrifice their liberty, happiness and life "because of [their] sacred love of the people." Curiously, here, as in Théâtre du Soleil's earlier productions, the conclusion is far from an unequivocal victory for the Left. It mourns immense loss, even as it praises those lost. One cannot accuse the company of untoward optimism in its depiction of history.


## Memory as an Act of Resistance
## Theatre History as an Act of Memory

Still, the concluding scene's list of Nazi victims, the song and the whole production of *Mephisto* offer a restitution of honor to those who chose to oppose the Nazis. While Höfgen and his real-life counterpart(s) thrived under Hitler and survived the war, they remained vulnerable to the reversals of history, which can be made or rewritten and corrected by plays like this one. Théâtre du Soleil has chosen neither Höfgen's career nor Otto Ulrich's as its model (though its sympathies with Ulrich are undeniable). By reconstructing fragments of both careers, the ensemble has operated somewhat like the historical materialist praised by Walter Benjamin in his "Theses on the Philosophy of History":

> To articulate the past historically does not mean to recognize it "the way it really was." It means to seize hold of a memory as it flashes up at the moment of danger. . . . Only that historian will have the gift of fanning the spark of hope in the past who is firmly convinced that even the dead will not be safe from the enemy if he [barbarism, fascism] wins.[10]

Seizing hold of memories may mean recalling the names of Nazi victims, or withholding the names of underground resistance members—both of which Otto Ulrich does in the play—or reciting the words and enacting the images of a play such as *Mephisto*; the actor in his role, the historian in his (or hers), the resistance fighter in his (or hers) practices the same art here, when attempting to rescue the dead from the oblivion to which fascism would consign them along with the living.

# —13—
# Lotte Goslar's 'Circus Scene'

Lotte Goslar is a clown who dances. In her stage world a young ballerina refuses to obey her teacher; life-size toy soldiers shoot each other to music box accompaniment; a talent show contestant plays the violin with her feet; and a grandmother dances into heaven. Most of these comic scenes make no overt political statement, and Lotte Goslar does not think of herself as "a political person;" but during her fifty-year career she has performed in some of Europe's finest political cabarets. After permanently leaving Germany in 1933, at the age of sixteen, she danced comic solos as part of the Peppermill Revue, the anti-fascist cabaret show directed by Erika Mann, in tours across Europe. (The Peppermill subsequently served as a model for the cabaret featured in both the film and the play *Mephisto*, based on Klaus Mann's novel.) Goslar also performed with the Liberated Theatre, a satiric, anti-fascist group in Prague, before coming to New York with the Peppermill in 1938.[1] There she continued to dance solo. In 1943 she joined the Turnabout Theatre in Hollywood and met Bertolt Brecht through their mutual acquaintances, Elsa Lanchester and Charles Laughton.

After Brecht saw one of Goslar's performances, he asked her to choreograph the carnival scene in his *Galileo*. This she did to his satisfaction in 1947. By her own account, she added one character to Brecht's play: in her interpretation, the street singers who mock Galileo through their ballads are joined by a hungry little girl who cannot dance. The singers have beaten the girl into learning some steps to illustrate their songs. The tiny girl epitomizes the sort of reluctant dancer who still appears in Goslar's repertoire. Brecht liked her choreography of the street singing and carnival frolicking enough that he subsequently invited Goslar to become the Berliner Ensemble's choreographer in 1951. She declined the invitation, preferring to stay in the United States.

Goslar accepted another offering from Brecht, however. In 1947, without any prompting from her, he wrote a pantomine scenario for Goslar to perform, and dedicated it to her. The one-page scenario is still performed by her American company, Lotte Goslar's Pantomime Circus, a group which she formed in 1954 and which premiered at the Jacob's Pillow Dance Festival in Massachusetts. Goslar is the only artist who holds the rights to perform the scenario, which remains unpublished. When I discussed the scene with her at her country home in West Cornwall, Connecticut, in 1984, she graciously related the entire performance history of *Circus Scene*.

On paper, the scene reads almost like a parable by Franz Kafka. It describes "a much discussed scene of horror" which occurs "in a circus in A. [an unnamed city or country]." A clown is locked inside a cage with a lion. According to Goslar he is a "cheap little clown who entertains in between acts, and has fallen asleep." Once locked inside, he wakes, sees the lion and is mesmerized by its stare. The lion then compels the clown to perform tricks as if he (the clown) were a trained animal; the clown jumps upon platforms, balances on top of a ball and crawls up a ladder, under the direction of the paw-pounding lion. The scene ends when the spell is broken. The lion removes his eyes from the clown for a moment, and the clown, sensing his temporary freedom, jumps onto the lion and bites him to death. The murder of the lion is not a simple act of self-defense; Brecht's scenario suggests that the clown's rescue was near. Circus employees armed with pistols and iron hooks rush in just as the clown is killing the lion.

The scene is a curious example of Brecht's continuing interest in clowns. Smith, the clown in *The Baden Learning Play*, is far different from the nameless clown in *Circus Scene*. As discussed earlier, Smith is a passive victim, never resisting the torture inflicted on him. The transformation of an innocent clown into a fighter in *Circus Scene* is closer in tone to Brecht's *A Man's a Man*, in which the army turns the clownlike porter Galy Gay into a "human fighting machine." For this reason, James Lyon compares *A Man's a Man* to the later *Circus Scene* in his brief commentary on the scenario.[2]

Brecht's scenario formed the basis for the pantomime, but Goslar added important elements not mentioned in the script at all: choreography, music, costumes and new characters—spectators who participate in the story by locking the clown in the cage and enjoying his predicament. She also chose to divide the lion's role among four dancers, turning the animal into a collective character she compares to a "lynching party, or Nazis."

*Lotte Goslar in performance. Inset:  Brecht and Goslar discussing his* Galileo *in Los Angeles, 1947.*

## The Men in the Lion Suit

Brecht himself was aware of something human about the lion—or something inhuman about the clown. As Goslar discovered in carefully studying Brecht's scenario, he refers to the clown as "the beast" ("Bestie") toward the end of the story. At first she thought that Brecht had made a mistake; but then she became convinced, with the advice of her friend, the German writer Hans Sahl, that Brecht meant it. The clown, in Brecht's own words, is transformed into the beast.

Goslar suggests the clown's transformation into a lion by having the clown take up and wield a whip which is worn as a tail by the lion until the closing moments. The whip-tailed lion is an abstraction, represented by four dancers, and it is primarily through the lion that Goslar demonstrates the affinity between man and beast. By dividing the role of the lion among four men and keeping the animal's human components quite visible, she suggests that a man can be part lion—if not wholly bestial. "I did not want a funny lion," Goslar declares. "I wanted it to be a powerful, dangerous unit." The four men "don't really look like a lion, but somehow convey an image of a lion. They [are] the front, the sides and the tail end—with a whip instead of a tail. There is a mane. A lion has only four legs, of course, and here were eight legs. So four of the legs [in the costumes Goslar designed] were yellow and the four meant to be invisible were black. When the lion is bitten by the clown, you see the four yellow legs [one on each dancer] move in a death agony." In this scene, as Brecht once said of epic acting, "there are no illusions that the player is identical with the character."[3]

## The Audience on the Stage

Although Lotte Goslar was given the circus scenario by Brecht in 1947, it was not publicly performed until 1972, at the ANTA Marathon Dance Festival in New York. The choreographer explains the delay this way:

> For many years I did not do anything with it. The main reason was the music. I totally work out of music. I never work with an idea first; music comes first, it has an atmosphere, suggests something vicious or friendly or loving or ridiculous. And if I like the music, and I am induced to do something, some images come up. If they connect with the thoughts that I have had, it can become a number that also says something. . . I called Lotte Lenya [actress and widow of composer Kurt Weill, who wrote music for other Brecht texts]—years after I had the script—and asked her whether Weill had any music not well known that I could use. She contacted the publisher, and they wrote her that there was one piece called "Café Royale." When I finally obtained it, the music was not at all what I wanted. Around the same period I heard another composition and

> I knew immediately that "this is the entire scene." It is by Mâche, and he com-
> posed it entirely with voices. You don't hear any real words. It sounds as if you
> are standing in the center of the circus ring and you hear the din of the voices,
> you hear laughter, screaming, shushing, everything, but it is just noise.

The voices represent the circus audience rather than the clown or lion. Goslar
decided to give the audience a physical role in the piece as well as a vocal
one. Brecht's scenario only twice refers to the spectators who "witness a strange
happening" as they watch the lion gaze at the clown and tame him. Goslar
gives form to the spectators' gazes as well as their voices, by placing performers
onstage to represent the circus audience. They watch the scene of horror after
one of their members initiates it, by locking the cage in which the clown
has fallen asleep. Goslar recalls that she cast an audience in the scene, "because
I am very much interested in human relations, what people do to each other,
good or bad." She continues:

> I know a lot of circus people, especially from the Ringling Brothers, and they
> have told me that when the aerialists work without a net they are paid time-
> and-a-half. I think that is an indictment of humanity; it means that more peo-
> ple will come to see the show when it is announced that there will be no net.
> I love to see the Chinese circus, where everybody is on a rope; they do the most
> fabulous things but you know they cannot get crushed in a fall.
>     So the spectators are sitting there and whenever the clown is in danger,
> this is what they want to see. Toward the middle of the scene, the clown is high
> up on the ladder and the lion has come apart, and two [parts of the lion] are
> climbing up, hitting [the clown]. It is almost as if [the clown] is doing a dance
> up there while trying to avoid being hit, and the spectators in the scene ap-
> plaud. [None of this crowd reaction is mentioned in Brecht's outline]. The head
> of the lion goes up alone and gives the clown one last hit. The clown almost
> falls off but he is hanging there, dangling, and then his shoes come off and his
> pants come off and the [onstage] audience laughs, because they find it funny.
> I think Brecht would have liked this staging. At the very end, once the lion is
> dead, the clown steps over him and turns around to look at the onstage spec-
> tators who had tormented him. Now they are all afraid; now they all know it
> can happen to them. He steps forward, tears out the lion's tale (a whip), looks
> from one side to the other into the real audience and swings his whip as the
> light pins down his face.

The audiences onstage and off are linked by the clown's gaze in Goslar's production. These visual references to the audience, which she added to Brecht's
outline, implement some of the playwright's own ideas about audience identification with onstage characters. Spectatorship, by its very nature, allows,
applauds and gratefully accepts the torment of the clown. Goslar says that
the *spectators* torment the clown, it should be noted. They side with the lion;
his gaze, which embodies a demand for thrills, and his enjoyment of the clown
act, might be likened to theirs. "The whole thing is really a power game,"
adds Goslar.

There is a hint of what Wilhelm Reich has called "the mass psychology of fascism" hidden in Brecht's *Circus Scene,* and Goslar reveals it through her depiction of audience involvement. The mesmerizing gaze turns the clown into a slave and the lion into a spectator; and it might be the same gaze that Brecht had seen in the faces of "drugged" spectators for whom theatre is a narcotic.[4] In his *Short Organon,* Brecht condemns such spells cast in the theatre, where spectators "look at the stage as if in a trance; an expression which comes from the Middle Ages, the days of witches and priests . . . . These people seem relieved of activity, and like men to whom something is being done."[5] Without recalling that Brecht wrote this, Goslar, too, compared the spectators in her *Clown Scene* to families in which parents carried children on their shoulders to see witch burnings. The trance described by Brecht in the *Short Organon* fits the passive state of the mesmerized circus clown. The clown's closing stares imply that his experience could become the spectators', and that they are potentially as vulnerable as he has been.

Although Brecht carefully avoids any explicit geographical or political references in his outline, and Goslar does the same in her choreography, it might be assumed that Brecht was writing about the predicament of those who would resist the spell and mass psychology of fascism; in order to defeat it, not only would they have to refuse its commands; they might also have to turn upon it with bestial force. James Lyon notes that late in Brecht's life the playwright "was fond of saying that in capitalistic society, if one fights a tiger, one becomes a tiger, i.e., that one assumes the characteristics of one's oppressors."[6] *Circus Scene* certainly dramatizes this. It also suggests that dangerous spells can be cast in the world of art and showmanship, and in life, too.

Lotte Goslar has created many clowns in her life. She does not find the clown in *Circus Scene* particularly funny. "The whole scene is serious," she insists, adding that if it has a few funny moments, "they are only funny because the fear has been overemphasized. At one point, when the lion suddenly looks at the clown for the first time, the clown's reaction is one of fear. He wants to chase the lion away, so he runs toward him and tries to chase him; this always gets a laugh, and should, because it is futile." A clown scene with only a few laughs seems particularly appropriate for our bloodthirsty age, when we tend to encourage death-defying bravado, if not murder, in the circus as elsewhere.

## The Clown with a Whip

Goslar says she has been tempted to play the role of the clown in the scene herself, but has always felt "this should be played by a man. Most of the time for me a clown is an 'it,' a figure. In this case, the scene involves a man, who could have some strength against superstrength, the lion. A woman would be more vulnerable somehow." Few clowns have been less vulnerable than the one who holds the whip at the end of the Goslar/Brecht *Circus Scene*.

The ending Goslar devised for the scene has a curious antecedent in her own life, incidentally. She recalls that the Peppermill Revue never returned to Zurich after the Nazis disrupted a show there. Tear gas and clubbing filled the auditorium, while on stage the master of ceremonies, Erika Mann, stood alone. Mann was dressed as a stormtrooper but "in fairy tale terms," according to Goslar. The program was called "Fairy Tales," and the group had turned tales from Grimm and Andersen into satiric political commentaries. Mann's stormtrooper was dressed in a silver jacket, a parody of the Nazi look. Whip in hand, she stared outward while Swiss socialists fought the fascists in the theatre aisles. I suspect that during this battle Lotte Goslar first envisioned the clown with the whip, years before she relocated him in Brecht's *Circus Scene*.

# $-|4$

# **Pierrot in the Great War**

## Theatre Workshop's 'Oh, What a Lovely War!'

During World War I, British music halls often presented pro-war propaganda in the form of songs and sketches. The poet and war veteran Siegfried Sassoon criticized these revues in a poem he wrote in 1916:

*Blighters*

The House is crammed; tier beyond tier they grin
And cackle at the show, while prancing ranks
Of Harlots shrill the chorus, drunk with din;
"We're sure the Kaiser loves the dear old Tanks!"

I'd like to see a Tank come down the stalls,
Lurching to rag-time tunes, or 'Home, sweet Home',
And there'd be no more jokes in music-halls
To mock the riddled corpses round Bapaume.[1]

Sassoon's opposition to shows that treated war as an occasion for song and dance gained a contemporary counterpart in 1963, when the Theatre Workshop of East London, England, created *Oh, What a Lovely War!* The songs and sketches comprising the play might have fit into a wartime music hall, except that instead of celebrating "The Great War," they conveyed its horror and dangers. The event was a kind of anti-music hall show. In *Oh,*

*What a Lovely War!* the Theatre Workshop revived a popular form for purposes antithetical to those it had served in the First World War.

*Oh, What a Lovely War!* can be seen as part of the Theatre Workshop's continuing concern with war and its recurrent satire of political leaders. In 1938, Workshop founder and director Joan Littlewood adapted and staged the novel *The Adventures of the Good Soldier Schweyk*, as Piscator and Brecht had done in 1928. The company presented Brecht's exploration of war and business, *Mother Courage*, in 1955. (One scene in *Oh, What a Lovely War!* pays homage to *Mother Courage* by stealing some ideas from it; Brecht's depiction of people who are afraid peace may break out and ruin their profitable businesses is repeated with variation in the Theatre Workshop play.) In 1958 the ensemble premiered Brendan Behan's *The Hostage*, which satirizes aspects of the ongoing war between British troops and the Irish Republican Army. As a play in this anti-war tradition, *Oh, What a Lovely War!* was less timely and angry than some earlier Theatre Workshop productions had been, as well as some later ones such as *MacBird* (1967) and *Mrs. Wilson's Diary* (based on fictitious *Private Eye* columns attributed to the British Prime Minister's wife in 1967). But it was extremely popular due—at least to some extent—to its clown show format.

The scenes in *Oh, What a Lovely War!* are set in the framework of a pierrot show, a popular British entertainment which existed during and after the period of the First World War. A pierrot troupe called "The Merry Roosters" served as a model; the play's Master of Ceremonies calls his group "The Merry Roosters" shortly after he introduces the show.

As the title "pierrot show" implies, characters in it dress somewhat like pierrot clowns in loose white blouses with wide sleeves and huge buttons, white trousers, large ruffled collars and black fool's caps or straw boaters. Traditionally, the English pierrot is a loud, physically active clown, as Champfleury and Baudelaire note when comparing the late nineteenth-century French and English versions of the pierrot:

> The English Pierrot is by no means the personage pale as the moon, mysterious as silence, supple and mute as the serpent, lean and long as a pole, to which we were accustomed by [the 19th-century French clown] Deburau. The English Pierrot enters the house like a tempest, falls like a bale, and shakes the house when he laughs—he is the vertigo of hyperbole.[2]

This clamorous style of comedy is consonant with the unabashedly sentimental and patriotic songs, dance and comic sketches of the British music hall.

In his history of the Theatre Workshop, Howard Goorney includes an explanation from the company's director, Joan Littlewood, about the choice of the pierrot show structure for *Oh, What a Lovely War!*:

> She said we are not doing a show about the First World War. We are finding a background for the songs, and these have a period of history which can be

presented without the realistic background that you would need in a film. Here we are on the stage, The Clowns, and never in the course of the evening are we going to forget that the audience are out there. Tonight we are going to present to you "The War Game." We've got songs, dances, a few battles, a few jokes . . . .[3]

Littlewood's contention that the show was not about the First World War is curious, and could account for a certain ambiguity of purpose in the evening, which certainly *appears* to be about World War I. She is more plausible when suggesting that the pierrot show style gave her actors an alternative to the conventions of realistic or documentary theatre. The clown costumes, the songs and sketches, the direct addresses to the audience helped Theatre Workshop evoke the extinct spirit of a wartime music hall. But the topics of the evening—military slaughter across Europe and its profitability for munitions manufacturers and glory-seeking statesmen—do not easily lend themselves to comedy, and the content undermines the form to some extent, as the structure juxtaposes silly, romantic songs and patriotic rhetoric with non-music hall documentation of massive deaths and unnecessary conflict.

The Theatre Workshop had employed variety show forms a number of times prior to its collective creation of *Oh, What a Lovely War!*. Brendan Behan's *The Hostage* is the most notable antecedent; it, too, drew on music hall traditions, allowing actors to address the audience directly, and sing and dance their way through a topical satire about war in Ireland. One of the songs in *Oh, What a Lovely War!* previously appeared in *The Hostage*. "Oh death, where is thy sting-a-ling-a-ling/Oh grave, thy victory?" was performed at the end of Behan's play, following the death of a young British soldier who had been kidnapped by Irish Republican Army rebels in Dublin. The refrain appears in *Oh, What a Lovely War!* after a series of scenes depicting troops dying in battle. The chorus of dancing, singing soldiers is conducted by an actor representing Field Marshall Haig, who dons a pierrot hat to conduct. The transformation of the Field Marshall into a clown (at any rate, the placement of a clown's hat on him) is directly in line with the tradition of anti-militaristic satire practiced by Durov and his pig.

## Pierrot in the War Games

But it is far less timely to turn the Field Marshall into a clown half a century after his war, than to turn a pig into a helmeted representative of the Kaiser before the war; and it is far less dangerous. The clown imagery in *Oh, What a Lovely War!* is tame and non-topical for the most part. One exception occurs in Act II when three pierrots put on the hats of army generals (one British, one German, one French) and comically outbid each other's estimates of the year their war will end. "We'll sew the entire thing up by 1918," says one pierrot. *"Neunzehn hundert, neunzehn* [1919]," says another. Their bids continue through the year 1964, and end with the comment, "Plenty more where they came from." This comic banter was first staged in 1963; the reference to 1964 suggests that the war among clown-generals had not yet ceased when the play opened; that, in a sense, the militarism of the pre-war years continues, in new forms, today. *Oh, What a Lovely War!* reopened the battles of World War I on a London stage, and then toured them in Germany, Scotland and America. In another sense, however, the play may be as indecisive as the clown-generals are about historical dates. While specific names and events of the war are projected over the stage in news headlines, the episodic scenes lack the unity and purpose that the pierrot show frame might have provided.

The pierrot imagery in *Oh, What a Lovely War!* is more decorative than functional. Actors replace parts of their pierrot costumes with military clothing—army hats, for example; but the actors never make reference to their semi-comic appearances. The implication that generals may be fools or clowns is only implicit. More conducive to the music-hall, episodic structure of the play—and its satiric spirit—is the game introduced by the Master of Ceremonies: "the ever-popular War Game." Especially in Act I, sketches are presented as parts of this game. It is a game in which scenes are sportively played out as the contestants fight for high stakes—for nations and the wealth of nations.

The game metaphor fades away during the course of the first act, however, and it is barely mentioned in Act II. It remains simply a metaphor, and does not become a fully formed and executed game. Perhaps the company invoked the idea of a game only to engage the audience in its presentational style—to encourage a sense of sports spectatorship in the audience and accustom spectators to a non-realistic acting style. After references to games called "Find the Thief," "The Plans," and "Find the Anarchist" in Act I, Act II opens with the last reference to a game in the play: "Find the Biggest Profiteer." Apparently, further mention of games once existed in the production. Actress Frances Cuka describes the lost lines about the War Game in Howard Goorney's book, *The Theatre Workshop Story:*

> When I saw [*Oh, What a Lovely War!*] at Stratford Victor Spinetti made the closing speech which went something like, "The war game is being played all over the world, by all ages, there's a pack for all the family. It's been going on for a long time and it's still going on. Goodnight." This cynical speech, which followed the charge of the French soldiers, was quite frightening and you were left crying your heart out. When I saw it again the the West End, I was shocked by the change of the ending. After Victor's speech the entire cast came on singing "Oh, What a Lovely War" followed by a reprise of the songs. All frightfully hearty and calculated to send the audience home happy. I think it was George Sewell who said, "The Management didn't take kindly to a down ending." As far as I knew Joan [Littlewood], and Gerry [Raffles, the financial director] were the Management, having rented the theatre . . . .[4]

The "charge of the French soldiers" mentioned by Cuka begins comically, as men "advance toward the footlights" while bleating like sheep; they are then machine-gunned to death, an ending far more sobering than the cheerful medley of songs which concludes the present text.

## Pierrot Missing in Action

The speech Cuka attributed to Spinetti does not appear at all in the published Methuen edition of the play. The cut is significant; it removes one of few speeches—along with the exchange about the ending of World War I—which linked past history to the immediate present. For the most part, the extant version looks only backward, presenting scenes and statistics of a war long over, and old songs. The bravado of the generals and the sentimentality and greed of their backers are continually undercut by reports of massive war deaths, but most of the presentation verges on nostalgia; the first World War was cruel and senseless except to those at the top, but above all it *was*, and is no more, the play implies. The pierrot show framework serves largely to stress the past tense of events. While the humor and gaiety are undercut by war scenes, the play's comic conventions are static and ornamental. Unlike Brecht's production of his *Baden Learning Play*, where projections showing slaughtered men were preceded by the sawing apart of the giant clown, in *Oh, What a Lovely War!* the cruelty of war is not evoked through physical clowning, despite the presence of the pierrots.

The play proved to be a tremendous commercial success in London, playing for a year at Wyndham's Theatre in the West End. It is tempting to accuse Joan Littlewood and company of war profiteering in their own way. The accusation would outrage many people who saw the play and enjoyed it, but at the very least the Theatre Workshop might be said to have subverted popular entertainment forms such as the pierrot show for profit as well as political purposes. There is nothing inherently wrong with commercial success, although Cuka's recollection of the play suggests that its bite was defanged to suit commercial specifications. But some critics suggest that even before the play was changed, it was too accommodating.

In a 1968 essay on political theatre, playwright David Edgar writes that while *Oh, What a Lovely War!* has "indeed drawn successfully on other popular-cultural forms," its form, "a basically Italian form, translated into British seaside entertainment," is "actually peripheral to the urban British working class."[5] There is some irony in his accusation, since the Theatre Workshop began in the 1940s and '50s specifically as a space for working-class drama. It may be irrelevant that when the play opened in London's West End, it was attended by a wealthier sector of society. Could the cast choose its audience? Ewan MacColl, one founder of the Workshop (and Joan Littlewood's former husband), thought that the success of the play spelled the end of everything their theatre had been seeking. He writes:

The wrong kind of good write-up from the critics produced a situation where you couldn't get near the Theatre Royal [in Stratford] for Bentleys and Mercedes, with the result that working-class people in the area felt "This is not for us." They felt uncomfortable in that sort of society and just didn't come. It is sometimes said that shows like . . . *Lovely War* were the high point of Theatre Workshop's existence. I think they were the low point. They symbolized the ultimate failure of Theatre Workshop. Here was a show, *Oh, What a Lovely War!*, which was ostensibly an anti-war show. Yet it was running in the West End. You had, for example, a retired general in the audience saying "Good show, damn good show, that is the real thing." I maintain that a theatre which sets out to deal with a social and human problem like war and which leaves the audience feeling nice and comfy, in a rosy glow of nostalgia, is not doing its job, it has failed. Theatre, when it is dealing with social issues, should hurt; you should leave the theatre feeling curious. It was at this point we could say farewell to the dream of creating a working-class theatre.[6]

Even if working class spectators never saw the play, it does not follow that it failed as political theatre; but MacColl's accusation could apply regardless of who saw the play, if its impact on its audiences was too gentle and cheerful.

Playwright John McGrath offers a more favorable evaluation of the play in his book *A Good Night Out*. McGrath himself has created plays for social club performance throughout England and Scotland, and he defends the use of popular entertainment forms against detractors like Edgar and MacColl. He writes:

It is true that in the mid-50s the Theatre Royal was not crowded with merry Cockneys, and that Rolls Royces were to be seen outside the door—mostly those of West End managers come to rip off the show [in this case, *The Hostage*]—this is not the whole story. Their work touring round the Manchester area gave [Littlewood], and her company, a real basis for creating theatre for popular audiences . . . . What was striking about [*Oh, What a Lovely War!*] was the way Joan and the company had worked together with great confidence in a style that had developed from the popular forms, and were able to use them and the language they created to go beyond a mere imitation of a Pierrot show, or a collection of variety tricks. Because the subject of the show, the unspeakable waste of so many human lives to help the ruling classes of Europe to settle a quarrel over exploiting and killing even more human beings—this subject would exert an immense pressure on whatever form were to be employed. In this instance, it forced Joan and the company to create an immensely powerful piece of theatre.[7]

McGrath goes on to outline the popularity and influence of the play and the Theatre Workshop's other productions on later political theatre endeavors, including his own. He is particularly impressed—and rightly so—by the company's collaborative methods and its "house-style that would pull in a working-class audience."

The popularity of *Oh, What a Lovely War!* in the mid-sixties cannot be denied. Of all the plays discussed so far in this book, the Theatre Workshop's production was the most successful in a traditional commercial venue. The "popular" elements of the play—those derived from music hall and working-class entertainments—undoubtedly contributed to its commercial success. If, as MacColl argues, audiences left the play "feeling nice and comfy, in a rosy glow of nostalgia," the renewal of pierrot show conventions may have been too faithful to the spirit of their antecedents, reviving the same sort of naive and patriotic sentiments soldiers felt as they sang and marched off to the trenches in France. Perhaps, as Siegfried Sassoon wrote, only by sending a tank into the theatre stalls, having it lurch to ragtime tunes, could a cast truly stop the "jokes in music-halls" which "mock the riddled corpses round Bapaume."

# ─15

# Trevor Griffiths' 'Comedians'
## Grock and Anti-Grock

T revor Griffiths opens his play *The Party* with a peculiar prologue. An impersonator of Groucho Marx comments on a huge portrait of Karl Marx. Groucho quotes the other Marx, ridiculing the author of *Capital* rather effectively by calling attention to his outmoded, awkward rhetoric. There is no further extension of this battle between Groucho and Karl in *The Party*, but in a sense Griffiths continues the discussion in a later play, *Comedians*. First staged in Nottingham, England in 1975, *Comedians* is a study of popular comedy from a Marxist perspective—it is Karl's turn to answer Groucho.

Griffiths has often referred to Marx and the Italian Communist theoretician and activist, Antonio Gramsci, in discussing the theatre; and as one who advocates "strategic penetration" of popular culture by writers on the left, the British playwright has attempted to represent politics through clowning. He has also been known to let clowns loose on the stage. While Brecht, Weiss and other leftist playwrights incorporated elements of circus clowning, Hanswurstian slapstick, and cabaret sketches in their scripts, Griffiths draws on a more contemporary and commercial form of clowning: that of stand-up comedy, which removes the clown from the circus ring and a cast of characters, and sets him on stage alone. If Brecht turned the stage into a dais, as Walter Benjamin once suggested, Griffiths goes further in *Comedians*, turning the dais over to clowns. He fills a classroom with aspiring comedians training for careers in British nightclubs. Theory and practice of comedy are presented first in "school" in Act I, then in a working-class club, between rounds of bingo, in Act II. The audience at the club prefers bingo to comedy, which indicates the diminishing importance of professional clowns in contemporary culture.

Griffiths discussed this change in an interview shortly before the play opened in 1975; he asked Stephen Dixon of the *Guardian*, "Have you ever wondered why the clown died? When you watch a circus on television nowadays and you see the clowns: don't you feel embarrassed? Once the clown liberated . . . ."[1]

*Comedians* suggests that clowning is now primarily an academic art, relegated to classroom study sessions while it dies as a popular art form. Even stand-up comedy in Griffiths' play serves educational ends, informing middle-class audiences attending *Comedians* that comedy has lost its vitality (which is not to say that the play itself lacks vitality; quite the contrary). *Comedians* reminds us that a once popular art dependent on live interaction between the comic and his audience has given way to dirty jokes, bingo and television.[2] It does so by briefly prompting the audience to interact with comedians, as they perform in Act II.

However, the nightclub acts that survive tend to be remnants of the past, conservative in their preservation of existing prejudices and old jokes. The old pro in *Comedians*, Eddie Waters, says to his students, "A comedian's joke has to do more than release tension, it has to liberate the will and desire, it has to change the situation." Waters recognizes that his students are not all able or willing to initiate change through humor. Some seek commercial success through recital of tried—and untrue—routines. When half of Waters' six-member class finds it opportune to recite a sexist joke in unison, the instructor ironically asks, "How can they say Music Hall is dead when jokes like that survive . . . down the ages?" This comment on the death of the music hall must have been doubly ironic to spectators who knew the background of Jimmy Jewel, the music hall veteran who created the role of Waters. As Waters he was criticizing students for reviving the sexism of the past—keeping alive the worst of music hall tradition. As Jimmy Jewel, though, he made it hard to deny some of music hall's best life had returned to the stage. Through the character of Waters, Griffiths questions whether comic tradition can be extended and renewed as a force for social and culture change—brought back with new lines as Jewel was—so that comedy does not merely reinforce existing prejudice.

## Grock and the Angry Young Clown

In the second act of *Comedians*, an angry young man named Gethin Price plays a tiny violin at the nightclub. As part of his act he burns his violin bow and smashes the instrument with "large sullen boots." Price acknowledges later that his routine was inspired by Grock, the Swiss clown famous prior to World War II. In circuses around the world, Grock would try to play a tiny violin, and conclude, "Ah, it's silly. I can't do it"[3] Frequently he managed to play the overture of *Traviata* on the instrument. "I don't think it's funny," Grock said of this feat in his autobiography, *Grock: King of the Clowns*. "On the contrary, it's unutterably sad, a poor little fiddle like that left all alone in a great big empty trunk. [I] take it out and play the overture [while my partner] sit[s] there and look[s] silly with astonishment."[4]

Price, too, provokes astonishment rather than laughter with his violin act. But his routine is far more violent than Grock's. The Swiss clown never destroyed his delicate violinette. Price's demolition act is closer to the fury of Peter Townsend of The Who; the British rock-and-roll musician often destroyed an electric guitar onstage in the 1960s. Price's assault on two suavely dressed mannequins resembling middle-class theatre patrons is reminiscent of Grock's act, but it, too, is transformed into something more destructive than the original. Griffiths reports:

*Grock, with his tiny violinette, preparing to enter the circus ring.*

Grock used to get a middle-class stereotype on stage and just reduce this person to nothing, to a point where it wasn't even funny, just painful. And the straight man would become so distressed that he would refuse to speak. Then Grock would become incredibly alone; in the fear of the void. And he'd try to make the man laugh, and finally manage it, and then the thing would be sealed and healed.[5]

Prices's act concludes without the healing or laughter of Grock's routine. Instead a trickle of blood flows down the white dress of the female mannequin on which he pins a flower; it appears he has stabbed her while trying to make amends for his rudeness. Price turns aspects of Grock's clowning—particularly the act of reconciliation—against themselves, simultaneously accepting and rejecting comedic tradition.

His appearance combines Grockian baggy trousers and white face with a British footballer's jersey and shaved head, for a similar clash of conventions. Grock himself was at times a sweet, endearing clown; Price is far less so. But he is a clown, or at least "half clown," according to the stage directions. Unlike his classmates, whose stand-up comedy is far removed from circus tradition, Price revives elements of circus mime, costume, musicianship and slapstick in his routine.

The contradictory conventions in Price's comedy parallel and amplify contradictions that recur throughout the play in a debate over the uses of popular culture. The uses advocated in *Comedians* extend in three directions, personified by Price, his teacher Eddie Waters and a nightclub booking agent, Bert Challenor. Challenor and Waters represent opposite positions as they advise the nightschool students about future careers in comedy. Challenor suggests acquiescence to audience prejudice, and compares a successful comedian–audience relationship to that of a manufacturer serving the commodities market: "They demand, we supply." Eddie Waters teaches his aspiring comedians a more subversive aesthetic philosophy:

A real comedian . . . dares to see what his listeners shy away from, fear to express . . . . A comedian's joke, has to do more than release tension, it has to liberate the will and desire, it has to change the situation.

Even Waters' aesthetic is somewhat restrained, more therapeutic than activist in orientation. By his definition, the comedian becomes a psychotherapist who sets the subconscious free so its fears can be comprehended and perhaps quelled. Elsewhere he says, "Comedy is medicine;" but his medicine is too patly prescribed, too full of homilies to be fully persuasive. In the last scene of the play, Waters confesses to Price that comedy may not always heal. He knows that pleasure may sometimes stem from brutality or violence, since (to his confoundment) he had an erection during a postwar visit to a concentration camp. His confession tends to affirm Price's vision of a world where the comedian wounds a spectator in the act of offering a gift; if there is any humor in this vision, it arises out of pain.

Price's aesthetic is never discursively explained; but he demonstrates it in his act. His anti-art and anti-audience behavior comes close to nihilism, as he smashes the violin and insults the two mannequins. These actions fly in the face of Waters' and Challenor's advice and constitute a third choice: that of breaking with existing popular culture in a rebellion that Griffiths has compared to revolution. When asked about *Comedians* the playwright responded not by discussing the alternative forms of humor he dramatized, but alternative political strategies:

> It's basically about two traditions—the social-democratic and the revolutionary tradition. It's about a tradition in culture . . . which is the persuasive, the rational, the humane tradition—arguing, educating for good, trying to change through education, through example. Set against that, there is a younger tradition, very violent, very angry, very disturbed, that says, "No, that isn't the way. That way we can look back down through history and see the objective compromises that emerge, stem necessarily from that tradition. We've got to restate in our terms what the world is like, what the world can be like." Basically, that is the confrontation. The play has been read as being about humour, as a play about comedians. At another level, it is probably that too.[6]

These different approaches to politics have their counterparts in Waters (the social democrat) and Price (the revolutionary), and in their different approaches to popular culture. Some of the aspiring comedians (McBrain, Samuels) simply repeat popular prejudices against ethnic minorities and women in their stage routines, because that is the type of act Bert Challenor books into clubs. Another student (Mick Connor) attempts to explode ethnic and sexist prejudice against the Irish through parody; he exaggerates stereotypes and their irrationality for satiric effect. His comedy is most faithful to Waters' philosophy.

Price is a disciple who betrays his master during the course of the play. Waters warns him against hatred in Act I, after he detects misogyny in the young man (whose wife recently left him, as we learn in the last scene): "People deserve respect because they are people, not because they are known to us. Hate your audience and you'll end up hating yourself." After seeing Price perform at the club, Waters tells him the act was "ugly. It was drowning in hate." Price rejects his teacher's homiletic pleas for "Love, care, concern." He argues that at times, comedy has to be fueled by hatred and ugliness:

> What do you know about the truth, Mr. Waters? You think the truth is beautiful? You've forgotten what it's like. You knew it when you started off . . . you knew it all right. Nobody hit harder than Eddie Waters, that's what they say. Because you were still in touch with what made you . . . hunger, diphtheria, filth, unemployment, penny clubs, means tests, bed bugs, head lice . . . . Was all that truth beautiful? . . . We're still caged, exploited, prodded and pulled at, milked,

fattened, slaughtered, cut up, fed out. We still don't belong to ourselves. Nothing's changed. You've just forgotten, that's all.[7]

## No Laughing Matter

In the closing scene Price argues for what could be termed "Comedy from Hunger," or even "Post-Holocaust Comedy," as the dialogue turns to Waters' memory of a concentration camp, and his inability to find anything funny after a visit to Buchenwald. Waters' description of Buchenwald and its punishment block as "a world like any other . . . . The logic of our world . . . extended," paraphrases a formula for humor ("Extend the logic of any particular world."); it implies that the Nazis followed a logic not unlike that of grotesque comedy, though the results were far from humorous. Price jests that, "A German joke is no laughing matter," and then praises Grock as the inspiration for his own post-holocaust sense of humor.

The praise tendered to Grock for his "hardness" which "wasn't even funny" suggests that postwar humor requires something besides love and concern; it seems to require a will to resist, the strength to say "no," as Brecht's clown plays suggest. Price vows that he will never line up to be gassed as Jews did; his attitude is a response to the history of fascism, as well as Grock's "hardness."

Although *Comedians* makes no reference to the fact, Grock met more than once with the leaders of Nazi Germany. An audience attending the play would probably have less knowledge than Price had about Grock's meetings with Hitler. But it should be noted here, at least as an aside, that the Swiss clown was initially rather ignorant of Nazism. In his autobiography Grock recounts a meeting with Nazi Minister of Propaganda Goebbels, who admired his comedy, as did Hitler. Grock had no idea who Goebbels was until the Nazi told him, much to Goebbels' amusement. He did know who Hitler was when Goebbels introduced the two. Grock, famous for reciting the question "Why?" at the most inappropriate moments, reports that when Hitler told him, "Herr Grock, this is the thirteenth time I have been to see you . . . and it will not, I hope, be the last," the clown "let slip unawares" the question "Why?" "There was a momentary quiver of his eyelids," reports Grock of the Führer, and it was "followed by a forced laugh."[8] Grock found such "puzzled faces" a "sheer delight," and, to his credit, for an instant he was able to startle a tyrant. Gethin Price, lacking a Hitler at his Manchester club, has to settle for the club audience as his nemesis. The mannequins and live spectators he insults are far less dangerous than a Nazi leader, but their world of bingo and business deals is one which he refuses to join.

(By contrast, Grock never fully refused Nazism. He continued to perform for German audiences long after his first meeting with Hitler in

1939—which calls into question the extent of his disrespect for Nazis. Unlike Karl Valentin, Brecht's favorite clown, Grock did not stop performing for Nazis during the war years.)

Much as Brecht derived some of his comic sensibility from the popular style of Valentin, Griffiths derives his from Grock. The British author's response to clown traditions is more skeptical than Brecht's, however. *Comedians* asks whether humor is still possible after Hitler and Buchenwald; Price's act verges on an oxymoron: humorless comedy. He recites sexist and racist jokes, but his macabre appearance and "hard" style of delivery undercut the sexism and racism, and prevent his audience from laughing at such jokes. His act kills prejudice—murders the old music hall, if you will. The truth is "a fist you hit with," in Price's view, and if there is any humor in his hard-hitting act, it lies in the act of destruction, which is reminiscent of Karl Valentin's tearing apart of the cabaret floorboards.

Trevor Griffiths' anti-clown is far removed from most of Brecht's comic figures. When Hitler threatened to end everything Brecht stood for, the playwright responded by constructing defenses against fascism with everything he had, including satire, in order to survive as an artist and a Marxist. Trevor Griffiths fits into a different tradition, one he once described as "a long and honorable tradition of Marxist attack inside bourgeois cultures and sub-cultures."[9] In *Comedians* Griffiths attacks bourgeois comedy and its audience from within the form itself. Price's fierce independence, his singular concept of comedy, places him in a vanguard position, answerable to no one. Isolated at the end of the play, after his wife has left him, after he declines to address spectators directly in the Manchester club, after he declines to share Waters' aesthetic philosophy, he is far more alone than Grock was after he had ridiculed someone in his act. Price's statement to Waters that he will not consent to being gassed, as Jews did in Germany, is far more vehement in tone than any earlier clown's refusal to obey authority. His declaration of independence is better suited to a revolutionary than a clown.

If Price were to continue to perform, he would no doubt be an avant-garde artist comparable to a character in another Griffiths play. In *Occupations,* Italian Communist Party founder Antonio Gramsci tells striking workers that, "A revolutionary movement can only be led by a revolutionary vanguard, with no commitment to prior consultation, with no apparatus of representative assemblies." The position is also reminiscent of Ibsen's Dr. Stockmann, who declares that "the strongest man is he who stands alone."

Gramsci's description of a revolutionary may fit Price, but it does not necessarily describe Trevor Griffiths. Griffiths' attitude toward comedy and politics is exemplified by Waters as well as Price. Through Waters he expresses doubts about the social usefulness of humor in dark times; perhaps humor simply amuses the ruling class, as Grock amused Hitler, and offers pleasure as Buchenwald offered Waters cause for an erection. The final moments of

*Comedians* place Waters' concept of comedy in a somewhat more optimistic light, however. The closing lines imply that therapeutic humor will continue to emerge from the most desperate of circumstances, and that there will still be a need for teachers of comedy. After Price leaves the classroom Waters talks to an Asian immigrant who had quietly watched the comedians rehearse earlier in the evening. The Asian offers to tell a joke, says, "it's very funny, it's very, very funny," and follows this self-confident preface with an excruciatingly grim anecdote. While the punch line is amusing, the opening passage of the joke is far from humorous. It is outrageous and funny that anyone would dare to begin a "very, very funny" joke this way: "A man has many children, wife, in the South. His crop fail, he have nothing, the skin shrivel on his children's ribs, wife's milk dries. They lie outside the house starving . . . ."

Adversity is the mother of humor, it seems. Waters offers the Asian an invitation to enroll in his comedy class. The play ends with the implication that comedy will continue to be born out of "hunger, diptheria, filth, unemployment, bedbugs, head lice," as Price had said it would, and that the new generation of comedians will include new ethnic minorities—Pakistanis and Indians who want to be assimilated—at the same time that Gethin Price seeks an alternative to assimilation.

## The Greatly Exaggerated Death of the Clown

Griffiths wrote *Comedians* with meticulous attention to detail. The play is immersed in local references to working-class Manchester and its culture. Its realistic time frame calls for a clock to display "real time" on the classroom wall. Ethnic and class affiliations of all of the characters are carefully delineated, as Griffiths' comedians reveal their personal backgrounds through humor. If, as Austin Quigly suggests, the play explores comic stereotyping through its characters' response to ethnic prejudice (as they exaggerate prejudice to explode it, or pander to it),[10] it also counters such stereotyping through its panoply of minute detail. It is revealing that the author of a play whose style approaches naturalism says that the "death of the clown" in contemporary culture might be attributed to "our social imagination . . . hammered by naturalism until we rejected the surreal or expressionist."[11] In *Comedians* Griffiths uses naturalistic techniques to approach the surreal, as embodied by Gethin Price and his variation of Grock. In the tradition of those who attack bourgeois cultures and subcultures from within, Griffiths subverts naturalistic theatre, leading spectators from the realistic into the clownishly surreal. The author is no Gethin Price, pulling out a delicate violin only to smash it; but Trevor Griffiths questions the dominance of naturalism, and the dreary imaginations that accompany it, within the delicately constructed, realistic framework of *Comedians*.

# —16

# **Dario Fo**
## The Clown As Counter-Informer

---

*"Fo is a great actor, a great director, and a great
clown, the last great clown of our time."*

—Franco Zeffirelli

For the past decade Dario Fo has been Europe's most popular political satirist. In his plays as well as in his own performances, the Italian artist offers his audiences a unique form of humor that might be called "documentary clowning." Extending the new naiveté that Wekwerth attributed to Brecht's plays, Fo creates stage fools whose innocence (or pretense of it) enables them to question the statements of diplomats, generals, historians and other sources of authority. As the "innocent" questioning progresses, the centers of authority look more foolish than their comic interrogators. The naive questions in Fo's plays, as in Brecht's, frequently recall the naiveté of Marx asking why enormous overproduction exists side by side with hunger, or why owners of factories should profit from other people's labor.

Fo's questions about history are not limited to the recent past, however. He has become, among other things, an expert on medieval literature; in pursuit of suppressed and lost stories told by medieval minstrels (*giullari*), he reconstructed a large collection of folk tales under the title *Mistero Buffo*. These tales recount Church history from a perspective radically different from that disseminated by the Vatican; they report miracles through the voices of ordinary people—from the perspective of the underclass, which Brecht, too, represented in his stage clowning.

Fo has been performing these medieval tales in one-man shows since 1969, and he has simultaneously been creating topical, satiric plays in collaboration with several theatre collectives. The plays, too, tend to be based on documents and historical events. Fo's best known farce, *Accidental Death of an Anarchist* (1970) draws on police and court testimony concerning the death of anarchist Giuseppe Pinelli; the man's alleged suicide in a Milan police station was actually a murder, according to Fo's play and facts released around the same time that Fo created the play.

Other popular satires based on actual events in Italy include *We Can't Pay, We Won't Pay!* (1974), which was inspired by an outbreak of shoplifting in the wake of high grocery prices in Milan; and *Klaxons, Trumpets and Raspberries* (1980), which responded to the kidnapping and murder of Prime Minister Aldo Moro. With his wife, actress Franca Rame, Fo has also created a series of one-character plays about women: they portray such figures as a housewife imprisoned by her jealous husband; the mother of a terrorist in search of her son; and Medea, the Greek heroine who murders her children to free herself from her husband. Since his 1953 cabaret revue *A Finger in the Eye*, Fo has created dozens of other plays and revues, only a few of which have been performed in America.

## Clowns and Circus Elephants at War

Fo's political satire has affinities with Brecht and the circus as well as Italian comic tradition. "Like Fellini," notes Richard Sogliuzzo, "Fo adores the circus: his productions are circuses in miniature; raucous music, clowns, acrobats, songs, dances, mimes, an Italian *Hellzapoppin*."[1] Politics and the circus are united most overtly in his play called *Throw the Lady Out* (1967-68).[2] The "lady" of the title is an ailing, elderly woman said to own the circus in which the play is set; but she is also Lady Liberty, or the United States in symbolic form, and her circus is an empire collapsing like a big tent as it loses wars abroad. Even the torch of freedom appears to be lost; at one point in Act I, the old lady is dressed like the Statue of Liberty, but she holds a Coke bottle instead of a torch. Originally the play was a response to the liberties America had taken in Vietnam, and the Warren Commission's report on the Kennedy assassination; Fo revised it for television in 1976, so the satire is now less directly related to events of the late 1960s.

"It's an allegory," characters announce from time to time, mocking their own play's symbols. But *Throw the Lady Out* is less a coherent allegory than a series of circus clown acts which caricature military and government officials. Every character's first name is "Clown" ("Clown Bob," "Clown Franca"), and "Clown Dario" is one of the ringleaders in this story about clowns whose allegiance to the circus changes as the circus' owner changes. After

*Dario Fo and drawings of title characters in an Elizabethan play,* Nobody and Somebody.

the old lady who owns the circus dies and her niece is assassinated, a military man named Valerio dresses in drag and claims that he is the "new old lady" in charge of the big top.

While the play never overtly says so, the militarization of the circus by Valerio corresponds to the military policies of America since its entry into

Vietnam. Valerio vows to send elephants and clowns to distant lands in order to prop up foreign governments. Clown Dario protests: "Elephants?! Colonel, we signed an elephant nonproliferation treaty, and we mean to keep it. Use conventional animals only." The military training the clowns undergo ridicules national preparation for a war in Vietnam or Central America or some other region America has not yet entered, and gives this play its resonance and timeliness. One grotesquely comic scene features pregnant women simultaneously knitting and training their unborn infants for military service by shouting orders at their wombs. After this we see a mother accompany her grown son to the battlefront; presumably, mothers will come to approve of war as long as it does not separate them from their sons. "Sh-h-h! Not so loud. My boy's asleep," Clown Franca tells enemy forces at the front. The play ends with grim humor, as a talking skull appears on television and announces to the soldiers, "Courage boys, we're behind you 100 percent."

The circus antics in *Throw the Lady Out* form a series of comic commentaries on American domestic and foreign policy, and militarism in general. What is more, they imply that politicans and military men are sometimes best represented by clowns. The combination of politics and clowning in this work is less precise in its documentation of actual events—and less biting in its satire—than later Fo plays, where the clown figure is not announced as such. But *Throw the Lady Out* does represent a culmination and turning point in Fo's career. It was written at a time when he decided to abandon conventional theatre circuits and go on tour with his own political "circus," addressing audiences which were neither middle-class nor habitual theatregoers. *Throw the Lady Out* was Fo's last bourgeois extravaganza; the actors took fifty-five days to learn the clown routines, including trapeze artistry. Subsequent Fo works have been staged more simply—sometimes written and staged in a few days for performance during factory occupations or political trials.

Around the time Fo wrote *Throw the Lady Out*, an increasing awareness of cultural and political upheaval around Europe—including protests against America's military presence in Vietnam—led the satirist to declare that he would no longer be a "jester of the bourgeoisie." Rather than entertain audiences whose values they did not share, Fo and Rame gave up a handsome income performing for conventional theatregoers to start over again. The couple subsequently performed for factory strikers, students, small villages, and rarely for the wealthier sectors of society. Their popularity has grown steadily; both perform one-person shows and new plays for large audiences which fill the sports stadiums, assembly halls, open air piazzas and circus tents on their tour circuit. While Fo has not written another full-length play about the circus since *Throw the Lady Out*, he has turned leading political and social figures into fools—or even characters beneath the contempt of fools—in his recent plays.

Fo's decision to create working-class theatre may have been influenced by his personal background as well as his changing political consciousness. He was born in 1926 in a small town in Lombardy, and comes from a working-class family; his father was a railroad worker. The satirist's own life has been immersed in the arts, beginning with study of painting and architecture in Milan, and the writing of satirical sketches in the 1940s. Since then he and Rame have created plays with theatre collectives, the most recent of which is La Comune, based in Milan. His satires have won Fo enemies as well as friends. The Italian Communist Party (PCI) ended two years of support for him in 1970 because he ridiculed it along with such other venerable institutions as the Catholic Church, the Christian Democrats, Christopher Columbus and the American CIA. Fo and Rame belong to no political party at present, and they consider themselves "unchained dogs," free to attack anyone in power. In turn, those in power have attacked them through harassment and censorship. Fo once noted that *Accidental Death of an Anarchist* was so successful in its exposure of state repression that it "produced a violent reaction in the centers of power. . . . We were subjected to provocation and persecution of all kinds, sometimes more grotesque and comical in their repressive stupidity than the very farce we were performing."[3]

## Fo Discovers America

Even the U.S. Department of State was to play a role in this continuing "farce," by twice denying Fo and Rame entry into America. The official reasons it offered for the first visa denial in 1980 had to do with the couple's membership in *Soccorso Rosso* (Red Aid), a group which is, in fact, only slightly to the left of Amnesty International. The group's legal aid to political prisoners in Italy hardly amounts to the "support for terrorism" cited by the State Department. Fo may be a heterodox Marxist, but he is no advocate of terrorist violence or kidnapping; on the contrary, he ridicules such actions in his plays. Admittedly, his reasons for opposing terrorist violence are not the same as the State Department's; he objects to terrorism because it serves the state, providing the government with an excuse to increase its repression and control over dissenters.

Fo and Rame were finally permitted to enter America in 1984, to attend the New York premiere of *Accidental Death of an Anarchist*. But the two have yet to perform their own works in the United States. At a New York press converence in November of 1984, Fo exhibited his characteristic wit as he thanked Ronald Reagan for all the publicity he had brought the couple. A few years before granting the visas, Reagan had phoned the artists in Italy, quipped Fo, and promised to deny them entry visas in order to make them better known. "From an actor of his [Reagan's] caliber, we couldn't expect anything less," Fo observed. After inventing this tongue-in-cheek publicity theory, the playwright seriously thanked the American cultural groups and individuals who had pressured the State Department for his and Rame's admission to the country. It should be noted that the man famous for his mimickry of leading politicians was able to enter America only *after* the 1984 election; if President Reagan feared that the Italian actor's arrival during the campaign might cost him some votes, his fears were not wholly unwarranted. Dario Fo confessed that having finally arrived in "the land where an actor can become President," he would be interested in running for President himself next time he visits.

## Forbidden Brecht

During his New York press conference Fo also discussed the production of his play on Broadway, "the bastion of capitalism." He insisted that the location of the play's production is less important than accurate presentation of his ideas on stage, wherever they are staged. He added that Brecht, too, has been staged on Broadway, "and I don't think any member of the Berliner Ensemble complained."[4] Brecht's theatre served as a model for Fo in this respect and others; but there was some irony hidden in his New York reference to the Berliner Ensemble. The company founded by Brecht objected to Fo's production plans for *The Threepenny Opera*. Fo's proposal to adapt Brecht's musical, and his subsequent writing of *The Sneering Opera*, reveal his own sensibility as well as his ambivalent relationship to Brecht's comedy.

Fo's theatre is no mere derivative of Brecht's, of course. The satirist is eclectic in his research, drawing on many comic and political traditions, which he renews with his own sense of slapstick and topical satire. His creation of *The Sneering Opera* began after the Berliner Ensemble invited Fo to direct *The Threepenny Opera*. He agreed to stage Brecht's play if some changes could be made in the text. After all, thought Fo, Brecht himself had warned that the classical status of plays is often an inhibiting factor in the staging of them; directors have too much respect for the classics. In Fo's own translation of Brecht: "Escape the terrorism of the classics."[5] (The reference to terrorism is more Fo's than Brecht's; while Fo has been wrongly accused by the U.S. State Department of supporting Italian political terrorism, it might be more accurate to accuse him of escaping cultural terrorism, if by that we mean disrespect for over-revered plays.) Apparently the Berliner Ensemble found Fo's attitude toward Brecht's text to be too irreverent; they declined to let the Italian author alter it as he proposed. Were Brecht still alive, reasoned Fo, he surely would have introduced into his play more recent issues, the problems associated with drugs, kidnappings, dehumanized sex, mass media, pop psychoanalysis. With these issues in mind Fo subsequently wrote and staged

*The Sneering Opera* in Turin, Italy, in the spring of 1981. He based the work on the libretto for John Gay's *The Beggar's Opera*, which had also been Brecht's source for *The Threepenny Opera*. Like both of the earlier works, Fo's play focuses on Macheath, a gangster who is rescued from hanging in the closing scene when he is granted an official pardon.

Fo's Macheath is a friend of policemen and politicians; and like the earlier versions, Fo's satire suggests that the qualities of politicians, businessmen and criminals are indistinguishable at times. The plays by Gay, Brecht and Fo all feature a number of songs. In place of the parodic opera ballads of Gay or the jazz-and-tango influenced songs of Brecht, however, Fo modeled his lyrics after the rock, reggae and blues songs of Frank Zappa, Patti Smith, Allen Ginsberg and other contemporary artists. His characters are based to some extent on *commedia dell'arte* stock types. The most significant departure from Gay and Brecht follows from Fo's decision to examine the effects of technology and industry on modern life. In his preface he notes, "The dominant element is the automatized, mechanical structure of conveyor belts, elevators."[6] He quotes Michel Foucault's statement that today the factory serves as a structural constant or model for jails, barracks, offices and department stores. In this regard Fo's play may be more consciously Marxist than Brecht's; it dramatizes the dehumanizing, commodity-and-profit-oriented aspects of industry that Marx analyzed so carefully in *Capital*. His opera suggests, with more topicality and contemporaneity than Brecht's version of Gay's libretto, that the factory and its products dominate our society. Industry's captains, selling unneeded commodities to people who can't afford them, may be the greatest criminals of our age.

This perspective is most evident in the wedding scene. When Brecht first dramatized Macheath's wedding to Polly Peachum (a scene only mentioned and never shown in *The Beggar's Opera*), he set it in an abandoned stable. Macheath's gang furnishes the stable with stolen goods, the style of which attests to their middle-class aspirations; they want Louis Quatorze and Chippendale chairs, like any respectable bourgeois family, but they steal theirs instead of buying them. In Fo's version, Macheath marries Polly in an abandoned industrial hangar. When Polly protests that she had hoped for a church wedding, Macheath tells her that they are in something better than a church: a cathedral of the new religion, in which production is love and profit is life.

The wedding scene suggests that factory life (along with the addictive drugs that the London gang uses) has dulled the senses of Mack and his cohorts, lulled them into a false idyll of abundance and freedom from labor, due to labor-saving machines. The gang is more awed by the wonders of industry than Macheath. The wedding gifts they roll in on an assembly-line conveyor belt include four dishwashers, three washing machines, eight stoves, six refrigerators, seven TV sets. Less than pleased by the abundance of appliances, Polly asks Mack whether he plans to open a restaurant business and

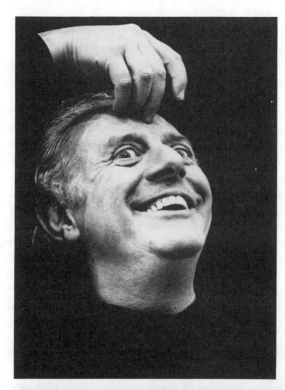

*Left: Dario Fo. Below: a scene from* The Sneering Opera, *written and directed by Fo and first produced at the Teatro Stabile, Torino, Italy, 1981.*

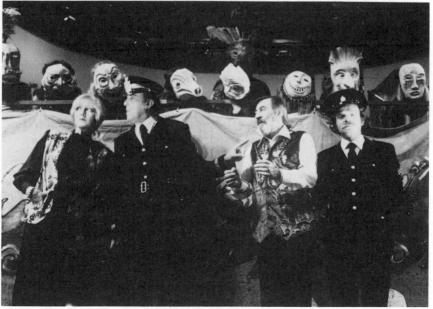

spend the rest of his life in a kitchen. One of the gangsters compares the scene favorably to a household appliance fair.

Macheath is not opposed to industrial commodities per se, but he yearns for more distinctive articles than the mass-produced items that his gang delivers. Like Brecht's Macheath, this one complains that the gifts lack style; he notes that there is not one piece by a well-known designer. Perhaps he would not complain were he given a refrigerator designed by Yves St. Laurent.

Fo is no stranger to the inside of factories, having performed his plays in plants occupied by striking workers. In *The Sneering Opera*'s wedding scene the situation is slightly different, however: the factory is occupied by Mafia-style gangsters, admirers of industry and its products. They value the products enough to steal them in large quantities; and this may be the only way, short of owning a factory, that they can acquire the products of labor without having to suffer the indignities of wage labor. The satiric scene of occupation is Fo's own form of protest against factory ownership; the factory he depicts is a place where men profit from the labor of others—a normal factory scene—except that here the profiteers are thieves rather than industrialists. The narcoticizing, dulling effect of consumer products (such as TV) on the public is ironically complemented by the admiration that drug addicts and pushers express for these products. Fo continues here a practice that Walter Benjamin attributed to Brecht, when he noted that the author of *The Threepenny Novel*, "makes visible the element of crime hidden in all business."[7]

Another important difference between Fo's version of *The Beggar's Opera* and Brecht's is the depiction of Macheath. While Brecht notes that the gang leader aspires to become a banker, and should be as staid and portly as the figure portrayed in Hogarth's painting of Gay's play, Fo bases his gangster on recent events and living people; his satire is not only as current as the daily news, it has been lifted *from* the news. Satire need not compete with reality in such cases; it merely has to document it. Fo explained the "documentary" nature of his portrait of Macheath in a 1983 interview with Steve Grant and Tony Mitchell:

> Mackie is like an Italian gangster—he doesn't have to act like an aristocrat and a snob, he is one naturally. Just like Cutole and other sensational Mafia bosses—they don't have to imitate aristocrats, they have their own aristocratic style and real relations with important politicans. When Cutole was in prison he had two restaurants working exclusively for him, and he had three walls of his cell knocked down because he needed an apartment, and he needed at least ten bottles of champagne per day, and only two bottles of whiskey, because he prefers cognac. . . . He turned his prison cell into an office where he held court and received people who asked him for favors. He was a go-between with the Mafia in getting Cirillo released. In brief, this ensemble of characters is the new Mackie

Messer. He's not in the least bloodthirsty—he looks like an accountant. . . . When you read about murders in the newspapers—three dead outside a cinema, another person decapitated, this is the same guy as Cutole who's responsible.[8]

## A Comedy of Terrors

Though many of Fo's political satires are derived from current events, they are not merely journalistic documents. Fo reconstructs events—or spins out sequels to events—in a manner that recalls Marx's idea about history repeating itself as farce. History turns into farce with a vengeance in Fo's *Klaxons, Trumpets and Raspberries,* renamed *About Face* for its American premiere at the Yale Repertory Theatre in 1983. Written soon after the kidnapping and murder of Italian Prime Minister Aldo Moro, the play angered some of Fo's countrymen, as it irreverently suggested that Moro's murder served the interests of business and the state.

Fo opens his play by imagining what might happen if terrorists tried to kidnap one of the wealthiest men in Italy, Fiat company owner Gianni Agnelli. The result is a grotesque farce of mistaken identities and Keystone Kop-style routines. The real Agnelli has yet to be kidnapped in fact, and in Fo's play the terrorists fail to kidnap him. The play asserts that enormous wealth makes men like Agnelli virtually invulnerable to terrorism—that to some extent terrorism serves these men by strengthening state repression of threats against wealth and power. This, then, is the folly of terrorism.

In the play's first scene Antonio, a worker in a Fiat plant, recounts how he inadvertently rescued the factory owner from a kidnapping. Antonio learns the identity of the man he rescued hours after he leaves the man in a hospital. Agnelli's face has been disfigured and his memory temporarily lost in a car crash during his kidnapping. Hospital surgeons remodel the unknown patient's face to match a photograph of Antonio, who has fled for fear of arrest. When Agnelli is ready to leave the hospital, Antonio's wife assumes that the recuperating amnesiac is her husband and takes him home. For a time Agnelli lives a worker's life, complete with exposure to assembly-line labor and police surveillance; as an amnesiac, his character becomes another naive, questioning clown who cannot understand his past life as an industrialist. Agnelli's memory slowly returns, however, and by the end of the play, after a series of almost documentary references to the Red Brigades' kidnapping of Aldo Moro, Agnelli realizes that he is more important than the murdered Prime Minister—because the leaders of Italy free political prisoners to rescue him—something they would not do for Moro. "I am the State," Agnelli declares, when fully aware of his former identity. In what may be one of the most humorous dramatic contexts ever conceived for the writings of Karl Marx, Fo's Agnelli asks the policemen around him:

Haven't you read your Karl Marx? Yes, I know. Nowadays it's only us top level industrial management people who bother to read *Das Kapital*, especially the bit where it says that "the true source of power is economic and financial, public holdings, the stock exchange, banks and merchandizers—in short, capital. And then there's another bit which children should be made to learn by heart and sing in rounds: "The sacred laws of the state are written on bank notes—economic rules. Governments and institutions merely prop up this state." . . . Do you realize what that means? Aldo Moro was sacrificed to preserve the respectability of the financial state, not the propper-uppers. Who gives a damn about them? Get this into your thick skulls—I am the State![9]

Here, as elsewhere, Fo's detailed sociological analysis verges on ponderous solemnity; if not for the fantastic, farcical context of mistaken identities, secret policemen hidden inside the TV set and washing machine, etc., the irony of such a monologue might be missed, or mistaken for mere rhetoric. Instead, it is seen against its comic background as the explosion of rhetorical banalities that it is. Agnelli's declaration of "statehood" ends as he ascends to heaven in priestly garb: an apotheosis more likely to elicit laughter than reverence. (Incidentally, the statements attributed to Marx in his closing speech may have been invented by Fo. More than one Marxist scholar has been unable to locate the quotations in Marx's own writing. Or perhaps Fo's Agnelli has not read Marx.)

In Milan, Fo played the roles of both Agnelli and Antonio, a virtuoso doubling which suggested that if not for their faces, property and armed force, all men might be equal. Fo's decision to portray both a wealthy industrialist and one of his employees is symptomatic of a comic, consciously practiced schizophrenia that pervades his satire. He embraces class enemies as collaborators in farce, presses them into his service, impersonates them and articulates their contradictory roles with immense humor. In *Accidental Death of an Anarchist*, Fo performed a larger number of roles—a maniac, a police inspector, a high court judge and a bishop. He kept disowning or temporarily exchanging one persona for another, so that the maniac's opening confession might well be Dario Fo's personal testimony; he claims to suffer from a psychic disorder, "histromania," a compulsion to play multiple roles.

This "disorder" is not new for Fo. He traces his performance and playwriting styles back to the storytelling of medieval minstrels. His characters continually tell one another stories, impersonating their subjects as they describe them. Fo also sees in his theatre an affinity with Brecht's epic style. Brecht had asked his actors to rehearse their roles "in the third person," narrating their stories at the same time they enacted them. Fo's plays, too, call for epic acting insofar as they require similar "stepping out of character."

Discussing the connection between his work and Brecht's in a 1976 essay on popular culture, Fo noted that in bourgeois theatre spectators accept the fourth-wall convention and identify with the actor's representation of a single character.[10] In popular and Brechtian theatre, rather than seeing isolated individuals on stage, the audience sees a "chorality." Any character portrayed by an actor becomes a pretext for speaking as many people, stepping out of character and directly addressing spectators. The imaginary fourth wall, the "delegated space" between audience and actors, is destroyed. The audience, like the actors, can no longer remain isolated under these circumstances.

## Law's Disorder

Individuals inadvertently create a collective identity in *Accidental Death of an Anarchist*. As the police trade alibis in their Milan station and mimic each other in retelling stories, they reveal a collective aspect of character; one character frequently steals or learns gestures and words from another. Fo further destroys the "delegated space" of actor and audience in such situations by resisting the notion that character and language are private property. His plays portray redistribution of property—consumer goods in *We Can't Pay* and the intellectual property of alibis and state secrets in *Accidental Death of an Anarchist*. This becomes a central action which parallels the redistribution of individual characters' language and gestures.

As noted earlier, *Accidental Death of an Anarchist* is based on an actual incident in which an Italian anarchist accused of terrorism was said to have jumped to his death from the fourth floor of a Milan precinct station. We now know, and Fo suspected as much when his collective first performed the play, that the anarchist, Giuseppe Pinelli, was pushed to his death by the police.

The subject may not sound like promising material for a farce, but Fo turned it into an extremely topical political satire in 1970. In his preface he called the play "an exercise in counter-information," noting that all references to the death are based on authentic documents—transcripts of investigations carried out by judges as well as police reports.[11] Fo's role as a clownish "counter-informer" went beyond documentation of known facts, however. When he first performed the play, he was able to add new material nightly; informed sources leaked him evidence not yet known to the public. The play functioned as a corrective to state secrecy and police suppression of evidence. Many of Fo's other plays also provide "counter-information;" even if they do not uncover state secrets, they re-examine public events and leaders with a critical attitude absent from corporate-owned mass media.

Now that the Pinelli case is past history, and the anarchist's innocence has been proved, the facts are not so urgent or controversial. Yet the play still functions as a complex, comic statement on state secrecy and abuse of power. While it was once a political rallying point for opponents of state repression and was seen as such by over half a million Italians, Fo's play remains popular in other countries because it suggests that forms of law and power are based on controlled information—state secrets which lose force once they are revealed, shared and "democratized."

The play's central character, the maniacal buffoon originally portrayed by Fo himself, mocks the state's control of information by pretending to be a high court judge. He is the epitome of a "documentary clown," turning state evidence around to make it testify against the state. In his disguise, the buffoon encourages police officers to compose their alibis against accusations that they murdered Pinelli. The Italian government itself inadvertently did exactly that in 1970, exposing its manipulative control of information by issuing contradictory reports and offering specious conclusions. Parodying the judicial process to expose it more fully, Fo juxtaposes the contradictions of various "official" reports for comic effect.

By impersonating authorities, inventing a number of alibis, encouraging the policemen to speak lines and lies he has given them, confusing them so that they don't know which thoughts are theirs and which are the impostor judge's, Fo literally makes a charade of the police description of the murder. In doing so, he intimates that the state itself requires a series of charades, cover-ups and manipulations in order to perpetuate its abusive power structure.

The capacity of Fo's buffoon to impersonate policemen, anarchists, a judge and a bishop, fosters a comic, carnival vision of society in which (as Bakhtin said of Rabelais' carnivalesque world), people become interchangeable within their mass body.[12] Fo himself is capable of becoming a one-man carnival who amply represents the collectivity; in one scene of *Mistero Buffo*, he portrays fifteen different characters by himself. Through a variety of gestures and speeches he expresses the responses of a crowd watching the miracle of Lazarus' resurrection. Fo's ability to perform crowd scenes solo may be one reason that French critic Bernard Dort has praised the "ubiquity" of this "epic actor." In describing Fo's performance in *Mistero Buffo*, Dort calls it the opposite of a personal display; Fo was not on stage to show himself, but rather to show many others.

His ubiquitous style of theatre is also evident in Fo's playwriting, where characters alter society, at least temporarily, by transforming themselves and creating new personae. Given the proper words and gestures, Fo's characters can change from factory owners into factory workers and from policemen into anarchists. The first act of *Accidental Death* ends with the police singing a favorite hymn of anarchists, because the buffoon has convinced them that it will make them look more human and sympathetic to the public: "I beg of you! For your own good . . . so the investigation will turn out in your favor. . . . Sing!" And they sing:

The whole world is our homeland.
Our law is liberty.

And through our thought
This world of ours shall finally be free.[13]

## The Miraculous Cabbage

The grotesque situations in which Fo's characters find themselves could be
described as Rabelaisian. Bakhtin notes that in Rabelais' world, the grotesque
"discloses the potentiality of an entirely different world, of another way of
life . . . a return to Saturn's golden age . . . [requiring] bodily participation
in the potentiality of another world."[14] The policemen who sing an anarchist
song briefly enter another world—that of their victim. But far more grotesque
transformations occur in other Fo scenes. A police officer harassing pregnant-
looking women appears to experience an hysterical pregnancy himself in *We
Can't Pay, We Won't Pay!* Several other "pregnancies" rapidly start and stop
in the course of the play, when a "golden age" of fertility and plenitude arises
at a time many people cannot afford to pay their grocery bills. In fact, it
is because they cannot afford groceries that the golden age and bodily transformations begin. Groups of women openly steal foodstuffs to protest the high
cost of necessities; they then stuff the goods under their coats to hide the loot
from husbands and policemen. The women claim that their bulging bellies
are pregnancies, and their naive husbands almost instantly accept the roles
of worried, expectant fathers. As noted previously, Fo's satire is based on actual events in Milan, where massive "proletarian shopping" (shoplifting) began
after grocery prices skyrocketed in 1974. The efforts of the women to hide
their stolen goods result in a farcical vision of urban Saturnalia, a world of
miraculous pregnancies and free groceries, sometimes both at once. When
the bulging bellies of Antonia and Margherita are discovered to hold bags
of salad, not unborn children, they claim a miracle has occurred. The police
inspector searching for stolen goods must accept their word or risk committing a sacrilege:

> *Inspector:* Oh yes? The cabbage miracle. Where are the roses?
> *Margherita:* Who can afford roses? They're very expensive.
> *Antonia:* In hard times, one makes what miracles one can. With the
> veg you've got handy. Anyway, miracles aren't illegal, you know. Also,
> there's no law that says a person can't carry a mixed salad on their
> belly.[15]

The satire here ridicules religion in an age of consumer capitalism. It
is an age of democracy where "miracles" can be purchased in any grocery
store, but the greatest miracle is that one can afford to pay the bill. In *We
Can't Pay, We Won't Pay!* the humor is less exotic than, say, the episode in
Rabelais' *Gargantua and Pantagruel*, in which Gargantua eats six pilgrims

in a salad because they had hidden under giant lettuce leaves in a garden to escape their enemies. Rabelais' grotesquery has given way to antic transformations more suitable for an age of inflation, shoplifting and "miracle" salads.

Fo's utopian satire offers us small miracles: policemen turning into anarchists and unborn children turning into food. The playwright knows and freely admits that his satire cannot achieve larger miracles. One speech in *Accidental Death of an Anarchist* questions the play's efficacy as a social corrective, and inadvertently explains its success at box offices years after it was written. Having revealed Italian political scandals, the buffoonish impostor in the play informs us, "The average citizen doesn't stand to gain anything from the disappearance of dirty deals. No, he's satisfied to see them denounced, to see a scandal break out so that people can talk about it. For him, that's real freedom and the best of all possible worlds."

If Fo understands the limits of his art, he also knows the source of its appeal. The buffoon in *Accidental Death of an Anarchist* tells us that his hobby is "the theatre of reality, so my fellow artists must be real people, unaware that they are acting in my productions, which is handy, as I've got no cash to pay them." The law officers who hear him, along with the audience, willingly become this masterful charlatan's co-conspirators, his "fellow artists," as he winks at both groups in turn, confides his impostures and scandals to listeners and asks them to approve of his disguises. His need for audience acceptance is complemented by his listeners' desire to be part of a political conspiracy, to hear secrets of state whispered aloud. The spontaneous and intimate sense of conspiracy between the satirist and his audience cannot be achieved as easily on electronic media as on stage, in person—especially if the person is a comic performer as gifted as Dario Fo.

While Fo's plays allow the audience to eavesdrop on dirty political deals or parodies of them, the playwright resists passivity and voyeurism in spectators. Like the maniac in *Accidental Death*, he, too, uses "real people" as his "fellow artists" by involving the audience and actors in playwriting and incorporating their suggestions into works-in-progress. Plays such as *Accidental Death of an Anarchist* have acquired several different endings as a result of Fo's exchanges with the audience. Other plays, such as *The Boss's Funeral*, contain an "unwritten" last act; instead of finishing the story, Fo and his cast discuss the play and its political issues with the audience. In this way he allows spectators to "enter" (his word) the performance and modify it; they, too, become agents of change.

"In this way his performance becomes a discussion [about social conditions] with the audience he is addressing," Brecht wrote of an epic actor's technique.[16] This can be said of Fo's performance style, too, although his style differs markedly from that of Brecht's epic theatre by responding to recent events with farcical "counter-information." And while both playwrights have tried to break through the fourth wall with the help of jesters and direct address, Fo has gone one step further "out of character." He ends by leaving his comic personae behind to become Dario Fo, listener, conversationalist, debater, political organizer. When he engages in these democratic, post-performance dialogues there is no longer any need for that perpetual outcast and renegade, the political clown.

# -17-

# The Jokers of Augusto Boal

"The walls must be torn down," writes Augusto Boal in a preface to his essay "The Poetics of the Oppressed."[1] The Brazilian director and playwright laments the loss of carnival conditions that existed in ancient theatre festivals, where everyone participated and there were no spectators. Boal calls for new forms of theatre without spectators; his forum theatre, invisible theatre and "Joker System" all parallel contemporary uses of clowning by breaking through the imaginary fourth wall in order to involve spectators directly in the theatrical event.

Once asked what writers or types of theatre influenced him most, Boal replied, "There were two major influences on my theatre . . . Bertolt Brecht and the circus."[2] He went on to say that Brecht had taught his own country's authors that "our obligation was to shed light on reality, not only to reflect and to interpret reality, but to try to change it." This sense of obligation, along with the influence of "the clownish acts performed at the circus" as well as the "tradition of political vaudeville" and carnival in Brazil, can be detected in Boal's theatre practices.

Boal began to develop his methods of play production while at the Arena Theatre of Sao Paulo from 1956 to 1971. He is an extremely articulate man of the theatre, and in several books he thoroughly explains his theories and practice, placing his ideas in the sociological and historical contexts of their origin. Some of the essays collected in *The Theatre of the Oppressed* were written in the late 1960s, after the 1966 onset of military rule in Brazil. Even before his arrest in 1971, Boal had to face military censorship and other forms of government harrassment which also influenced his thinking. His opposition to Brazilian government militarism, and other nations' colonialism, led him in a political direction similar to Brecht's, and like Brecht, Boal faced government persecution and forced exile. He has conducted workshops in other Latin American countries since leaving Brazil in 1971, and has more recently led exploratory workshops in Paris, where he heads an institute for research in Theatre of the Oppressed.

In his book bearing that name, Boal's extension of Brecht's theories is carefully delineated. His techniques encourage spectators to become participants in a play—or at least active and audible respondents to the actors—rather than passive and overly empathic voyeurs. While Brecht sought to alter spectator sensibility through new acting and staging methods, Boal goes directly to the audience's role and attempts to change it, or even abolish it, so that spectators become actors and co-authors in a collaborative art.

## A Politician Takes the Stage

In Boal's "forum theatre" spectators are invited to replace actors during the performance of scenarios that are devised collaboratively; they are encouraged to devise and act out different solutions or endings to the situation in progress. The event is tremendously democratic, and potentially satiric, as Boal demonstrates in one anecdote he tells about a forum theatre performance in Sicily. In a village there the local population found itself unable to speak freely with the mayor. One villager represented the mayor in a forum theatre workshop conducted by Boal, and the other villagers found themselves able, at last, to say what they wanted to the mayor (or his stand-in). The mayor—who was in the audience—stopped the performance and replaced his representative with himself, because, according to Boal, "the villager who played [the mayor] was not defending him so well."[3] In this case the forum achieved what everyday life could not; it allowed the villagers to speak freely and directly to their mayor, and forced him to defend himself in front of all those assembled. By performing in scenarios that deal with their own problems, the people who attend Boal's forum theatre workshops are helped to confront and find solutions for those problems. (The example described here recalls a legend about the ancient Athenian tyrant, Kleon, who reportedly sat in the front row of a theatre while Aristophanes impersonated and ridiculed him on stage in *The Knights*; Kleon waited until the festival was over before he responded by harrassing Aristophanes.) In Sicily the boundary between life and art was virtually eliminated in a public square, as the mayor became more fully responsive to local opinion. Boal adds that forum theatre does not fully abolish the separation between the staged scene and the audience; it simply makes them interpenetrate more. The spectator does not have to watch passively all the time, and the actor does not have to act all the time. It is democratic, he says, in the sense that "one can speak, propose ideas."[4]

## The Stage Disappears

The public also participates in a staged event in Boal's "invisible theatre," although in this case the public remains unaware that the event is theatre at all. The Brazilian director invented the concept of "invisible theatre" when government censorship necessitated a political theatre form which could pass for everyday life. Instead of announcing that a scene is being staged, Boal and his associates stage an event—a quarrel, for example—in a public space: a restaurant, a bus, a museum. As spectators witness the action and are drawn into it either verbally or physically, they become unwitting actors. One invisible theatre performance began when Boal's actors dined in an expensive Brazilian restaurant. Given the bill, one actor claimed he could not afford to pay it and loudly discussed the high cost of food. Actors planted elsewhere in the restaurant took up the discussion and collected money to help pay the exorbitant bill. Most of the other diners had no idea that they were witnessing a staged drama, and participating in it, as they donated money and joined the debate over the cost of living and national economic policies. Unlike some forms of "guerrilla theatre," this performance in no way assaulted its audience or invaded territory foreign to its concerns. Where would it be more appropriate to discuss the cost of food than inside an expensive restaurant? Like Boal's other forms of theatre, this one moves toward an interchangeability of actor and spectator, of theatre space and public space. "The spectator can become an actor, the actor can become a spectator," says Boal.[5]

To European and North American critics, some of Boal's theatre practices may appear to be closer to therapy than theatre. The instant transformation of spectators into actors who improvise dialogue could encourage simplification to excess, with unrehearsed or amateur acting and one-dimensional characters and plot. Such simplicity serves a purpose, however, when Boal seeks to create forms of expression for segments of the Third World population that have no prior exposure to formal theatre. Instead of imposing culture from "above," as colonizers impose their way of life on conquered subjects, Boal encourages cultural creation by those who need their own forum, offering them a chance to address their problems—or their village mayor—in their own language.

This encouragement of indigenous culture is indebted to Brazilian educator Paulo Freire's practices, described in *Pedagogy of the Oppressed*;

and it shares Freire's commitment to education. The replacement of passive spectatorship is part of a larger political aim: to convey a sense of self-determination to the audience, letting the people sense their own creativity as well as their potential power to effect change. In *Pedagogy of the Oppressed*, Freire writes of the conflict the oppressed face in the choice "between ejecting the oppressor or not ejecting him; between human solidarity or alienation; between following prescriptions or having choices; between acting or having the illusions of acting through the action of the oppressors; between speaking out or being silent, castrated in their power to create and re-create, in their power to transform the world."[6] These same choices are offered to spectators, in non-coercive rehearsal form, by Boal's theatre; here, too, people can become actors, speak out and engage in what Freire calls "critical and liberating dialogue" so as to "intervene critically in the situation which surrounds them."[7] Boal's methods challenge the spectator's actual situation in a performance, and not just his consciousness of that performance; this is rehearsal for life, as Boal seeks changes of situation and not merely changes of consciousness.

## The Joker Without a Joke

Boal developed his "Joker System" in order to place a representative of the audience on stage. The "joker" to which the system's title refers is something like the court jester pictured in modern playing cards. He is the "wild card," which is to say, he can play any part in one of Boal's productions. He is ubiquitous, changing roles more often than Dario Fo, but for similar purposes. The joker serves as master of ceremonies, commenting on the action as it proceeds. One of his multiple functions recalls the 1920 entry in Brecht's diary, previously quoted, in which the German playwright vowed, if he ever controlled a theatre, to hire two clowns and have them pretend to be spectators during intermissions, when they would exchange opinions about the play and the audience. When Augusto Boal was devising his Joker System in the mid-1960s, his familiarity with the writings of Brecht and with clowns led him to practice what Brecht had only dreamed of.

Encouraging spectators to ask questions of characters or to replace them and play out their roles, fosters in them a critical attitude—the same attitude that Brecht was after in 1920, when he wrote in his diary that things "need to be criticized," and vowed that clowns would be his theatre's critics. Boal, too, attributes this critical attitude to clowns:

> For me, the clowns don't represent reality with realism, but as they see it. They magnify, they deform reality. I have always thought that realism serves to hide reality, instead of showing it, and I don't like realism. . . . Instead of showing the appearance of things, we should show how they really are. In French we

say: *"Au lieu de montrer les choses vraies, montrez comment les choses sont vrai-
ment."* ("Instead of showing true things, show how things are true.") I believe
that the clowns don't approach a character in a realistic way, but in a deformed
way. They try to show what is essential to them, and then magnify [it]. What
I try to do in theatre is the same; not to show a correct image, but the deformed
image. . . . [Clowns] deform because they choose a few elements and eliminate
the rest. . . . That's what we try to do.[8]

Boal's Joker undercuts appearances and realism by functioning as exactly the opposite of a protagonist, a person who "has only the character's
level of consciousness, not the actor's."[9] The Joker, says Boal, "can play any
role, including the protagonist, master of ceremonies, lecturer, judge,
*raissoneur*, stagehand; he can interrupt the action, repeat certain actions in
order to demonstrate them better, use slides, films, diagrams, statistics."[10]

However, for all his changes and display of alternative roles, the Joker
as Boal describes him is not necessarily comic or satiric. It would be misleading
to equate the term "Joker" with "clown." (In Spanish the word Boal uses is
*comodin*, meaning "playing card joker" or "something of general utility.")
Humor—or lack of it—is not crucial to the system. More important is the
behavior of the actor and audience which the system fosters; in this area his
system extends Brecht's development of a naive, fairground or carnival theatre
style, and a "critical attitude." The Joker is less a conventional clown than
a Brechtian epic actor. As Brecht describes it:

The actor does not allow himself to become transformed on stage into the
character he is portraying. He is not Lear, Harpagon, Schweyk; he shows
them. . . . Because he doesn't identify himself with [the characters] he can pick
a definite attitude to adopt toward the character whom he portrays, can show
what he thinks of him and invite the spectator, who is likewise not asked to identify himself, to criticize the character portrayed. . . . The attitude which he adopts
is a socially critical one. . . . His performance becomes a discussion (about social
conditions) with the audience he is addressing. He prompts the spectator to justify
or abolish these conditions according to what class he belongs to.[11]

Brecht's concept of "discussion with the audience" is odd; it implies that
spectators will silently, mentally converse with the actors as a result of the
socially critical attitude imparted to them in the performance. Boal takes the
idea of mutual dialogue literally, encouraging the audience to engage audibly
in dialogue with actors through planned interventions. Boal also resists audiences' identification with specific characters by having them ask questions
about the characters.

These questions are addressed directly to the characters (not the actors
portraying the characters) by either the Joker or the audience members
themselves. There is necessarily an element of naiveté in a process which encourages the illusion that spectators can talk to characters in a play: but the
situation is not that different from a sports event in which spectators call out

words of encouragement to their favorite players. In fact, Boal compares his interview sessions between the Joker and the characters to halftime interviews with players conducted by sportscasters during soccer games.

His analogy between theatre and sports contests recalls Brecht's own comparisons between sporting events (especially boxing) and the theatre of his day. In sports contests the audience knows the rules and everyone is an expert or a judge, noted Brecht; Boal, too, encourages a sense of participatory democracy in his audience, as everyone becomes a friendly interrogator. Boal goes so far as to call the Joker a judge. Everyone else then becomes part of his tribunal, since the Joker represents all spectators and speaks for them; the Joker "belongs to the universe of the audience," says Boal, and "asks those questions the audience wants answered."[12]

The potential for role exchange here suggests that just as the Joker can be anyone in a play, anyone in the audience can be a Joker. The plan promises a new, democratic and celebratory art in which ordinary people approach the ancient, first impulses of theatre as Boal defines them: "Free people singing in the open air. The carnival. The feast."[13]

# -18

# American Folly
'MacBird,' The San Francisco
Mime Troupe,
El Teatro Campesino
and The Plutonium Players

*"All my humor is based on destruction and despair. If the whole world were tranquil, without disease and violence, I'd be standing in the breadline right back of J. Edgar Hoover."*

—Lenny Bruce[1]

T he "disease and violence" to which Lenny Bruce responded with satire also influenced American political theatre during the 1960s. Much as the Federal Theatre Project emerged in the 1930s in response to the Great Depression, a later generation of artists responded to political crises in the 1960s. Its audience and writers shared a common history of support for the Civil Rights movement, the Vietnam anti-war movement and the unionism of the United Farm Workers. But as the most destructive "disease and violence" of that period diminished, after American troops were withdrawn from Vietnam, the intensity of our political activism and the forcefulness of our political satire also waned.

America's Left has no continuing public discourse comparable to that in Europe, where socialists and communists openly debate in the parliaments and theatre artists continue the same debates, using other means, on the stage. The legacy of McCarthyism and the lack of a broad-based socialist movement inhibit such public discourse in America. "Marxism" and "socialism" have virtually become dirty words within the mainstream, and have remained minority group philosophies since the late 1940s. Instead of creating plays as part of an ongoing debate, American creators of political theatre respond to events on an impromptu basis: like Lenny Bruce they thrive on crises—

"disease and violence." And for the most part these responses occur outside mainstream commercial theatre.

Robert Brustein once observed, "Direct confrontation of American life—banished from our stage—has had to find refuge in 'illegitimate' theatrical entertainments like the monologues of Mort Sahl, the nightclub skits of May and Nichols."[2] "Direct confrontation of American life" can now be seen on occasion at resident theatres which did not exist in Sahl and Bruce's heyday, but political satire still rarely appears on American stages.[3]

## Into the Breach with 'MacBird'

*MacBird*, the most widely discussed American political satire of the sixties, was first professionally performed in a New York nightclub, the Village Gate, in 1967. The popularity of Barbara Garson's play suggests that under certain conditions satire can have an impact on America's consciousness; the main prerequisites are an unpopular war, an unpopular President (these two are almost always around) and a caricaturist willing to defile leading statesmen. The formula has always served political cartoonists well; playwrights have seemed less eager to follow it, for reasons to be discussed shortly.

Garson's satire draws on Shakespeare's *Macbeth*, using its plot of power and betrayal to parody contemporary American political figures. Shakespeare's language is distorted, transformed into speeches written for impersonators of Lyndon B. Johnson and his Cabinet. The play shows Johnson arranging for the assassination of John F. Kennedy, so that he might accede to the Presidency. While the accusation against Johnson was as preposterous when it was written as it is now, the substitution of LBJ for Macbeth became a provocative metaphor for the White House as a source of state violence. If LBJ did not murder JFK to become President, he did sustain his own power—and what he thought was America's power—through escalation of a war that killed hundreds of thousands of Asians in Vietnam.

In Garson's hands Johnson becomes a stock dramatic figure: a sadistic if stupid braggart soldier representative, in the Ubu Roi tradition, of unrestrained appetite for power. He is a power-hungry assassin who claims that his "Pox Americana is what all the freedom-loving world desires." The primitive weaponry (lance, spiked shoulder pads) and archaic language of a Texan turned Scottish king provide a useful alternative to the veneer of civility and restraint shown in televised press conferences of the sixties, in which the President humbly claimed, "We seek no wider war," while all the time widening the war.

Garson's transformation of a revered tragedy into crude, topical satire caused a fury of debate among American critics; some discussed the play's merits as if all of Western aesthetics, not Johnson's war or "Great Society" policy, were under attack. Richard Gilman accused Garson of nihilism and, worse yet, of having fun: "This little nihilist from Berkeley sits down and without disturbing herself in the least proceeds to fashion a piece about which the most frequent admiring description is that it is 'fun.' "[4] While fun is not in itself a measure of success or failure (although Brecht once said that theatre "has got to have" fun), it is also not a quality usually associated with politics or political theatre in America. Perhaps our government has gone so awry that only a satirist like Garson, Lenny Bruce or Abbie Hoffman can find any "fun" in politics.

MacBird was also attacked for its departure from historically proven facts and from the logic of Shakespeare's plot, as if it were up to Garson to preserve decorum and veracity even though she saw the White House losing them. Much as the anti-war movement was asked to stop being negative about American policy, and propose instead an alternative in positive terms ("Get the troops out!" was not considered positive enough), Garson was chided for doing no more than desecrating Shakespeare, LBJ and other hot- and cold-war politicians. In retrospect, her achievement was singular; as stage satire of a President the play has not been surpassed.

At the same time, MacBird is now terribly out of date; the heat and laughter it generated would not return were the play revived. It was not a play for all time, but for a day, as some imitator of Shakespeare might say. In a sense, the greatest impact of a play like MacBird stems from the fact that it has been performed at all.

The simple act of stepping on stage to impersonate a man in power and ridicule him is so rare in our society that this in itself becomes a political act, an unusual critique of power. When, in MacBird, the actor Stacy Keach impersonated Lyndon Johnson, his specific words were less important than the image of a Texas assassin dressed for battle in baseball catcher's mask, spiked shoulder pads and chest protector. An image of power had been captured, dressed in comic military costume and forced to act out someone else's battle plan—which ended in defeat. (The act could have been Durov's except that an actor in comic battle gear, rather than a pig in a helmet, portrayed the state's ruler.) The humor and "offense" grew first and foremost from the author's concept: Cast LBJ as Macbeth, move the politician from his Oval Office television cameras to a nightclub stage and let him wield state violence as a glorified spear-carrier.

If it appears on stage at all, American political satire tends to derive its potency from this transfer of power from press conference to stage play: the very act of impersonating a president or general is the most forceful part of the show. This act of transfer may account for audience enthusiasm about plays like MacBird which seem unimpressive on the page.

The assumption of power by an actor in such plays also initiates a leveling process noted previously in reference to Brecht's Arturo Ui. A disruption comparable to those in Brecht's epic theatre occurs in *MacBird* when Stacy Keach's clowning breaks the illusion that he is Macbeth or LBJ. In breaking his own illusion of power, by juxtaposing LBJ with Macbeth, Shakespeare's seriousness with Garson's parody, Keach hints that the power of actual leaders might also be an illusion: a role that can be laughed at or taken away by ordinary people like those watching Keach's usurpation of the throne.

*MacBird* and other American political satires thrive on this mimicry of statemen's roles, but they do not often merit attention as dramatic literature; they lack the wit and complexity of satire contained in foreign plays, because our leaders also tend to lack these qualities. American Presidents lend themselves to cartoons and skits but not to detailed stage portraits, most probably due to the nature of American political rhetoric which tends to move away from complexity and toward "freedom or tyranny" simplicity. Unless debate depolarizes and enriches our language so that substantive discussion of such concepts as "socialism" and "unilateral disarmament" become more commonplace in the language of politicians, it is unlikely that American playwrights will create complex drama critical of those in power.

The present limits of our political vocabulary might also account for the continuing popularity of Presidential mimics, who offer spectators slight variations on the political imagery and language of Presidential press conferences and photo opportunities. Politicians holding lesser offices (or none at all) rarely receive such attention on the stage except, perhaps, within the context of a San Francisco Mime Troupe play.

At present, mainstream American playwrights are more inclined to focus on public events only when those events affect private life. An ensemble like the 26-year-old collective San Francisco Mime Troupe, however, is better prepared to consider extra-personal issues because it can create within its own artistic community the leftwing political discussion missing from society at large—and then bring that discussion to the public.


## Follow the Marching Gorilla

The San Francisco Mime Troupe initially derived its terms of discourse from the political activism of the sixties. Both Garson and the Mime Troupe developed their satiric sensibilities in the San Francisco Bay area when the Vietnam anti-war movement arose. Their drama owes some of its flair to the theatricality that surfaced in mass protests and street theatre of the period. The Mime Troupe participated in parades with a "Gorilla Marching Band," featuring a rag-tag group of musicians and a bass drum with a gorilla painted on it: a far cry from the assaults on spectators launched by some "guerrilla theatre" groups in the sixties. Garson had written *MacBird* for a Berkeley Vietnam Day rally; the Mime Troupe prepared a puppet show for a Vietnam Day march in 1965. Conspiracy buffs might trace the origins of this outspoken political theatre back to the Free Speech Movement which began in 1964 at Berkeley, when University of California students objected to the campus administration's suppression of student political groups. A sit-in at Berkeley's Sproul Hall and other, subsequent defenses of free speech may have encouraged West Coast theatre artists to address political issues with the same fervor and inventiveness they saw employed by the Free Speech activists. What is more, the audiences for these artists were prepared for political plays by rallies which addressed many of the same issues as their plays, similarly criticizing those in power.

In its first decade the Mime Troupe updated and politicized several *commedia dell'arte* scenarios. One of its *commedia* productions, based on Goldoni's *L'Amant Militaire*, was an anti-war and anti-pacifist satire which toured the country in 1967, at the same time Barbara Garson's *MacBird* was moving to New York and national attention. *MacBird* ridicules the men who brought America into Vietnam. *L'Amant Militaire* attacks not only the rhetoric and lies of American generals, but also those of American leftists whose naive opposition to the war in Vietnam proved ineffectual. The play exemplifies a practice the Mime Troupe has continued throughout its history: criticizing the Left—its own audience—when it sees fit, as well as turning its barbs on its opponents.

In *L'Amant Militaire*, Italians residing in the town of "Spinacholla" resist a Spanish army maneuver—"Operation Guinea Wrangle"—designed to end Italian rebellion against foreign invaders. The analogy between Spain's occupation army in Italy and America's in Vietnam needs little elaboration, especially since the language of the generals is calculated to sound so American. Eventually a female impersonator of the Pope intervenes to save his—or her—countrymen from the Spaniards. But first, two Italian women naively endeavor to sweet-talk the Spanish generals into peace:

> We will speak to them, we will speak [to the generals], Corallina, and the sweet voice of reason will silence the thunder of battle.[5]

Rosalinda's innocent faith in reason and pacifism fails to bring peace. A more militant message is delivered by the puppet Punch, who speaks for the Mime Troupe as a whole when he advocates draft resistance and condemns war-profiteering. These views are not espoused in Goldoni's original text, of course; but Goldoni himself was anti-militaristic, if not anti-pacifist, in his version. According to J.S. Kennard, in his book *Goldoni and the Venice of His Time*, the playwright "sapped" militarism "at its base by showing a number of officers utterly deprived of the spirit that ennobles their profession. . . . Like many other Venetians of his time, Goldoni did not see the possible use of war as a means to promote welfare or progress. . . . No Goldoni character glorifies the military profession."[6]

*Pantalone and the General in the San Francisco Mime Troupe's L' Amant Militaire, 1967.*

While the Mime Troupe drew on earlier anti-militaristic comedy for its caricatures in *L'Amant Militaire,* the play's closing advice is more representative of the 1960s, when the radical group Students for a Democratic Society advocated participatory democracy. The servant woman Corallina impersonates the Pope and enters to rescue her countrymen by announcing, "Listen my friends—you want something done? Well, then, do it yourselves." Her message suggests that anti-war resistance cannot be provided by a play, or by an actor telling spectators what to do; the answer must be found in collective action, participatory democracy, possibly of the variety embodied by the Mime Troupe itself in its cheerful, collective creations.

## Peace Prize for Christmas Bombing

The physical acting style of Mime Troupe company members is often more comic than their dialogue. (It would be difficult, in any case, to find punchlines for characters whose deeds include ordering the Christmas bombing of Hanoi and then winning the Nobel Peace Prize.) But Mime Troupe satire depends less on comic dialogue than on impersonating men in power, ultimately turning them into clowns through physical humor.

Dialogue was never the strongest feature of Italian *commedia* either;

like *commedia* scenarios, which were built around character types and comic business rather than dialogue or plot, the Mime Troupe's first *commedia*-based works, as well as its later works based on other forms, offer variations on stock characters. The paunch of a fat Mime Troupe industrialist, the sunglassy stare of an FBI agent in a raincoat, reveal their characters quickly through costume and gesture. The characters are flamboyant, with features as distinctive and emblematic as the wrinkled neck and bouffant hair of an aged, Sunset Boulevard president in a political cartoon.

Until recently all Mime Troupe plays were rehearsed for performance outdoors on a portable platform stage, which required sacrifice of subtlety in gesture and speech. The broad physical comedy of Italian *commedia* is well suited to the larger-than-life style needed for open-air productions.

The Troupe's non-realistic acting style also adapts Brecht's technique of Epic Theatre, breaking the illusion of the performance with songs, puns, asides and diatribes which depart from the narrative and comment on it. In one sequence of *L'Amant Militaire*, a braggart general switches from an Italian dialect to Lyndon Johnson's Texas accent and style of rhetoric. This is followed by commentary by the puppet Punch, who quotes Al Capone's warning against Bolshevism. In the course of two speeches, the Mime Troupe's satire passes from Renaissance Italian characterization to mockery of the President of the United States to Punch-and-Judy puppetry imbued with the historical consciousness of a Chicago gangster. The array of sources is dazzling, and ultimately funnier by virtue of its juxtapositions than because of any single technique or joke. Purity of style has never been a Mime Troupe aim. Quite the contrary: the group purposely eschews consistency of style within its plays, and changes styles from play to play, seeing the means of performance as less important than the reality it addresses. In short, the ensemble takes politics more seriously than it takes any single style of theatre. As founder R.G. Davis notes in his history of the Mime Troupe, "Our *commedias* were bound by real politics, thus satire was our forte, not slapstick. We always related our joke to something tangible, rather than developing comedy from fantasy."

Art that criticizes reality and comments on it—instead of imitating it, glorifying it or ignoring it—is not widespread among American theatre groups. The Mime Troupe, although it becomes more widely recognized with each successive production or tour, remains one of the few American companies to undertake such tasks in its satires.

## Punch Says War Is No Clown Show

At one point in *L'Amant Militaire* the clown Arlecchino is crucified, and Punch notes that the scene is full of "good old hard-hitting realism." But Punch himself, and the puppetry that makes him live, represent an alternative to stage realism. Violence and its rhetoric are not portrayed realistically in the play; when Punch counsels the audience to resist war the implication is that a play, even a realistically performed one, cannot stop war. Only political activism can begin to do that. Theatre, because it is a place where puppets and buffoons oppose the American armed forces, is frivolous. As Punch warns, "You know the war is just a little bit tougher than this clown show."

Models for the Mime Troupe's puppets and clowns have been recruited from several sources other than Italian *commedia*. The foremost recruiting ground for these comic types is the American government, at home and abroad. Army officers, conservative politicians and presidents display the traits most often mimicked by the Mime Troupe. These plays often put government and corporate rhetoric in the mouths of buffoons, as earlier political satires have done. There is no need to refute the arguments of generals and multinational corporation presidents if you can make them sound foolish in their own language. Listen to a few Mime Troupe military generals in *L'Amant Militaire* and you overhear an only slightly revised version of a Pentagon press briefing:

> It [is] the fundamental policy of the Spanish government to pursue peace with every available weapon.
>
> We have complete control of the cities and towns, and our pacification teams are running over the countryside. The rebels are being rolled back, they're hurting, they're on the defensive, as if proved by the growing number of their attacks.

The satire here is not deep; it rarely transcends surface, clichéd phrases of political and military leaders. But the phrasing and context are comic, undercutting (or overthrowing?) the characters from a leftist perspective.

Other sources of inspiration for the Mime Troupe are the political consciousness and dramaturgies of Brecht and Fo. Both of these authors have had their plays adapted to Mime Troupe needs, filtered through its Americanized preference for physical comedy and satire (which Brecht and Fo anticipated in their own ways.) The company combined its own style with that of Brecht's Epic Theatre when staging his *The Exception and the Rule, The Mother* and *Turandot*. It also staged Dario Fo's farce *We Can't Pay! We Won't Pay!*, and Mime Troupe writer Joan Holden adapted Fo's *Accidental Death of an Anarchist* for another Bay Area theatre, the Eureka. Although direct steals from Brecht and Fo are rare, one can detect Brechtian irony— *Threepenny*-like parody of Biblical rhetoric in Alonso's line in *L'Amant Militaire*: "It was grief that killed Caesar. And Socrates—Coriolanus—Our Lord—Richard Nixon, alas. History groans with examples of greatness betrayed by the mob." Larger debts to Fo and Brecht are evident in the Mime Troupe's commitment to foster social change and to create awareness of the need for change by portraying social struggles on stage.

## Twenty-six Years of Folly (1959-1985)

In recent years the Mime Troupe has incorporated some qualities of comic strips and popular music in its plays—finding models of entertainment in forms more contemporary than Italian *commedia*. The songs range from union organizing chants to reggae, rock and blues. The comic strip *Terry and the Pirates*, with its spies and military intrigue, provided imagery for *The Dragon Lady's Revenge* (1971). *Superman* served as a model for Factwino, the super-intelligent protagonist of *The Factwino Trilogy* (1980-82) and an opera, called *Factwino: The Opera*, based on the same material (1985). One stage direction describes the title character as an "elderly Negro in comic book outfit."

The most significant shift in Mime Troupe history occurred after its founder R.G. Davis left the company in the late 1960s; around the time of his departure Davis wrote that the ensemble was suffering from "participatory democracy (inherited from the Students for a Democratic Society)." He continued, "As distinctions between expertise and will dissolved due to pressure from participatory democracy and idealistic fantasy, the antagonism between professional performer and amateur participating member increased."[7] If, as Davis contends, the Mime Troupe was a microcosm of the anti-war movement, its difficulties in decision-making may well reflect those experienced by the American Left at large in the late sixties. It should be noted that the Mime Troupe has survived Davis's departure, however; since he left, multiracial and feminist emphases have become more pronounced in plays concerned with feminism (*The Independent Female*), American intervention in Central America (*Last Tango in Huahuatenango*), the Moral Majority (*Factwino Meets the Moral Majority*), the electoral process (*1985*) and the closing of steel plants (*Steeltown*).

While the Troupe has developed a national following through years of touring, and an especially loyal following at its home base in San Francisco, its actors often find themselves preaching to the converted. As Theodore Shank notes, the company promotes "the feeling of being the good minority standing against the evil Establishment. Such easy moral distinctions suggest one of the reasons stereotype *commedia*-like characters and symbolic characters are so often used."[8] The feeling of being "the good minority" can too easily become self-congratulatory and encourage complacency rather than activism among its adherents. Critic Lee Baxandall was particularly disturbed by this tendency in the Mime Troupe's production of Brecht's *The Mother* in 1975; his open letter to the Troupe feared that they were clearing "every obstacle from the immediate (unthinking) response of (their) left but naive audience . . . I don't think you originally intended to be mere cheerleaders of a futile revolutionary fantasy."[9] Baxandall also expressed concern that the Troupe might be "locked" into "the structure of a skillful brightly-colored poster" which it imposed on Brecht's play, even though the play "demands a realist, if cheerful and stylized, performance."

Revolutionary posturing suits the Mime Troupe's broad, exaggerated style of acting, and its depiction of Brecht's flag-waving revolutionaries in *The Mother*, as well as Central American guerrillas and defiant union strikers in other plays, might easily be seen as cheerleading for a revolution. Such stiff, rhetorical poses are more removed from American life today than they were in the 1960s, when "revolutionary" was a term used to describe new cars as well as radical political plans. It may well be that the Mime Troupe's style was better suited to the sixties than it is to the present. Troupe members are, in fact, aware of the need to change with the times. Joan Holden has said that in the group's recent plays, *Steeltown* and *1985*, "the psychology's more realistic [and the works are] less agit-prop and more particular." She explains, "The politics of the sixties and ours in the seventies were very programmatic. We knew what the issues were, we were Marxists, the message was clear, the foreign models were clear. We're still Marxists, but the models aren't clear anymore."[10]

As an adversary critic of local and national government for a quarter of a century, the Mime Troupe continues to advocate social change along socialist, democratic and Marxist lines—wide rather than narrow lines, based on responses to specific events and politicians. Its adversary stance was reaffirmed in 1984 when the ensemble was awarded its first federal grant by the National Endowment for the Arts, and longtime Troupe member Daniel Chumley vowed, "We'll bite the hand that feeds us." Despite its increased budget and dependence on subsidy, the Mime Troupe still functions as a counter-cultural and alternative political voice, outside the mainstream of commercial entertainment and outside of mainstream American acting styles as practiced by the disciples of Stanislavsky and Lee Strasberg.

If the Troupe's material once flattered the Left community with fantasies of success, it does so no longer. Recent plays like *Steeltown* have no happy ending, and promise no easy and rosy future through socialism. However, the San Francisco Mime Troupe does still provide an otherwise elusive sense of solidarity and community to a following that has yet to develop a powerful cultural network in America. The Left has had to settle for alternative theatre groups and small touring troupes as its spokespersons, and it will continue to do so until it acquires more influence among politicians and larger cultural institutions. Popular theatre techniques derived from *commedia*, comic strips and rock music concerts do not guarantee widespread popularity in our culture, where ninety-eight percent of the population attends no theatre at all. The Mime Troupe is still competing for a small percentage of that small percentage of theatregoers; but it also continues to support the formation of mass movements against militarism, sexism and racism—movements which promote Mime Troupe ideas about social change more widely than any stage play could. In that sense, the group's plays are only the first act of a larger program to change society.

## "Somewhere Between Brecht and Cantinflas"
## The Clowns of El Teatro Campesino

The Mime Troupe has also served as the training ground for a number of actors who left and developed their own varieties of political satire. The most notable Mime Troupe alumnus is Luis Valdez, founder of El Teatro Campesino. The clowns of El Teatro Campesino first appeared in Delano, California in 1965, at a time when the union now known as the United Farm Workers was organizing Mexican American laborers in the region. The group began as a theatre by and for farmworkers, and its satires were directed at farm owners during the early years of the U.F.W.'s struggle for recognition. Luis Valdez founded the ensemble after studying playwriting at San Jose College and performing roles for the San Francisco Mime Troupe. Valdez's background in theatre led him to draw on past stage traditions as well as the immediate experience of farm workers. Models for El Teatro Campesino's plays include the Mexican comedian Cantinflas, the San Francisco Mime Troupe and Bertolt Brecht. (Valdez himself once described El Teatro Campesino as a group of farmworkers "somewhere between Cantinflas and Brecht.")

When Valdez decided to form a theatre to support the strikers in Delano, Cesar Chavez and other union leaders encouraged him. Initially the group performed short one-act plays called *actos*, which were designed to inspire workers and student supporters on the picket lines and at union rallies. The actos were agit-prop skits which used highly topical satire to address the concerns of strikers. The plays had to be brief and sharp so as to fit into larger programs at rallies; it was essential that they get ideas across quickly and graphically to farm workers who might never have seen any theatre before, or felt any need for it.

The Campesino actors found slapstick to be the most effective means of conveying their ideas. Its broad, optimistic humor raised union morale while advocating distinct forms of action. Valdez once explained the company's preference for slapstick:

> Our comic images are directed at the farm worker; they're supposed to represent the reality that he sees. It's not a naturalistic representation; most of the time it's a symbolic, emblematic presentation of what the farm worker feels. But we can't be stuffy about it, so we use slapstick.
>
> If you think that DiGiorgio [a ranch owner] is living and standing on the backs of his farm workers, you can show it with humor. You get "DiGiorgio" to stand on the backs of two farm workers, and there it is and nobody will refute you. [11]

## Cantinflas Meets the United Farm Workers

In his book *Alternative American Theatre*, Theodore Shank observes that El Teatro Campesino took Cantinflas as their model for "broad energetic movements that could convey a situation even without words."[12] This view gives Cantinflas slightly less credit than he deserves. Besides frenetic physical action, the comedian also excels at verbal humor.

Cantinflas, a Latin American successor to Chaplin's Little Tramp, was called "the world's greatest comedian" by Chaplin himself. (This was some time after the Little Tramp had retired, of course.) Like the character he portrays, Cantinflas began his life in poverty. He was born in 1911 in Mexico City, and worked as a singer, dancer and comedian in a tent show *(carpa)* before starting a film career in 1940. In films he became one of the world's highest paid actors. (He never hoarded his wealth, but gave away large sums to the poor.)

His name was Mario Moreno, until a *carpa* heckler shouted *"En la cantina tu inflas"* ("When you drink you talk big!") during a performance. He shortened that phrase into a stage name, and the word has now become both a verb and noun in Mexico. To say little while talking a lot is to "cantinflear." A popular clown is now called a "Cantinflas."

Unlike Chaplin's silent clown, Cantinflas became famous primarily for his comic monologues. Mexican audiences would wildly applaud and laugh at his nonsequiturs, gibberish and other verbal evasions. Critic Richard Condon suggests that the Mexican clown spoke this way less as wily self-defense than out of childlike innocence:

> Cantinflas is innocence; he is not aware of injustice . . . . No matter how severe the crisis, Cantinflas recognizes no crisis . . . . He is not aware of the chance of punishment; he is aware only of the fun a fellow can have while talking for the sake of words and sounds themselves. Senators do it all the time.[13]

Like senators who filibuster, however, Cantinflas occasionally ends up saving himself and his friends through his comic, confusing speeches. In one film he escapes conviction for murder by talking gibberish to the judge and jury, until they too begin to talk gibberish.[14]

This verbal facility, combined with his slapstick escapes from danger, allow the "little man" to out-maneuver people more socially respected or better educated than he. His victories may be implausible, but they offer a fantasy of success which has amused and comforted many lower-class Mexicans.

In Campesino's *actos* it is the figure of authority—the boss, army general or government advisor—who speaks most of the comic, Cantinflas-like gibberish. The group's political clowns, much like those created by the San Francisco Mime Troupe, are comic exaggerations and stereotypes of people in power. Campesino clown speeches tend to be more fanciful and humorously long-winded—more Cantinflaseque—than their Mime Troupe counterparts.

Gibberish and other comic evasions form the excuses of farm owners who oppose the union in plays such as *The Two Faces of the Boss* (1965). Patroncito, the two-faced boss, becomes a buffoon as he defends land ownership. It is doubtful that any boss was ever this envious of his workers. He tells a worker:

> I'm going to let you in on a little secret. Sometimes I sit up there in my office and think to myself: I wish I was a Mexican . . . . Just one of my own boys. Riding in the trucks, hair flying in the wind, feeling all that freedom, coming out here in the fields, working under the green vines, smoking a cigarette, my hands in the cool soft earth, underneath the blue skies, with white clouds drifting by, looking at the mountains, listening to the birdies sing.[15]

What is so difficult about the boss's own life?

> They say I'm greedy, that I'm rich. Well, let me tell you, boy, I got problems. No free housing for me, Pancho. I gotta pay for what I got. You see that car? How much you think a Lincoln Continental costs? Cash! $12,000! Ever write out a check for $12,000, boy?
>
> *Farmworker*: No señor.
>
> *Patroncito*: Well, lemme tell you, it hurts. It hurts right here! (slaps his wallet in his hind pocket) And what for? I don't need a car like that. I could throw it away!

The boss continues to complain about his high cost of living and finds the self-pity so convincing that he asks a scab worker to take his place, to suffer the role of "Rancher for a Day." The farmworker not only accepts the role; he refuses to trade back, keeps the property, wears the owner's pig-faced mask and calls in the police to harass the boss when he claims *he* is the real landowner. As a policeman drags the owner away, he calls out for help from union organizer Cesar Chavez; at last he sees why the workers need a union to defend their rights.

In other Campesino *actos*, other figures of authority are buffoons: a nonunion contractor in *Quinta Temporada*; a Pentagon general and a grower in *Vietnam Campesino*; a secretary to Governor Ronald Reagan in *Los Vendidos*; Chicano armed militants in *The Militants*. They too betray their greed and racism through outrageous actions and ridiculous self-justifications.

## From Cantinflas to Brecht

In a 1983 interview Valdez acknowledged that his scenes about "out-witting the power" have affinity with the comedy of Brecht as well as Cantinflas. He noted that Cantinflas was identifying with the low man on the totem pole.

He was the victim of fate, and yet trying to survive in his own way, using his wits; out-witting the rich, outwitting the powerful, doing a double-talk that everybody knew was nonsense but it was imitative of education, it was imitative of being powerful. And so he became a very popular hero, and a magical hero to watch. There is some of that character . . . of the harlequin character in Brecht's world, here and there . . . . that rawness that was in Cantinflas, the fact that he could take a pair of ragged pants and turn them into a clown's costume, his guaraches, his little hat—that was inherent in Brecht: the triumph of the tramp, because Brecht was an intellectual tramp.[16]

Like the actors who take the roles of Brecht's protagonists, Cantinflas establishes a distance between himself and his character—the rich person he imitates. He remains identifiable with the poor and powerless throughout, as he steals gestures and language which are not his in order to survive. Much as a real farm owner depends on poor Mexican Americans to create his wealth, a farm owner on El Teatro Campesino's stage depends for his existence on the labors of the Mexican American actor who portrays him. In this sense, the "rich" men on the stage owe their survival to the theatre ensemble. The act of impersonation becomes a temporary, comic upsetting of power relations, as poor farmworkers control the boss by *becoming* the boss onstage.

This carnivalesque reversal of boss and worker roles can be found in other modern political plays, including Fo's *About Face* and Brecht's *Puntila*, as noted earlier. The recurrence of this motif in the work of satirists may be due to a perception they share with Marx about capital's dependency on labor. The farcical switches of identity dramatize an interdependency of labor and capital, worker and boss, which those who rule would often prefer to obscure or deny.

El Teatro Campesino itself has been extremely dependent on the experience of farm workers (their labor, if you will.) Their struggle for social and economic justice accounts for the strong political consciousness in the *actos*, which are far different in this regard from what Richard Condon describes as the comic "innocence of Cantinflas."

## One, Two, Many Teatros

By 1970 the farmworkers and El Teatro Campesino began to see their struggle against farm owners as part of a larger movement against racism and war. The company's *Vietnam Campesino* satirized the Pentagon's alliance with lettuce growers, by revealing that at the same time the U.S. Army was sending Mexican Americans to their deaths in Vietnam, it was buying lettuce grown in non-union fields. In the play, a caricature Army commander, General Defense, tells lettuce-grower Butt Anglo:

You spray pesticides, and I bomb Vietnam . . . . So what if we've killed the people? We've saved the country from Communism . . . . So what if you've poisoned the farmworkers? You've saved the crop from Communism.

These preposterous arguments on behalf of the "military-agricultural complex" might rival Cantinflas' gibberish, but unfortunately, the logic is derived from actual events rather than a film comedian's imagination.

Perhaps the career of Cantinflas inspired Campesino actors more than the substance of his routines. His success as an actor proved that a Mexican (and by extension, a Mexican American) could become a highly popular comedian, and do so by siding with, and favorably portraying, the lower classes. El Teatro Campesino itself has now become a model of success in the arts, showing scores of other Mexican American theatres that it is possible to act professionally in America regardless of ethnic background, and to express one's own cultural and political identity through the medium of theatre.[17]

## From Clown Outfits to Zoot Suits

In 1978 El Teatro Campesino won national attention for its production of a musical history play, *Zoot Suit*, which opened at Los Angeles's Mark Taper Forum, then moved to Broadway and was finally made into a Hollywood film. The play, written by Luis Valdez, is based on documents and news reports of the early 1940s; it focuses on the so-called Sleepy Lagoon murder trial which took place in Los Angeles. Seventeen Mexican Americans were placed on trial for a murder they did not commit; although the court would never admit it, the defendants were also on trial because of their minority group affiliation, and their gang's habit of dressing like the *Pachuco*. *El Pachuco*, a mythic figure who appears as a character in the play, is a street-smart, defiant Latino dressed in a zoot suit with square shoulders and baggy trousers. Despite the odd costume, *Pachuco* is no clown.[18] He represents the independence and self-respect of Mexican Americans, who have often been denied these rights by members of the dominant culture.

In writing *Zoot Suit* Valdez revived a neglected chapter in the Mexican American struggle to preserve an independent cultural identity and resist assimilation and racism; but the play itself went through a process of cultural assimilation en route to Broadway. The satire and bilingual dialogue which had distinguished earlier works by El Teatro Campesino receded in favor of gratuitous romantic intrigue and slick dance choreography. Despite these concessions to a Broadway musical formula, the play failed to earn a profit in New York. It was well received by Mexican Americans and others in Los Angeles but the film based on it, like the Broadway production, turned out to be less successful than its creators hoped.

One critic of *Zoot Suit* was Valdez' longtime associate and former direc-

*Left: Socorro Valdez as La Muerte (Death) in El Teatro Campesino's* La Carpa de los Rasquachis (The Tent of the Underdogs), *a 1972 play about a field worker. Right: Edward James Olmos as* El Pachuco *and Daniel Valdez in El Teatro Campesino's* Zoot Suit, *written and directed by Luis Valdez and produced in 1978 at the Mark Taper Forum.*

tor, San Francisco Mime Troupe founder R.G. Davis. He accused the playwright of compromising his identity and political commitment in pursuit of profit. An essay by Davis and Betty Diamond argues, "When a cultural nationalist [such as Valdez] goes to Broadway to reach a wider audience, his message, which previously gained much of its force from its cultural specificity, must be diluted."[19] The "cultural nationalism" to which Davis refers also constituted a dilution of earlier Campesino aims insofar as it removed the theatre group from struggles alongside unions and the anti-war movement, placing it in the less activist role of investigator of ethnic and cultural history.

One could argue, on the other hand, that plays such as *Zoot Suit* are a logical extension of Campesino's previous work. Once the union had won its biggest struggle for recognition by farm owners, Valdez and his company decided to expand the range of Mexican American life portrayed in their art. In the early 1970s Valdez wrote:

> We wanted to concern ourselves with the cultural as well as the economic oppression of our people, whose consciousness as well as their land had been invaded by the Anglo. In Del Ray we give 'History Happenings': successive chapters

of Mexican and American history in *actos* and puppet shows, with music, free to the community . . . . We will consider our job done when every one of our people has regained his sense of personal dignity and pride in his history, his culture and his race.[20]

After *Zoot Suit* Valdez and his company returned to more community-oriented projects in the small town of San Juan Bautista. El Teatro Campesino now performs there regularly for Mexican Americans and others in the region. Some of its recent works, called *corridos*, are small, one-act musicals based on folk ballads. New Campesino plays rely less on satire than the earlier ones, as they explore mythology, religion, culture and Mexican American history. As the actors move into a more conventional theatre structure, away from the picket lines and outdoor rallies where the company began, and away from the need for provocative stage equivalents of rallying cries, there have been few Pentagon generals, boycotted lettuce growers and similar clowns on El Teatro Campesino's stage.

## The Plutonium Players

Halfway through the decade of the 1980s, it has become clear that the constituency that re-elected Ronald Reagan is large, influential and not going away. The Moral Majority and proponents of increased defense spending at the expense of social programs are active and not likely to change their positions as a result of satire from the left. If you cannot beat them, perhaps you can join them and laugh with them—or so goes the facetious conclusion of the Plutonium Players, a group of satirists which formed in San Francisco in 1977, as the Theatre Collective of People Against Nuclear Power.

The group's satire garnered national attention in 1980 when it took the form of a "Reagan for Shah" campaign, which called on the President of the United States to assume a position better suited to his patrician and militaristic leanings. The campaign began at a "Rally to Stop the Peace," a mock-protest against an anti-war teach-in on the Berkeley campus. "Reagan for Shah" was the first of many slogans the group now known as the Plutonium Players employed to mock American conservatism by clownishly embracing it to excess. Other mock-organizations founded by the Players have been less widely publicized, but their names, too, embrace the most extreme aspects of militarism and patriarchy as if there is nothing better. Although they exist primarily in name, on the Players' press releases and in mock-indoctrination lectures, the groups include the National Association of Grenade Owners (favoring legalization of grenades for personal self-defense and hunting), Another Mother for World Domination, and Voice of the Unconceived ("Sperms and Eggs Are People Too," they claim).

By creating these imaginary organizations and holding rallies for them, the Plutonium Players more or less capture their enemy; they make supporters of Ronald Reagan, of Moral Majority leader Jerry Falwell and anti-feminist Phyllis Schlafly, appear ridiculous by speaking for them, moving the logic, rhetoric and even the dress code of these figures beyond plausibility. In fact, the Players do not often have to exaggerate all that far beyond their models to make their satiric points. Their slight variations on existing organization titles have resulted in The Moral Monopoly ("We have a monopoly on morality"), Ladies Against Women's Men's Auxiliary, Students for War, Millionaire Mommies with Nannies Against State Childcare, the Lt. Calley Institute for Boys, Citizens Against a Girl V.P., the Committee to Intervene Anywhere (C.I.A.), the Nancy for Queen Fan Club and China Friendship League, and the Moral Sorority.

The Players' best-known "organization" by far is Ladies Against Women, an anti-feminist bevy of three women—or, rather, ladies—and two men who greet Phyllis Schlafly and Jerry Falwell at rallies across the United States. Decked out in 1950s dresses, pillbox hats, white gloves and leopardskin furs, the ladies carry signs declaring "I'd Rather Be Ironing" and "Make America a Man Again." L.A.W. held a bake sale in Dallas during the 1984 Republican Convention; the ostensible purpose of such a sale, with cake prices running into billions of dollars, is to end the Federal deficit through contributions from the private sector.

The ladies have been seen in many other cities, too, because the Plutonium Players encourage small groups outside the Berkeley area to imitate their act; in fact, they send out scripts to prospective followers. This may be one of the few occasions in history when an American political organization has expanded its membership by giving out stage directions; but why not do so in a decade when politics and theatre have become virtually inseparable? Any woman can particpate in this amalgam of politics and clowning, and become a "Lady": all she needs are a few homely clothes and a picket sign. In this sense the theatre of the Plutonium Players is democratic and highly participatory. (Men can join the Men's Auxiliary of Ladies Against Women, of course.)

The group has also presented a parodic indoctrination session, called "An Evening of Consciousness Lowering," to prospective members in the Bay Area and on a national tour. The two-hour, indoor event features comic lessons in baking (instructions on making a Hostess Twinkie); clothing (L.A.W. supporters are encouraged to wear South African diamonds and alligator purses); and persuading men to lift heavy objects. The Ladies also give improvised advice to troubled (i.e., liberated) audience members. While the parodic lecture-demonstration is amusing, L.A.W.'s outdoor rallies remain its most innovative form of political satire. The bake sales and picket lines merge realism with cynicism, satire with political endorsement, and tongues with cheeks, as the Players cheer on national leaders of the Right while thoroughly

*A message to the author from Ladies Against Women, and a bake sale held by the group in Dallas during the 1984 Republican Convention. Proceeds were used to help reduce the federal deficit.*

supporting the Left. Like the Mime Troupe, El Teatro Campesino and the cast of *MacBird*, they turn national leaders into clowns. They depart from the other groups, though, by disguising their outdoor performances as street demonstrations. The political theatre of the sixties, which derived so much of its vitality from the anti-war marches and rallies of the period, has come full circle with the Plutonium Players. While street protests once functioned as theatre, in the hands of the Plutoniums theatre becomes a political demonstration.

The next logical step in their masquerade might be an invitation from President Reagan to join the White House staff as speech writers. The President has a sense of humor of his own, of course, as his public jests about ducking assassination bullets and bombing Russia have demonstrated. The satirists from Berkeley need Reagan in the White House to provide them with material—it was he, after all, who provided the impetus for their first national campaign (promoting Reagan for Shah). But why might Reagan need the Plutoniums? Well, short of announcing that he has decided to become the new Shah of Iran, he couldn't come up with a better punchline than a statement that they are his kind of ladies.

# —19

# A Day at the Circus with Bread and Puppet Theatre

Inside a grove of trees on a hot summer day, a jazz saxaphone laments the military destruction of a Latin American village. The event is portrayed by small puppets—cardboard birds of prey which swoop down on clay peasant figurines and their cardboard homes. A life-sized, *papier-mâché* puppet known as Uncle Fatso impersonates the President of the United States during this scene; the fat, cigar-wielding businessman in red, white and blue top hat recites fragments of Ronald Reagan's pronouncements on Latin America. Part of his argument justifying military invasion is quoted directly from a Presidential radio broadcast of only a day earlier (August 15, 1983). The ease with which White House statements can be adopted for the sake of parody by a *papier-mâché* figurehead is startling. This scene, performed as a sideshow at an outdoor circus in Glover, Vermont, represents in abbreviated form the parodic sensibility of the Bread and Puppet Theatre. It distorts and exaggerates both everyday life and politics, creating a puppet equivalent of political cartoons.

Alternately larger and smaller, more gray and more colorful than life, the puppets encourage a sense of humility, even awe, in their audience; man is not the measure of all things when he is only five inches high—a huge, floating white bird made of cloth dwarfs him.

Besides presenting alternatives to the everyday sizes and shapes of life,

Bread and Puppet brings a festival spirit to its performances. The puppets are often designed and arranged in scenarios which commemorate special occasions such as the life, death and resurrection of El Salvador's Archbishop Oscar Romero; he was brought back to life as a huge, twelve-foot-tall puppet at the 1984 summer circus. These scenes take place on farmland in Vermont and in anti-war parades nationwide, in which spectators are free to walk around—and walk away if so inclined. There is no illusion of permanence or a captive audience on these occasions; rather, the company creates a sense of spontaneity, a freedom from confined and confining spaces.

Since Peter Schumann founded the Bread and Puppet Theatre in 1962 (after immigrating from Germany a year earlier), the theatre has moved from a loft on Manhattan's Lower East Side to a fairbooth at Coney Island to a barn on a Vermont farm, in between tours and residencies at other locations across the Americas and Europe. Bread and Puppet can perform anywhere because it consists largely of puppets, designed by Schumann and his associates, that can be carried or worn by almost anyone. The human composition of the group therefore tends to change, expanding even to a contingent of hundreds for parades such as the June 12, 1982 march to the United Nations advocating nuclear disarmament. Besides contributing banners, masks and floats to political demonstrations, Bread and Puppet tours its plays and annually offers a festival, "Our Domestic Resurrection Circus," at its home in Glover, Cate Farm.

*Bread and Puppet Theatre on parade.*

The circus in Glover parodies most other circuses. Peter Schumann once noted that the commercial circus is "a very empty business of superlatives that are added to each other to create some kind of tickle that people don't need for their lives. It says something that is not very useful anymore."[1] The Glover circus is, in his view, quite another kind of event. He explains:

> [It's an effort] to find a new way of doing circus that is more human, that is not merely a collection of superlatives, of extraordinary feats arbitrarily mixed together, but something that becomes a story of the world circus. We don't use circus techniques: the heaviest acrobatics done in our circus is a somersault. Or the horse is done by somebody putting on a horse mask. In that respect, it's only a parody of a circus . . . . I guess the circus we do is a little bit like the gigantic pageants performed all over the United States on pieces of American history . . . .[2]

Bread and Puppet's annual circus fuses the theatricality of street demonstrations with elements of outdoor history pageants and parades. The festival's "domestic resurrection" reference implies a renewal of life at home, here on earth, as opposed to otherworldly religious salvation. But a pantheistic reverence for life is evident in some Bread and Puppet scenarios praising earth, water and sky at a time when the ecosphere is threatened with destruction.

The hills and pine trees on Cate Farm serve as scenery for a few of the events Schumann stages. Most of the props and puppets also reflect a preference for art that employs natural and everyday materials. Clay, *papier-mâché*, raw canvas, wood from nearby trees are shaped into a variety of puppets and banners. The simplicity and almost primitive "homemade" quality of Bread and Puppet creations results from Schumann's desire that art be accessible to all people. For the same reason, there is no admission charge at the Cate Farm festival. Another indication of the group's interest in accessible art is its recent opening of a "cheap art" store annex, where colorful banners and posters are sold for almost nothing.

The puppet shows, which take place at various locations around the farm, literally surround spectators, involving them personally in the spectacle. One senses that he could simply walk into the barn, ask to join a puppet show and some mask or float would be found for his use. (In fact, many volunteers do rehearse with Schumann and join the festival as performers— but they usually arrive and start work weeks before the circus begins, not during its performances. It is not quite that spontaneous.)

The 1983 circus offered a variety of popular entertainments: poetry readings, music, juggling and plays with puppets of all sizes. More than ten thousand spectators roamed from one event to another across green fields and forests in the two-day pastoral celebration of counter-cultural art and anti-war politics. (The events are "counter-cultural" in that they offer their simple forms as alternatives to the expensive spectacles sold in much of mainstream culture: they are differentiated as much as they can be from the "empty business of superlatives" Schumann has renounced.)

Each day of the circus begins with a series of "sideshows," short plays and other events located all around the farm. One five-minute scene, "Bubble Trouble," shows Uncle Sam's greedy relative Uncle Fatso playing with cardboard cutouts of American battleships. He sits in a large cutout of a tub. The ships are threatening to invade Nicaragua, it is announced, and the plug ought to be pulled immediately from Uncle Fatso's tub. It is, and Uncle Fatso goes down the drain along with his ships.

One of the most amusing sideshows involves no puppets, only twenty pre-teen children and comedian Paul Zaloom, who has helped them write and stage a satire of their relationship to parents. The children play all the roles, ridiculing themselves and adults in what could be called a liberated children's theatre, of, by and for children (although adults can certainly appreciate it too.)

Bread and Puppet plays often resemble children's stories; the vocabulary is limited, but out of it the company constructs vivid, imaginative fantasies. These rarely approach agit-prop didacticism—even when the scenarios are political allegories. The Circus offers more than plays, however. The setting constitutes an alternative, cartoon world where for two days almost everything, including food, is free. The event often seems a large-scale parody of the everyday world.

## Garlic-Buttered Bread and Circus

A "Bread Store" on the farm offers free, delicious sourdough bread to all its customers—the same homebaked bread that the company distributes free to its audiences after its performances on tour. Behind a wooden counter, a baker pretends to compete for customers, advertising the virtues of his garlic-buttered slices over the plain slices around the corner. More than 6,000 ears of cooked corn are also given away. Bread and Puppet Theatre lives up to its title fully, providing food as well as art. "We sometimes give you a piece of bread along with the puppet show," Schumann says, "because our bread and theatre belong together. For a long time the theatre arts have been separated from the stomach . . . . The old rites of baking, eating and offering bread were forgotten. Bread shall remind you of the sacrament of eating."[3]

Although Brecht objected to what he called "culinary theatre," in which acting is digested as if it were a pleasurable and easily absorbed meal, Schumann's concept of bread and theatre is closer to Brecht's wry *Threepenny Opera* dictum: "First comes the food, then the morality." Bread and Puppet offers both, though not necessarily in that order.

In the afternoon the main circus event is another form of parody: a *papier-mâché,* cloth and wood circus menagerie, complete with dancing bears (actors in bear suits) wearing tutus, tigers (actors in tiger suits) jumping through a ring of (red paper) flames, Olympic games with giant puppets competing at boxing and shot-put. Schumann, dressed as a friendly Uncle Sam, dances on stilts fifteen feet high. The fall of the Roman Empire takes place, briefly, in a comic history pageant featuring "bread and circus" gladiators thrown to lions, Caesar being assassinated and—of course—Nero fiddling. The Empire ends with an invasion by Northern barbarians—who arrive in a Volkswagon bus, one hundred percent parodic Aryans, dressed in Viking helmets and bathing suits.

"Bread and Circus" is known as a term for Roman Empire spectacles designed to placate civil discontent, but Bread and Puppet's "bread and circus" offers just the opposite sort of entertainment. Perhaps that is why it chooses to include a parody of an ancient Roman festival.

## The Papier-Mâché War to End All Wars

The 1983 Circus closed with an evening pageant that used the surrounding landscape as its setting. Across the hills a military force moved toward a cardboard city, which it planned to destroy. Survivors of the war filled a cloth boat (an ark of refuge?) and sailed away to safety.

But the parade of militarism before the war affected a giant puppet couple in a different way. The two figures, a farmer and his wife resembling the couple in Grant Wood's famous American Gothic, were so saddened by the militarism passing before them that the wife set fire to a lifesized, *papier-mâché* jet plane which burned into the night as a finale. It was a silent, but eloquent image of resistance to militarism.

The 1984 and 1985 pageants, featured puppet shows about El Salvador, Guatamala, Nicaragua and other Latin American regions which many fear will become the United States' next "Vietnam." Several of these anti-war plays were subsequently taken on the road and performed in America and abroad. The newest works extend a repertoire of anti-war imagery which has become a trademark of Bread and Puppet scenarios since the period of American involvement in Vietnam. At anti-war marches in the sixties the puppets often led the parade. One of the company's most direct protests against war, a scene entitled "A Man Says Goodbye to His Mother," depicts a soldier in a gas mask who bombs a village with a plane, kills a child, destroys a house and finally is stabbed to death himself by the child's mother, who resembles the mother he left behind. The same primal story returns, with variation, in new Bread and Puppet shows reflecting current American military expeditions around the world; the Vietnam-era political puppet show has not gone out of date yet.

Peter Schumann's banners and puppets have been compared to the German Expressionist art that emerged around the time of the First World War. The nightmarish qualities of that style seem particularly strong in Schumann's depiction of war.[4] He also acknowledges a debt to Goya's scenes of war, which he has imitated in one puppet show simply titled *Goya*. His opposition to militarism can be traced back to his own family history in Germany: Schumann's family "fled from their home barely ahead of the Soviet army [in 1944], with the whole horizon ablaze behind them and other refugees clinging to the roof and windows of the last train," according to Edward Hoagland, who adds that Schumann remembers "the town on fire, the black smoke and explosions from the inferno of Breslau as it burned."[5] Childhood memories of escape from a bombing may account for what mask-maker Ralph Lee describes as Schumann's obsession with imagery of death and resurrection.

Schumann's puppets rarely speak up at war protests or circuses; at least not in voices of their own. They may take the words they do speak from Presidential radio broadcasts, if they need words. Curiously, Peter Schumann sees this form of caricature as "documentation," not "satire." He once told an interviewer:

> I dislike satire—it's too easy. When I use a [Lyndon] Johnson speech I use it for documentation, not satire. I like documented dialogue and narration; it has a substance that invented stuff can't have. I like to write with the help of a tape recorder—to hear what people really say.[6]

Most of the time the puppets are silent, which can mar a show by adding a vague mysticism to it; more often the silence intensifies the mournful sense of Schumann's apocalytic scenes. And then even the apocalypse is ridiculed; Florence Falk reports that one Domestic Resurrection Circus ringmaster introduced his audience to "the war you've all been waiting for—World War III," after which a roaring forty-foot green dragon (composed of people under a cloth cover) danced to strains of "When the Saints Go Marching In."[7] Whether the end arrives with mourning or dancing, the Bread and Puppet Theatre's apocalypses are usually followed by a moment of communion, as bread is passed among the spectators. Unmasked puppeteers, having portrayed the End of the World or some other horror, eat, converse with spectators and come back to life.

Bread and Puppet's circuses and plays will never stop a war by themselves, but they offer American dissenters the sense of a continuing anti-war culture as few other theatre groups do. Perhaps the interaction between the anti-war movement and Schumann's puppets was revealed most fully at Cornell University during the Vietnam war period. At that time Father Daniel Berrigan was fleeing the FBI. The fugitive from justice had committed the crime of destroying draft board records, and had decided to continue his resistance underground rather than go to prison. During the Bread and Puppet Theatre's performance at Cornell, Berrigan appeared, briefly addressed a sympathetic audience, and vanished among the masks and puppets surrounding him. Since then the activist-priest has been arrested, imprisoned and released several more times for anti-war protests. But it is tempting to imagine that Berrigan never left Bread and Puppet; that behind every mask, inside every dancing bear's suit, there is an anti-militarist who will march against war again—as soon as he leaves the circus.

# 20
# Trial by Satire
## From Brecht to the Green Party

*"You know how many princes, kings and republics
have been saved, how many battles won, how many
perplexities resolved by the advice, counsel and predictions of fools?"*

—Pantagruel[1]

### Brecht's Theatre of Trials

Writing about his 1932 conversations with Bertolt Brecht, the Soviet author
Sergei Tretyakov reported that Brecht planned to start a new theatre in Berlin
which would be devoted exclusively to the staging of famous courtroom trials.
Brecht never actually set this plan in motion, but his concept of trial as theatre
has recently been implemented, with some variation, by the Berliner Kommune and the Green Party in Germany, as well as by some Americans. Brecht
wanted his theatre to function like a courtroom, with two trials an evening,
each lasting an hour and a quarter. He explains:

> For example, we might perform the trial of Socrates, a witches' trial, the trial
> of Karl Marx's *Neue Rheinische Zeitung*, the trial of George Grosz on the charge
> of blasphemy for his cartoon of Christ in a gas mask . . . . Let us suppose that
> the trial of Socrates is over. We organize a short witches' trial where the judges
> are armored knights who condemn the witch to the stake. Then the trial of
> George Grosz begins, but we forget to remove the knights from the stage. When
> the indignant prosecutor storms at the artist for having insulted our mild and
> compassionate God a terrific racket breaks loose, as though two dozen five-gallon
> samovars were applauding. The noise is caused by the knights who are moved
> to applause by the defender of the defenseless God.[2]

As Tretyakov noted, Brecht's plan for staged trials is an elaboration of a tendency already evident in his plays; namely, his endeavors to create drama as convincing as court pleas and teach audiences to reach a verdict, "transforming the spectator's chair into that of the judge."

Two years before he spoke of "trial theatre" to Tretyakov, Brecht cast a large number of Berliners attending his *The Measures Taken* in the shared role of tribunal judge. In that play, several Communist Party agitators report their activities to a Moscow tribunal called the "Control Chorus." The chorus' role in the 1930 production was sung by 400 Berlin workers, all of whom became participants in the play's investigation of a murder.

The agitators re-enacted a propaganda campaign which had resulted in the death (was it suicide or murder?) of a comrade. As the Control Chorus, the Berlin workers witnessed the scenes and passed judgment on them in song. Of course, since the lyrics and music were written by Brecht and Hanns Eisler, there was no chance for spontaneous decisions during performance. There were, however, opportunities for chorus members to ask questions and suggest changes during the rehearsals; this they did and in this sense the production permitted spectators to become co-authors and/or judges in the tribunal.

Brecht never again experimented with workers as participants in this fashion, possibly because many years of exile and Nazi repression followed; whatever potential Brecht had found for collaboration with Berlin workers ended in 1933, when he had to flee the country and was separated from German-speaking audiences and actors. His subsequent scenarios for trials and judicial inquiries were less experimental and more cynical. Rather than encouraging ordinary people to become judges, plays such as *Arturo Ui, The Visions of Simone Machard, The Good Person of Setzuan, Galileo* and *The Caucasian Chalk Circle* portray mockeries of justice, courtroom scenes in which injustice and corruption usually triumph. At a time when militarism and fascism were taking over Europe, justice, Brecht felt, was best portrayed as unattainable and the judicial system as a farce or inquisition.

In 1934, while in exile in Denmark, Brecht still dreamed of courtrooms, but they were places of persecution. He told Walter Benjamin:

> I often imagine being interrogated by a tribunal. "Now tell us, Mr. Brecht, are you really in earnest?" I would have to admit that no, I'm not completely in earnest. I think too much about artistic problems, you know, about what is good for the theatre, to be completely in earnest.[3]

He had fled persecution from the Nazis, only to find it in America when the House Un-American Activities Committee questioned him about alleged Communist plans to infiltrate and take over the Hollywood film industry. The courtroom vision of his nightmares briefly came to life in Washington, D.C. in 1947, when Congressmen asked him, in effect, if he *was* completely in earnest. And, as in his dream, he said no, he was not in earnest; he joked with them about mistranslations of his plays and suggested that his lyrics about revolutionary leadership should not be taken too seriously. Robert Stripling, an investigator representing HUAC, read a lengthy excerpt from Sergei Tretyakov's memoir (published in Moscow) of conversations with Brecht, and asked if Brecht recalled that interview. Brecht answered, "no"—a one-word punch line that had the whole committee laughing. Brecht himself had the last laugh. Throughout the hearing he held a plane ticket to Europe in his pocket, and he left America soon after he was excused from the witness stand.

Brecht also displayed mistrust and facetiousness toward courts in his 1945 play, *The Caucasian Chalk Circle*. The play's central character is by no means autobiographical, yet the courtroom farce certainly reflects Brecht's own attitude toward justice in an age of fascism and world war. After the village scribe Azdak is arbitrarily appointed to the bench during a revolution in an ancient Caucasian city, he metes out legendary, unheard-of justice. Poor and defenseless villagers win complaints against the wealthy and powerful. But the golden age of justice, the utopian moment that Azdak represents, is depicted in terms far from earnest. The legendary judge is a buffoon, and even if his verdicts favoring the oppressed are just, they are also one long series of vaudeville turns. As critic and translator Eric Bentley has noted, Azdak is a modern Lord of Misrule, thriving in a revolution rather than a Saturnalian Feast of Fools; but like many festivals, the revolutionary golden age is short-lived. Azdak, temporary representative of the disenfranchised, abandons his position on the bench admitting, "I'm not cut out for a hero." He is too cowardly—or too interested in survival—to stand alone against the powerful for long. A choral singer concludes the play by saying that the people of Grusinia remember Azdak's judging as "a brief golden age, / Almost an age of justice."[4]

## Clowns in the Courtroom: Fo and Irwin

Brecht's portrayals of the judicial system in action were almost all geared toward audiences in legitimate theatre houses. Dario Fo's courtroom plays have been performed in less conventional theatre spaces (piazzas, political clubs) for working-class audiences. Besides satirizing an ongoing judicial inquiry in *Accidental Death of an Anarchist* (discussed earlier), Fo and his company have created other political trials in theatrical form, "a grotesque, critical form of theatre with songs" within hours of the original trials on which theirs are based, to let citizens outside the courtroom know what happened inside.[5] During a 1973 trial arising from a clash between police and workers, Fo's actors "represented the judge, the lawyers, the workers and the police, and . . . showed what would happen the next day." The audience was then able to attend "the more dramatic performance put on by the state the next day," make a comparison, and "realize the truth about the justice and the fascism in the whole event," according to Fo. On such occasions, Fo's theatre becomes an alternative system of judicial inquiry, able to cross-examine the state and its judges through clowning.

A few months after appearing on Broadway in Fo's *Accidental Death of an Anarchist,* American clown Bill Irwin devised his own parody of law and order. The program, a "work-in-progress" entitled *The Courtroom,* opened in New York in May 1985. A former member of San Francisco's Pickle Family Circus, Irwin has most recently been developing plays which combine traditional slapstick and mime with the innovations of postmodern dance, theatre and performance art. This fusion of forms, which has been described as "the new vaudeville," began when a number of performers trained by the Ringling Brothers clown school ran away from the circus.

After Bill Irwin and some of his colleagues attended the Ringling Clown College in Florida, they decided that large, three-ring arenas and the commercial packaging of humor were inimical to the extended gags and outrageous parodies of social manners that had attracted them to the profession in the first place. They subsequently found audiences for their alternative clowning in small, one-ring circuses such as the Big Apple Circus and the Pickle Family Circus, and at New York's Dance Theatre Workshop. Their merging of popular entertainment and experimental performance art offers them freedom to engage in social criticism in a way that they feel the Ringling Brothers circus clowns could not.

The new vaudeville's potential as a forum for social satire was amply demonstrated in Irwin's *The Courtroom.* For the event, he assembled an enormously gifted group of performers including clown and juggler Michael Moschen, tap dancer Brenda Bufalino, break dancer Rory Mitchell, ventriloquist and composer Doug Skinner, and fellow clown Bob Berky.

The succession of scenes features a silent Irwin as a stumbling, innocent dullard who enters the halls of justice in search of a bicycle license. Scheming lawyers seize him as a witness in a murder trial, ultimately conning him into playing stenographer, lawyer and judge as well. Half of the other cast members also take a turn as judge before the evening ends; and each time a new judge ascends the bench, objections are raised to his rule and lawyers throw the rascal out. Though Irwin's scenario is not overtly political—it never refers to specific world events—there is a political comment inherent in this portrayal of justice as shortlived and dismissible.

The men who portray lawyers in *The Courtroom* dress in oversized black-and-white plaid suits (Irwin wears yellow plaid), and look as if they might have stepped out of an R. Crumb comic or Hollywood gangster film. Their movements are more cartoon-like than human. When the gray-wigged judge tells the lawyers that they are overcharging their client, that their jobs might be done better by an arbitration board, the gentlemen fall flat on their backs in a dead faint.

Irwin's courtroom requires that its inhabitants perform odd and comic rituals in the name of the law. As one of the lawyers, Moschen tosses white rubber balls in an elaborate juggling routine meant to represent his arguments in the case; his presentation is hypnotic, dazzling, more impressive than a hundred legal briefs.

The other clown lawyers decide that they need more time to prepare arguments, and they draft Irwin to stall with "some sort of song and dance." The reluctant new lawyer, using top hat, cane and a jazz LP (labeled "Court Record"), performs some wonderfully comic tap and breakdancing routines, with the guidance of his colleagues. The dances, as well as the pratfalls, ventriloquism, double-takes, puns and slapstick chases performed by the ensemble, transform the tedium and obfuscation of legal proceedings into entertainment. At the same time, they imply that courtroom verdicts are more often influenced by lawyers' glibness and "fancy footwork" than by the truth of their arguments.

The mockery of courtroom behavior in *The Courtroom* is too mild and diffuse to be regarded as effective political satire; it could easily be enjoyed by members of the very professions whose manners it ridicules. Still, *The Courtroom* represents an interesting experiment in American theatre. Irwin merges popular dance forms and circus arts with a cartoonist's sense of political humor.

It is too early to say whether this work-in-progress will lead to political theatre as forceful as that of Dario Fo or Bertolt Brecht, which, as Irwin well knows, also owes a great debt to popular entertainment forms. Irwin's next project, appropriately enough, was the portrayal of Galy Gay, the innocent civilian lured into a foreign war in Brecht's *A Man's a Man*, at the La Jolla Playhouse in San Diego.

## The Trial of Fritz Teufel

Theatrical mockery of justice can also occur far from any stage, on streets and in courtrooms, as Durov demonstrated early in the century with his circus acts. One contemporary variant on Durov's street and courtroom satire is the theatre of the Berliner Kommune and its most prominent member, Fritz Teufel. (Teufel means "devil" in German; it appears that this man was destined to be notorious from birth.) Teufel and a friend were arrested and tried in Berlin for distribution of leaflets in 1968. Their leaflets proposed the burning down of Berlin deparment stores in order to bring the Vietnam War and its horrors home to the German public. Teufel and his colleague testified that their leaflets were satires, "modest proposals" in the tradition of Jonathan Swift, and their argument was supported by the testimony of various literary scholars and critics. The two satirists were acquitted.

According to critic Hans Mayer, the result of the episode was a fully realized play for the courtroom:

> Literature—a leaflet having satirical intent and not hiding its debt to Swift— had been treated as reality and alloyed into reality by the state's attorney. In turn-about the reality of the judicial jargon was displaced into literature, recast in the aesthetic realm. The play went beautifully, according to its wholly fresh playing rules, and could not have ended any other way but with a happy ending.[6]

Mayer sees Teufel's "theatre" as an extension of German traditions including marionette theatre, Yule mummeries and Hanswurstiana. Teufel falls into the Hanswurst tradition of clowning with this difference: He plays his scenarios of disruption not against neoclassical stage heroes, as did Hanswurst, but rather in courtrooms and on Berlin streets, against judges and generals.

Another admirer of Berliner Kommune activity, the playwright Peter Handke, wrote that Fritz Teufel freed theatre from the falsifications of fixed literary forms, such as Brecht's parable plays, where social commitment is turned into style or is subservient to it. Handke said he deplores artists who "manipulate one's commitment into a poem or . . . make literature out of it, instead of just saying it out loud." His essay on street theatre derides as "laughable" performers who "troop to the microphone, one after the other, each to deliver a Brechtian *aperçu* . . . in the most cultured possible tones."[7]

Handke is not opposed to street theatre per se—certainly not Teufel's variety of it—but rather to that which announces its performance in advance and consists of elegantly formed perceptions which diminish the event's capacity to shock and agitate. He finds the Berliner Kommune able to shock and agitate because it avoids "furnishing the ends of . . . performances with manufactured, ready-made recipes for the new order." Handke observes:

> Committed theatre these days doesn't happen in theatres (those falsifying domains of art where every word and movement is emptied of significance) but in lecture-halls, for instance, when a professor's microphone is taken away . . . and professors blink through burst-open doors, when leaflets flutter down on to the congregation from galleries, and revolutionaries take their small children with them to the lecture, when the [Berliner] Kommune theatricalizes real life by "terrorizing" it and quite rightly making fun of it.[8]

The last aspect, "making fun," is inseparable from other components of the Kommune's activity. Teufel has called himself a *spassgerilja* or "fun guerrilla," defined as one who kills by ridicule.[9] (He opposes armed terrorism, although he has been accused of several kidnappings.)

## Durov's Cart Minus Durov

The Berliner Kommune renewed the satiric tradition developed by Durov when his pig pulled him in a cart through the streets of Kharkov. Teufel, too, was pulled through the streets on a cart—though not by a pig. After he was arrested for the crime of throwing paint-filled eggs at the car of the Shah of Iran, (as well as throwing stones at the police, which he says he did not do), he spent two-and-a-half months in jail. He then began a probation period during which he was required to visit a Berlin prison twice a week. Teufel transformed the jaunt into highly popular street theatre: sitting high atop a cart and secured by a ball and chain, he had his friends push him to jail. A crowd assembled to watch the spectacle as Teufel rang the prison doorbell and demanded, "Take me back in." Rarely has a prisoner been this free to mock authority; to put on his own chains before the police do it and then set himself free in front of a prison.

He flaunted his freedom once too often, however. Teufel was supposed to stay in Berlin during his probation period, but he flew to Frankfurt to attend a meeting of Students for a Democratic Society. When the police searched they couldn't find him. He went to the Frankfurt police station with a crowd of 200 others, all shouting, "Take us all in, or leave us all alone." The police arrested three people in the crowd who had beards resembling Teufel's, but they didn't succeed in getting their man. He went back to Berlin where he stayed hidden underground. His career as a courtroom *farceur* unexpectedly ended when Teufel put on a disguise and went to a courtroom where a hearing on the anti-Shah demonstration was in progress. He was caught and re-arrested there, his identity no longer mistaken, his cry of "Take me in" no longer so amusing.

## The Youth International Party (Yippies) on Trial

Teufel's courtroom escapades have American parallels in the performances of "Yippies" Abbie Hoffman, Paul Krassner and Jerry Rubin in the late 1960s and early '70s. During the Yippie years of protest against U.S. Army presence in Vietnam, these activists also turned trials (their own, in Chicago in 1969, in particular) into satiric theatre events. From the transcript of their Chicago trial, in which Hoffman, Rubin and others were accused of inciting riots outside the Chicago Democratic Convention, a number of stage and television plays have been derived.

One of the plays, *The Chicago Conspiracy Trial* by Ron Sossi and Frank Condon, is compiled directly from transcripts of the testimony. The theatricality of politics is made quite clear when the poet Allen Ginsberg testifies. Asked if he recalls what Abbie Hoffmann said to him in February 1968, Ginsberg replies:

> Yippee! Among other things. He said that politics had become theatre and magic; that it was the manipulation of imagery through the mass media that was confusing and hypnotizing the people in the United States, and making them accept a war which they did not really believe in . . . .[10]

The Yippies, with fellow travelers Ginsberg, William Burroughs, Norman Mailer and Jean Genet, sought to counteract mass media manipulation of events with their own communications in public demonstrations, press conferences, essays and courtroom testimony. (The Yippies wrote no plays. Rubin, in his book *Do It!*, asked readers to become theatres as well as actors but not playwrights: "You are the stage. You are the actor . . . . There is no audience," he declared in a chapter titled "Revolution Is Theatre-in-the-Streets." Those who watched Rubin cavort in front of a camera, however, might question his own willingness to forget about audiences.)

What could have been the most interesting theatre event resulting from the Chicago trial never actually occurred. In 1970 the founder of the San Francisco Mime Troupe, R.G. Davis, planned to restage the trial, with most of its original defendants portraying themselves, for a national tour. The abridged, four-hour stage version of the conspiracy trial was to be performed in large assembly halls across America, to serve as a rallying point for leftists somewhat in the manner that Piscator and Brecht had envisioned political theatre might serve audiences in the 1920s. (Davis had previously studied Brecht's writings and staged several of his plays, so the similarity of the two directors' ideas is not accidental. Davis' casting assistant offered Chicago Judge Julius Hoffmann a chance to portray himself, in the same mocking spirit that Piscator invited Kaiser Wilhelm II to represent himself in *Rasputin*. Hoffman, like the Kaiser, declined.)

## Durov's Pig Minus Durov

Yippies Rubin and Hoffman also declared a pig named Pigasus as their candidate for President in 1968, continuing Durov's tradition of portraying politicians as barnyard animals (though Pigasus had not a fraction of the theatrical training of Durov's animals.) Rubin wrote an amusing memoir about the campaign which testifies that, in spite of his skill in public relations, when it came to pigs he was no Durov:

> We didn't know anything about pigs . . . . We piled into a car, $25 in our pockets, and we were on our way to heartland America, rural Illinois, to buy the next President of the United States . . . . The farmer told us to catch our own. We

looked at each other, uptight; none of us had ever had the opportunity to chase a pig before . . . . The goal was to take Pigasus to the Picasso statue in the Civic Center [Chicago] to declare his candidacy. Lawyers told us we would violate a disorderly conduct statute by bringing a farm animal into the city. What if Hubert Humphrey [the Democratic Presidential candidate] were bringing Ringling Bros., Barnum and Bailey Circus into the city as a political stunt? Would they arrest Hubert? All laws are political. Could we get Pigasus to the Civic Center before the cops snatched him? We had set up a big international press conference, so the cops were hip to it. It would be a coup for the cops to pick up Pigasus first, thwarting the dramatic myth that would go across the world.[11]

At the Civic Center the pig and its Yippie friends were thrown into a paddy wagon in front of a crowd "packed with TV, radio, newspapermen and FBI agents," according to Rubin. Similar arrests occurred throughout the 1968 campaign. Rubin reports that each time their candidate was arrested, the Yippies went to a farm and bought another one. Their satiric campaign extended Durov's circus act, with some important differences. The Yippies had none of Durov's skill as an animal trainer; they undoubtedly would have won more sympathy from the press, children and even law courts if their candidate had been as intelligent as Durov's trained pig. In other words, their circus skills were deplorable.

Rubin once called himself "the P.T. Barnum of the Revolution," and he may have been a promoter in Barnum's tradition. He turned himself and his friends into "freaks," creating their own sideshow with pigs, parades and media events designed to "freak out" the public. Like some of the attractions advertised by Barnum, the revolution promoted by Rubin never arrived. But he managed to promote his menagerie much more widely than Barnum or Durov could in their day. Durov's satire was directed at the circus-going public; that of the Yippies was meant to unsettle a national audience through the electronic and print media. In the "society of specatacle," as French political theorist Guy Debord has described the era, these activist-satirists created spectacle for mass audiences, on mass media which reached millions of spectators. What Rubin, Hoffman and friends often failed to acknowledge (as R.G. Davis notes in "Rethinking Guerrilla Theatre") is that the mass media select and control coverage of such comic protests, turning them into thirty-second news anecdotes or back-page amusement items, forgotten almost as soon as they are noticed, or sandwiched between advertisements to stimulate sales of consumer goods.

The efficacy of Yippie satire may have been summed up best by Abbie Hoffman in his autobiography, *Soon to Be a Major Motion Picture*. Hoffman says that he never thought the Yippies' guerilla theatre "could alone stop the war in Vietnam."[12] Rather, the group's actions extended the possibilities of "involving the senses and penetrating the symbolic world of fantasy (television's primary aim)." A broad-based national anti-war movement with a "strong appeal to reason . . . mobilizing pacifist resistance" was also needed, Hoffman felt, to end the American military presence in Vietnam.

## A Mock Trial for the Country's Leading Actor

Yippie fantasies in the sixties have been followed by some broader-based theatrical protests against war in the eighties. One recent event featured attorney William Kunstler, who had defended Hoffman and Rubin in Chicago in 1969. On June 9, 1984, Kunstler prosecuted the President of the United States. The trial, coordinated by the New York Coalition Against U.S. Intervention in Central America, charged Ronald Reagan and his associates— Henry Kissinger, Jeane Kirkpatrick and Caspar Weinberger—with the violation of the charters of the United Nations, Nuremberg and the Organization of American States, as well as the Constitution of the United States. Fifteen-foot-high, *papier-mâché* replicas of the defendants were borne through the city's streets along a parade route that led from United Nations Plaza to Times Square, where the mock-trial was staged outdoors.

Members of the coalition behind the event included Artists Call Against Intervention, Democratic Socialists of America, Harlem Fightback, Mobilization for Survival, New Jewish Agenda, Riverside Church Disarmament Program, the War Resister's League and Women's Strike for Peace, among others. In all, more than 100 peace, disarmament and anti-intervention organizations participated. On June 7, two days before the trial, the Coalition led a civil disobedience action in which 500 protesters temporarily shut down the Federal Building in New York City to protest American foreign policy and war preparation.

The June 9 event was half festive protest and half serious legal proceeding. Before the trial began at Times Square, ten thousand demonstrators witnessed a series of performances by actors, poets and dancers, and saw a display of colorful banners near the United Nations. The crowd then paraded with street dancers, banners and marching band behind a truck carrying the huge puppet defendants to Times Square's Armed Forces Recruitment Center.

The mock trial offered only the slightest pretense of fairness toward the accused. The four puppets "spoke" in their own defense briefly and comically, in taped statements prepared by voice impersonators. Most of the testimony came from poets, folksingers, political activists and one Guatamalan refugee masked to protect his identity; all objected to American foreign policy in Latin America. Kunstler served as master of ceremonies rather than a conventional prosecutor, and another attorney, Margaret Burnham, shared this role with him. The trial could correctly be perceived as a mockery of justice by friends of the Reagan Administration; victims of the Administration's foreign policy would no doubt reply that they have never seen anything but a mockery of

*Weinberger, Kissinger, Kirkpatrick and Reagan puppets on trial in Times Square, June 1984.*

justice in their own countries, either. The event had little if any impact upon world law, and the accused are unlikely to surrender for imprisonment, but the proceedings fused satire, theatre and political activism in a manner that could serve as a model for other protests, or so the sponsors hoped. The Center for Constitutional Rights' newsletter, published in June 1984, featured a copy of the June indictment against President Reagan and his colleagues, along with the following advertisement:

> It [the indictment] can be used as an organizing tool by everyone. "Serve" it on Reagan Administration officials when they come to your city, town or campus, or hold a mock trial to accuse the Administration of war crimes—then let the people decide.

The invitation comes very close to self-parody in its suggestion that anyone can hold a war crimes tribunal. Without the sanction of a larger community, preferably an international body such as the United Nations or the World Court, such calls for justice remain mere gestures: polite, legal and unheeded protests against military violence. In any case, this trial by theatre seemed a particularly appropriate means in 1984 to protest the policies of a former Hollywood actor; only the ratings could have been better.

## The Red-Nosed President and the Green Party

Late in 1983, preparing to protest the impending renomination of Ronald
Reagan in Dallas, a number of Americans who had been calling themselves
Yippies affiliated their group with Germany's Green Party. They later began
calling themselves the North American Green Party.[13] The affiliation is
tenuous but it suggests that these Americans see themselves as part of an international movement. (FBI agents might call it an international conspiracy.)
The German Green Party has gone somewhat further than the Yippies in
advancement of trial by satire, however; in 1983 its theatrical territory expanded to include the Bundestag (Germany's national parliament), when
twenty-seven of its members were elected to public office.

By now it should be clear that the term "political theatre," once applied
generally to theatre of a political nature, may today also apply to *politics*
of a *theatrical* nature. This is particularly evident in the Reagan Administration, with a former actor occupying the White House, utilizing his smile and
relaxed manner—his performance—as effectively as any legislative program
to gain the confidence of the American people.

Ronald Reagan has even been caricatured as a clown. The cover of the
August 1984 issue of the German journal *Stern* featured Reagan in a red put-
ty clown nose, along with a caption referring to his "deadly sense of humor."
The caption was inspired by his overheard radio warm-up, in which Reagan
joked that Russia had just been outlawed forever and U.S. bombing would
begin in five minutes. While the President's sense of humor backfired in that
particular instance, more often than not his affinity for the media and his
sense of humor have worked very effectively on his behalf, as have his army
of media advisors and the services of an advertising firm previously best known
for selling Pepsi Cola.

If today politics has become almost inseparable from theatrical performance, if our age has become one in which politicians must be actors, at
least there are alternatives to the genial, corporate salesman's acting style
which emanates from Washington. The spectacles of dissent created by Germany's Green Party *(Die Grünen)* provide a counter-example to the White
House. Instead of substituting individual charm and covert action for publicly
legislated policy, the Greens promote peace and new parliamentary laws
through group spectacle and, occasionally, song and satire. They are developing a new form of theatrical politics; one with a collective, group
hero/heroine—the Greens—whose media images and everyday practices embody the democratic impulses of its members. While certain spokespeople,
including American-educated Petra Kelly and East German exile Rudolph
Bahro, have been singled out as leaders by the press, the collective theatrical
actions of the Greens have received the most attention.

Their merging of the social and aesthetic realms can be traced back to

Brecht and Piscator, and constitutes an innovative extension of forms that those earlier activist-artists had developed in Weimar Germany. What Brecht once said of Piscator's theatre (where Brecht himself worked in the late 1920s) applies to the theatre of the Green Party: Its "images, statistics, slogans . . . enable its parliament, the audience, to reach political decisions . . . . [It] was not indifferent to applause, but it preferred a discussion. It didn't want only to provide its spectator with an experience but also to squeeze from him a practical decision to intervene actively in life."[14]

There can be no question that the Green Party's following has intervened actively in German life, especially since March 1983, when the Green list of alternative candidates won more than five percent of the popular vote nationally, entitling the Greens to seat twenty-seven delegates in the Bundestag. The electoral victory attested to increasingly popular support for the Greens' uncompromising opposition to nuclear missiles and nuclear power; its total of two million votes also indicated that, without the wealthy corporate backers who consistently favor larger parties, the extra-parliamentary Left can secure national attention—and even enter parliament—by offering new ideas through imaginative, highly theatrical campaigning.

The Green Party has repeatedly gained press coverage of its controversial speeches and rehearsed or staged events, which thrive on the novelty-seeking tendencies of mass media. These events might more properly be termed counter-plays than plays; they originate as responses to, and parodies of, government power displays. In the early seventies Robert Brustein criticized American leftists for their media showmanship, full of blustery rhetoric about revolution; it was, in Brustein's phrase, "revolution as theatre."[15] In the past decade, however, elected officials have also promoted their policies through theatrical "scenarios," although theirs hardly advocate revolution. The White House and Pentagon have spent billions to develop and publicize scenarios for a nuclear war in what they call the "theatre" of Europe; they opened their "nuclear-theatre" production with the installation of new missiles across the continent. The Administration saw the installation of the arsenal as a victory in itself: proof that no village in Europe is exempt from the presence of American bombs, which are stored or aimed anywhere the generals choose. In this context, the Green Party's theatrical demonstrations against the new missiles are not merely rhetoric; they function as counter-plays to what Greens, generals and presidents alike might term "an American show of force."

Some Green Party demonstrations have involved civil disobedience, continuing the tradition of non-violent protest developed by Thoreau, Gandhi, Martin Luther King, Jr., and, more recently, the Berrigan brothers. The acts of civil disobedience committed by Philip and Daniel Berrigan have included such highly theatrical rituals as pouring blood and ashes on military property and damaging a nuclear missile nose cone with a hammer—attempting to beat a nuclear "sword" into a plowshare—as part of a group known as the Plowshares Eight. They have transformed these protests into performances by recreating their trials and bearing witness anew in Daniel Berrigan's play *The Trial of the Catonsville Nine*, first produced in Los Angeles by the Mark Taper Forum, and in Emile de Antonio's film *In the King of Prussia* (in which the Berrigans re-enact the Plowshares Eight trial). The Berrigans' well-publicized trials for civil disobedience have undoubtedly inspired members of the Green Party, with whom they have met in Germany and America. One Berrigan-like protest conducted by the Greens took place at a reception for diplomats in Hesse, Germany in August 1983, when a Green Party deputy spilled a wine glass of blood on the uniform of an American Army general to protest "the insane armament of the American government and Reagan's aggressive behavior in Latin America." Another Green Party delegate, noting that "everything we do is symbolic theatre," went on to derogate this blood-spilling as mere "summer theatre."[16]

A difference between earlier protests and the one in Hesse is that the latter action was committed by a government official. Unlike the theatre of the Yippies and the Berrigans, recent Green protests have been, so to speak, endorsed by voters and sponsored by legislators. When legislators find it necessary to break the law, the press notices; and the Greens have concluded that such violation of the law may be necessary to resist militarism. Green Party Bundestag delegates have advocated civil disobedience to stop the installation of new missiles in their country, and have sponsored mass protests against the weapons. (Their attitude recalls Durov and Liebknecht's inventive resistance to German militarism eighty years earlier; but the performance arena has moved from circus ring and courtroom into the Bundestag and diplomatic circles.)

One of the Green Party's most impressive demonstrations took the form of a special war crimes tribunal. Other moments of theatre have been quieter and simpler. In 1983, when the Greens were about to enter the Bundestag for the first time, conservative incumbents feared that delegates wearing blue-jeans inside the usually staid chambers would profane the law and all it stood for. The Greens decided to make one concession to the conservatives; they agreed that one delegate—a woman—would enter Parliament in coat and tie. The others wore sweaters, jeans (and shoes as far as we know), and carried green plants to their desks, creating an atmosphere of unconventionality that received international media attention. They also placed signs reading "Nuclear Free Zone" on their Bundestag desks. Such gestures brought the theatricality of mass protests—marchers' slogans and props—into a new context; parliament itself became the setting for street theatre.

There is a drawback to such political theatre. The issues of ecology, disarmament and unemployment which motivate Green Party tactics usually receive attention only after the theatricality of the public spectacles themselves has been reviewed. A *Washington Post* report in February 1983 began by

*Left: Petra Kelly of the Greens, holding up a poster which asks, "Will you say you didn't know?" while participating in a West German parliamentary debate over the deployment of U.S. missiles. Right: Green Party poster celebrating the election of Greens to the European Parliament.*

describing a Green rally as "a reincarnation of the sixties as a parade of jugglers, gypsy violinists and rock bands shared the spotlight with anti-war activists preaching the gospel of pacifism;" the jugglers and violinists often receive far more attention than the speakers. Still, the shock tactics seem necessary to effect political change. "It takes an artist to shock people nowadays," says Brecht's Peachum in *The Threepenny Opera;* in today's art of politics perhaps it takes an elected official's violation of decorum or law to shock German statesmen and American military officials, so hardened are they (and the press) to other methods of dissent.

## The Greening of Bertolt Brecht

Quoting Brecht to explain Green Party policy is something that the Greens themselves have done repeatedly. In June 1982, Green Party theoretician Rudolf Bahro read from Brecht just before calling for a general strike, citing lines from Brecht's poem, "The Buddha's Parable of the Burning House."[17]

Addressed to those "no longer concerned with the art of submission/ Rather, with that of not submitting . . . and beseeching men to shake off/ Their human tormentors," the poem could well serve as the preface to a general strike. Petra Kelly has also drawn upon Brecht's writings in her speeches. A lecture in August 1981 which denounced chemical warfare began with Brecht's statement that "Carthage waged three wars; it was still powerful after the first, it was still habitable after the second, it was no more to be found after the third."[18]

More relevant to the collective character of Green Party actions are Brecht's calls for collective political work. On the cover of their Peace Manifesto, the Greens feature Brecht's declaration: "And if we all say no, war will be the past and peace the future." This plea for collective refusal of war pervades Green Party policies. Another statement concerning "mankind's memory" of war was part of the inaugural address opening the Green-sponsored nuclear war crimes tribunal in 1983. In her opening remarks Kelly said, "Bertolt Brecht was right when he wrote in 1952":

> Mankind's memory of the suffering people have already endured is astonishingly short. Our capacity to visualize future suffering is even more limited. The descriptions which New Yorkers received about the terrors of the atomic bomb apparently did not alarm them very much . . . . It is exactly this insensibility which we have to struggle against, as death is its most extreme consequence.[19]

Kelly added that the Greens were convening their tribunal to "resist this insensibility through non-violent means." In a sense, its purpose was to continue to do exactly what Brecht had urged.

## The Greens at Nuremberg, 1983

The Green Party tribunal had several antecedents, including the Nuremberg trials held after World War II under the auspices of the Allied powers. Insofar as the Green tribunal was not sponsored by a government but by a self-appointed judicial body, its form was closer to that of Bertrand Russell's 1967 War Crimes Tribunal in Stockholm, which found the United States guilty of genocide in Vietnam. One of the Russell tribunal judges, Jean-Paul Sartre, said, "The judges are everywhere; they are the peoples of the world, and in particular the American people. It is for them we are working."[20] His statement suggests that everyone is invited to judge these global issues; only massive public agreement with the verdicts will give the self-appointed courts legitimacy.

Sartre's statement also hints at a curious form of audience involvement and suspense that has accompanied the more recent tribunals in Nuremberg and New York. The suspense depends on whether spectators are willing to see themselves as judges, thereby lending legitimacy to the proceedings. Do the people of the United States or the U.S.S.R. want to judge their leaders outside of the existing legal channels? Suppose those who watch the proceedings of a tribunal or learn about the trial agree that the accused are guilty. The question remains: Who would enforce the legitimacy of the verdict?

The Greens drew on the internationally accepted legitimacy of the first Nuremberg tribunal by holding another war crimes tribunal at the same site. As William Sweet noted in the May 1983 issue of *The Progressive,* the Green Party tribunal began exactly fifty years and one month after Hitler came to power in Germany, in the same city where Nazi war criminals were placed on trial, after it had been leveled by American and British bombs. The setting resonated with history, and the Greens were determined not to forget the past—or let "mankind's memory" forget—as they evoked the possibility of new, more horrible war crimes.

The crimes investigated were those committed by the U.S., the U.S.S.R. and other nuclear powers in their preparations for nuclear war. The event primarily involved members of the international peace movement and the Greens. Its organizers—Kelly, Gert Bastian (a Green Party delegate and a former NATO general) and Joachim Wernicke (a West Berlin medical doctor)—asked government officials from the United States, Germany, Great Britain, France and the Soviet Union to participate, but they all refused. Among those who did testify were American anti-war veterans Daniel Ellsberg, Philip Berrigan, Barry Commoner, Richard Falk and Nobel laureate George Wald.

According to Joachim Wernicke, the tribunal was definitely not conceived as a theatre event, although there was about the proceedings an element of theatre. He explains:

> There was a real and prescheduled questioning of the witnesses, and the objective was to come to clear statements on a prepared list of claims regarding alleged war crimes . . . . [The theatrical elements] clouded the news coverage in the Federal Republic: Only one right wing newspaper, *Frankfurter Allegemeine,* found out about the real contents, as shown from a headline, "The Greens demand the right of emergency defense against the U.S."[21]

Despite Wernicke's concern about elements of "theatre" distracting from the issues, the hearings never became a circus or parody of justice. For the most part the proceedings were comic only by implication, in their condemnation of crimes yet to be committed (such as potential U.S. destruction of Germany by "limited" nuclear war). At the hearing Daniel Ellsberg said that when he had first read the Pentagon Papers years ago, uncovering plans to escalate to nuclear war in a Berlin crisis, he felt that he was reading "evidence for future war crimes trials," and it is just such "evidence" that the Greens collected at Nuremberg. The event ended with guests issuing the following declaration: "Any use and the threat of using atomic, biological and chemical weapons is contrary to international law and criminal."

While the Greens had planned the tribunal as a legal proceeding and not a theatre piece, one play was staged during the three days of hearings: Daniel Berrigan's courtroom documentary *The Trial of the Catonsville Nine*. It offered an example of American resistance to war and established a sense of solidarity between the Berrigans and the Greens in their efforts to create new, anti-militaristic laws through public testimony. The play also indirectly reaffirmed that more conventional forms of political theatre are not yet obsolete. Perhaps in the spirit of that play, we will have an opportunity to see a new theatrical effort, *The Greens at Nuremberg* or the like, at the next war crimes tribunal.

## Stand-up Comedy at Nuremberg

Any play written about the Green Party's Nuremberg tribunal would have to include the remarkable comedy act that took place during the proceedings, when former U.S. Central Intelligence agent Philip Agee delivered his testimony. After he left the CIA in the mid-seventies, Agee publicly revealed some of the illegal practices the agency had authorized against foreign governments; as a result of his confessions, Agee was banned from entry by several governments friendly to the United States—England, France, the Netherlands—as well as the U.S. itself. At the tribunal, he prefaced his testimony against American nuclear war preparations by recounting a dream about Vice President George Bush's 1983 trip to Europe. Bush (who was director of the CIA during Agee's term of employment) tried to persuade European leaders that it was in their interest, as well as America's, to deploy the new nuclear missiles in their territories. Here, in his own words, is Agee's dream:

> A couple of weeks ago, when Vice President Bush was here on tour, I had the craziest dream. Even now it seems almost real. Can you imagine? I had been appointed to introduce Bush in an enormous hall before six thousand people—the biggest performance of his European tour.
> I know it wasn't real, but there I was, about to introduce a man who has called me over the years: an anti-American, a traitor, a subversive, a villain for all seasons—all those compliments that produce such enormous satisfaction.
> Now I had the chance of a lifetime. Don't blow it, Phil. I kept telling myself, don't botch it this time. Suddenly I was out at the microphone, a huge orchestra behind me, and with all the flare and hype of a big-time television emcee:
> "Ladies and Gentlemen, you already know our next and featured entertainer a man who has rocketed to the top of all the lists. He's backed up tonight by this great band and by a chorus of 572 of the most beautiful creatures ever Made in U.S.A.
> "For their first number they're going to sing their latest mega-hit—you guessed it—their new rendition of that old Bill Haley favorite: Rockets Around the Clock! And now, Ladies and Gentlemen, from the people who gave you

Hiroshima and Nagasaki, let's give a big hand to George Bush and the Rockettes! Take it away, George!"

Huge ovation! Enormous applause! As I jogged off the stage, I suddenly realized where I was. I was at the national convention of the Chri . . . Chris . . . . Dem . . . oh, you know, one of the big parties here.[22]

Having described the Vice President's promotion of nuclear weapons as a great entertainer's performance, Agee stopped his own political routine to say that he had once dreamed nothing other than official versions of how the United States became the great world power, the leader of the Western Alliance and leader of the Free World, but his dreams have now become more critical of American military policies. Abbie Hoffman once said that repeated police harrassment of Agee had "trapped" the former CIA agent in a "Lenny Bruce routine," where small towns compete with large cities to harass the traveling comedian.[23] Perhaps Agee decided that if he were going to be harassed by police as Bruce was, he might attempt a few stand-up comedy routines of his own. His Nuremberg monologue about political entertainment underscores the festive, celebratory spirit latent in even the most serious Green Party events.

If it needs a specific Brechtian antecedent, the Nuremberg tribunal has one in Brecht's plan for a theatre of trials. The Greens have implemented that plan, except that the playwright had wanted to stage famous trials from the past; the Green Party staged one from the future. The tribunal was also a concrete step toward implementing the Greens' political platform, published in 1980, which included a call for "worldwide denunciation of all politicians, scientists, military strategists and technologists who plan, build, operate or support weapon systems or technologies leading to mass destruction and genocide. In the case of a war," the platform continued, "those responsible should be brought before an international tribunal. It is our intention to strive for the establishment of such a tribunal."[24]

While events such as the tribunal and their colorful entry into parliament win the Greens attention, the spectacles they create also serve their aims of democratized, participatory decision-making. They focus on the party as a whole rather than on any one speaker. The Greens are anti-State and against leaders—even of their own party, to a degree. (In 1984 a group of six women collectively became head speakers for the Party in Bonn, after it was decided individual speakers like Petra Kelly were being singled out too often and "worn out" by the press and politicians.) While the Greens have to run individual delegates for election, they devised a plan in which elected officials serve only half of the four-year term to which they are elected, then switch places with an assistant. The party's redistribution of power can also be seen in its anti-ageism. Its candidates for an election in Hamburg included two schoolchildren along with a teacher, a dockworker, a social worker and an editor.

## The Return of Danny the Red

The theatre of the Greens can also be seen as an open, participatory form of political action markedly different from the violent acts (or "closed theatre") of the German-based Baader-Meinhof terrorists a few years earlier. The terrorists' theory of vanguard politics, by which small, swift acts of warfare are supposed to inspire massive armed resistance or a general strike, resulted instead in increased repression of dissent by the state, and isolation, prison and death for the terrorists.

The Greens openly oppose both violence and the hierarchical and elitist leadership of government. They have risen to prominence primarily due to broad-based public support for their anti-nuclear, pro-environment activities. Theirs is an "open theatre" that anyone can join as marcher, voter or prospective Bundestag candidate. Their preference for grassroots democratic actions is part of a tradition that began in the late 1960s in France as well as Germany, and it is exemplified by the career of one Green activist in Frankfurt, Daniel Cohn-Bendit. "Danny the Red," as journalists have dubbed the red-haired man, was singled out by the press as the leader of France's general strike in May 1968. However, the striking students and groups of that period contend that they acted spontaneously, in concert but without a single, unifying program or leader, in a manner that foreshadowed current Green practices. "We are all Cohn-Bendit," students joked in 1968, in collective role-playing which anticipated the Greens' "open theatre."[26] And Cohn-Bendit agreed; they were all equal to him in one sense. In his book on the events of that May, *Obsolete Communism: The Left-Wing Alternative,* he wrote that a future movement extending the lessons of 1968 must resolve "to struggle against the formation of any kind of hierarchy . . . . To bring real politics into everyday life is to get rid of politicians."[27] Cohn-Bendit is now part of that "future movement" he called for; and his warnings have been heard by the Greens.[28]

The democracy of the Greens is so anti-authoritarian and anti-anthropocentric in its ecological commitment to all forms of life—human and other—that it verges on a parody of shared power at times. John Ely reported in *Radical America* that an especially ecologically conscious Green Party representative in his Baden-Wurtenberg state legislature announced to other legislators that he was the spokesperson (or is it "spokescreature?") for all German toads, who need to be protected from abuse in radioactive experiments. The announcement was meant to be sincere, not self-parodic, but it is clownish nonetheless. It recalls Vladimir Durov's defense of his pig Chuska in a Russian courtroom. "I want to prove that a pig can be useful not only after his death, when his meat is to be found on the dinner table, but also during his life," Durov argued in Kharkov, after being arrested for driving his pig-drawn cart through town. The Russian clown's political consciousness seems very much alive in Baden-Wurtenberg and other cities where the Greens actively promote their reverence for life in all its diverse forms. This reverence is exemplified by that solemn but comic defense of animal rights.[29]

## The Carnival in Parliament

Once every year since the 1949 founding of the Bundestag, West Germany's parliament has been visited by carnival revelers. The visitors are not ordinary citizens but elected delegates who abandon decorum and order for a day during the carnival season. This festive spirit in parliament has been extended considerably beyond the carnival season by the Green Party, since its delegates entered that august body.

If the Greens expand their performance arena even further by winning more votes, and hold larger protests in the future, the result could well be a cross between a carnival and a general strike like that of May 1968 in Paris: a political festival opposing "business as usual" and functioning, like the medieval clowns and fools described by Mikhail Bakhtin, as "the constant accredited representative of the carnival spirit in everyday life out of carnival season." More than once Rudolph Bahro has called on the Greens to promote an extraordinary general strike, a great moratorium "against going on in the same old way."[30] As part of an answer to the title of his essay "How Can We Stop the Apocalypse?" Bahro explains why he sees a need for such a moratorium:

> The counter-movement will either boycott elections and/or gain a potential foothold in parliament that is conceived right from the start as being there simply to disrupt the normal execution of the 'compulsion of things,' to tear away the curtain of justification and expand space for extra-parliamentary forces to put pressure on the institutions.[31]

The curtain has been torn away, perhaps, now that the Greens are inside the Bundestag, though the show goes on and the apocalypse is still in the wings. The disruptions mentioned by Bahro now come from some of the players *on* the stage—which is to say, in the Bundestag—as well as from outsiders.[32] The Greens are not merely stage actors or clowns, but they continue Durov's tradition by moving between carnival and parliament, satire and politics, as they defend toads and humans alike against extinction.

# Notes

## Chapter 1

1) Emanuel Dvinsky, *Durov and His Performing Animals*, p. 17. There are several different accounts of Durov's arrest. Laurence Senelick has concluded that Anatoly Durov, Vladimir's brother, was the one arrested for treasonous satire in Berlin, in an act with *two* pigs, and that Karl Liebknecht was not involved in the case. (See his "King of the Jesters, But Not the King's Jester," *Theater* magazine, Spring 1985, p. 100.) Anecdotes attest that both of the Durov brothers performed circus acts with a trained pig, and according to L.V. Smirnov, a researcher at the Leningrad Circus Museum, each brother declares in his own memoir that the *"Will helm"* incident involved him alone. Perhaps both of them were arrested for the same crime on different occasions. This is improbable. In a letter he sent me in 1985, Smirnov also notes that the Circus Museum in Leningrad has a July 2, 1892 Berlin Court document describing the release of Anatoly Durov from prison. It does not indicate exactly what crime he committed.

Vladimir Durov wrote a short pamphlet *(In a German Prison,* 1914) inspired by his two arrests in Berlin. (The second arrest had nothing to do with his circus acts; he was jailed while attempting to defend the rights of other Russians in pre-war Germany.) He reports that he met Karl Liebknecht on both occasions. I have taken Vladimir at his word, even though he once refers to Wilhelm Liebknecht (Karl's father) rather than Karl Liebknecht as his lawyer. He writes that after the *"Will helm"* incident, the lawyer visited his prison cell, smiled and said, "I thought you'd been exiled from here, dear sir!" "How glad I'd be," answered the clown, "if the German laws were so strictly carried out; then I wouldn't be in prison. All my life they've been exiling me from everywhere, and now they want to keep me!" (Trans. Laurence Senelick.) Liebknecht won Durov's case, according to this section of the pamphlet.

Confirmation that the lawyer's name was Karl Liebknecht is offered by Dvinsky and Rèmy *(Les Clowns,* p. 433). Towsen, in *Clowns,* also credits the *"Will helm"* incident to Vladimir, not Anatoly, and says that it occurred in 1907 (p. 316). Aleksandra Talanov, too, credits the *"Will helm"* satire to Vladimir in her biography of the Durov brothers (Moscow, 1971, untranslated). In any case, one or more of the two brothers was arrested for the crime described in my opening pages.

2) Karl Liebknecht, *Militarism and Anti-Militarism,* trans. Alexander Sirnis, p. 30.

3) The source here is Towsen's *Clowns,* p. 315. Laurence Senelick differs with Towsen, and argues that the claim "Jesters to His Majesty the People" would have been unthinkable as long as the Tzar was on the throne; use of the title would have amount to *lèse majesté,* preempting the Tzar's own title by calling the people "His Majesty."

4) Bertolt Brecht, "On Experimental Theatre," in *Brecht on Theatre,* pp. 130-31.

5) Brecht, "Short Description of a New Technique of Acting," in *Brecht on Theatre,* p. 139.

6) Brecht is quoted here by Martin Esslin in *Brecht: A Choice of Evils,* p. 53.

7) Enid Welsford, *The Fool: His Social and Literary History,* p. 28.

8) Mikhail Bakhtin, *Rabelais and His World,* p. 276.

9) Vladimir Durov, *My Circus Animals,* pp. 15-16.

10) Frank Wedekind, *Prosa,* pp. 294-95 (my translation).

11) Sol Gittleman, *Frank Wedekind,* p. x.

12) Wedekind, *Such Is Life (King Nicola),* in *Modern Continental Drama,* trans. by Francis T. Ziegler, p. 804.

13) If, in fact, Anatoly Durov was arrested for the *"Will helm"* satire in July 1892 (a possibility suggested in Note 1 above), then Durov's satire of the Kaiser could have occurred before Wedekind's.

14) Liebknecht, p. 161.

15) Bill Irwin, Paul Zaloom, the Flying Karamazov Brothers, Geoffrey Hoyle and other new American clowns have recently begun creating performance pieces comparable in length and format to the solos and extended acts of European clowns. Zaloom's satiric lectures based on U.S. government documents are the most politically topical of these shows. See Ron Jenkins' "Acrobats of the Soul" in *American Theatre,* March 1985. Also Pat Aufderheide's "Zaloom's Junky Comedy" in *In These Times,* June 12, 1985, p. 20.

16) Arnold Hauser, *The Social History of Art,* Vol. 1, p. 86. Hauser's definition applies to some *commedia dell'arte* troupes, but not those patronized by courts.

17) Bakhtin, p. 8.

18) *Ibid.*

19) Richard Findlater, *Joe Grimaldi,* p. 157.

20) Findlater, p. 143.

21) Dario Fo, "The Clown and Power" in *Clowns and Farceurs,* p. 83 (my translation).

22) Brecht, *Brecht on Theatre*, p. 6.
23) Augusto Boal, *The Theatre of the Oppressed*, p. 177.
24) Hans Mayer, "Culture, Property, Theatre," trans. Jack Zipes, in *Radical Perspectives in the Arts*, p. 318.
25) Bakhtin, p. 255.

## Chapter 2

1) Brecht, *Diaries, 1920-1922*, pp. 32-33.
2) Brecht, "Alienation Effects in Chinese Acting," in *Brecht on Theatre*, p. 91.
3) Ludwig Tieck, *Puss-in-Boots*, trans. Gerald Gillespie, p. 85.
4) Brecht is quoted here by Hans Mayer, "*Brechts Tod*," in *Theatre Heute*, March 1984, p. 2.
5) Martin Esslin, *Brecht: A Choice of Evils*, p. 99.
6) Robert Heitner, *German Tragedy in the Age of Enlightenment*, p. 5.
7) G.E. Lessing, *Hamburg Dramaturgy*, p. 48.
8) Tieck, p. 89.
9) Esslin, p. 99.
10) The source here is Denis Calandra's "Valentin and Brecht," in *The Drama Review*, No. 61, p. 95.
11) Brecht, "Karl Valentin," in *Prosa I*, p. 39.
12) Brecht, "A Radio Speech," in *Brecht on Theatre*, p. 19.
13) Karl Valentin, *Der Reparierte Scheinwerfer*, pp. 99-100 (my translation).
14) Sue-Ellen Case, "Introducing Karl Valentin," *Theater*, Fall/Winter 1981, p. 9.
15) Brecht, *The Messingkauf Dialogues*, trans. John Willett, p. 69.
16) Walter Benjamin, "Conversations with Brecht," in *Understanding Brecht*, p. 115.
17) Brecht, *Collected Plays*, Vol. II, p. 243.
18) Brecht, "Karl Valentin" in *Prosa I*, p. 39 (my translation).
19) Strehler is quoted here by Calandra in *The Drama Review*, No. 61, p. 96.
20) Brecht, *Schweyk in The Second World War*, trans. Max Knight and Joseph Fabry, *Collected Plays*, Vol. VII, p. 78.
21) Eric Bentley, *The Brecht Commentaries*, p. 174.
22) Benjamin, *Understanding Brecht*, p. 17.
23) Brecht, *Collected Plays*, Vol. II, p. 245.
24) Patti Parmalee, *Brecht in America*, p. 155.
25) Valentin, pp. 128-29 (my translation).
26) Brecht, *The Elephant Calf*, trans. Eric Bentley, p. 218.

## Chapter 3

1) Walter Benjamin, *Understanding Brecht*, p. 83.
2) John Willett, *The Theatre of Bertolt Brecht*, p. 144.
3) Hans Mayer, "*Brecht oder die plebjische tradition*," in *Anmerkungen Zu Brecht* (my translation), p. 10.
4) Karl Marx, *Capital*, pp. 102-03. All quotations taken from Ben Fowkes' translation.
5) Augusto Boal, *The Theatre of the Oppressed*, p. 84.
6) Brecht, "*Flüchlingsgespräche*" (*Conversations in Exile*), in *Prosa 2*, pp. 233-36.

7) Darko Suvin, "The Mirror and the Dynamo" in *Brecht*, ed. Erika Munk, p. 97.
8) Benjamin, p. 13.
9) Benjamin, *Illuminations*, pp. 262-63.
10) Brecht, *The Threepenny Opera*, trans. Eric Bentley, p. 92.
11) Brecht, *A Man's a Man*, trans. Eric Bentley, p. 172.
12) Benjamin, *Understanding Brecht*, p. 25.
13) Louis Althusser, *For Marx*, pp. 144-45.
14) Brecht, "Appendices to the Short Organon," in *Brecht on Theatre*, p. 277.
15) Terry Eagleton, *Walter Benjamin*, p. 161.
16) Hans Mayer, *Bertolt Brecht and the Tradition*, p. 159.
17) Brecht, *Puntila*, trans. Ralph Manheim, p. 172.

## Chapter 4

1) Frank Wedekind is quoted here by Sol Gittleman in *Frank Wedekind*, p. 21.
2) Brecht, "Frank Wedekind," in *Brecht on Theatre*, p. 3.
3) Lion Feuchtwanger, *Success*, trans. Willa and Edwin Muir, p. 223.
4) Lisa Appaignanesi, *Cabaret*, p. 141.
5) Wedekind, *Earth Spirit*, in *The Lulu Plays*, trans. Stephen Spender, p. 10.
6) Jonny Ebstein, *"Le Cirque Dans la Dramaturgie de F. Wedekind: Lulu,"* in *Du Cirque au Théâtre*, p. 77.
7) Sol Gittleman, *Frank Wedekind*, p. 13.
8) Gittleman, "Frank Wedekind and Bertolt Brecht," in *Modern Drama*, Vol. 10, No. 4, (1967), p. 404.
9) Brecht, *Baal*, trans. Ralph Manheim and William E. Smith, p. 16.

## Chapter 5

1) Lingen is quoted here by Ronald Hayman in *Brecht*, p. 143.
2) John Willett, *The Theatre of Bertolt Brecht*, p. 130.
3) Lotte Lenya, foreword to *The Threepenny Opera*, p. vii.
4) Brecht is quoted here by Frederic Ewen in *Bertolt Brecht*, p. 244.
5) Brecht, "Notes on the Berliner Ensemble Production [of *Puntila*]," in *Collected Plays*, Vol. VI, p. 415.
6) All references to *The Baden Learning Play* are based on Lee Baxandall's translation, included in *Brecht*, ed. Erika Munk, pp. 177-97.
7) Brecht is quoted here by Patti Parmalee, *Brecht in America*, p. 208.
8) Sergei Tretyakov, "Bert Brecht," in *Brecht As They Knew Him*, p. 71.
9) Brecht, "Editorial Notes," in *Collected Plays*, Vol. II, p. 246.

## Chapter 6

1) Carl Weber, *Hamletmachine and Other Texts for the Stage*, p. 120. When Müller was a dramaturg at the Berliner Ensemble in the early seventies, he persuaded the ensemble to stage an experimental production of *The Baden Learning Play*; without a doubt he admired Brecht's play.
2) Quoted by Weber, p. 18.

3) Heiner Müller, "The Walls of History," in *Semiotext[e]*, No. 11, p. 52.
4) Antonin Artaud, "The Theater and the Plague," in *The Theater and Its Double*, p. 29.


## Chapter 7

1) Brecht, "Geschichten von Hërr Keuner," *Prosa 2*, p. 106.
2) Brecht, *Diaries, 1920-1922*, p. 141.
3) Erwin Piscator, *The Political Theater*, p. 268.
4) Brecht, *Schweyk in the Second World War*, trans. Max Knight and Joseph Fabry, *Collected Plays*, Vol. VII, p. 40.
5) Brecht, quoted in Klaus Volker's *Brecht Chronicle*, p. 268.
6) Brecht, *Conversations in Exile*, trans. and adapt. Howard Brenton, unpublished at present. Copyright Stefan Brecht, 1981, quoted with permission. All dialogue taken from this version unless otherwise noted.
7) *Ibid.*
8) Brecht, quoted in *Volker*, p. 99.
9) *Ibid.*, p. 122.
10) Brecht, *Schweyk in the Second World War*, p. 98.
11) *Ibid.*, p. 80.
12) Brecht, *Conversations in Exile*.


## Chapter 8

1) Kott is quoted here by Eric Bentley in *Casebook on Waiting for Godot*, ed. Ruby Cohn, p. 66.
2) Hans Mayer, "Dogs, Beckett and Brecht," trans. Jack Zipes, in *Essays on Brecht: Theater and Politics*, p. 73.
3) *Ibid.*
4) Hugh Kenner, *Flaubert, Joyce and Beckett: The Stoic Comedians*, p. xiii.
5) Enid Welsford, *The Fool: His Social and Literary History*, p. 321.
6) Jacques Audiberti, in *Casebook on Waiting for Godot*, pp. 13-14.
7) Brecht, *Puntila and Matti His Hired Man*. All quotations from the play are taken from *Collected Plays*, Vol. VI. All quotations from *Waiting for Godot* are taken from the author's own translation, Grove Press, 1954.
8) Georg Lukacs, *Realism in Our Time*, p. 21.
9) Charles Chaplin, *My Autobiography*, p. 45.
10) Chaplin, p. 144.


## Chapter 9

1) Manfred Wekwerth, "Brecht Today" in *The Drama Review*, No. 37, p. 121.
2) Wekwerth, p. 123.
3) Heiner Müller, "The Walls of History," in *Semiotext[e]*, No. 11, p. 64.
4) Brecht, notes in *Collected Plays*, Vol. VI, p. 456.
5) Frederick Ewen, *Bertolt Brecht*, p. 375.

6) In fact, a counter-Reichstag trial was staged to protest the Nazi triumph in the 1933 Reichstag fire trial. (Thanks to Martin Esslin for this information.)

7) Brecht, "Prohibition of Theatre Criticism," in *Poems, 1913-1956*, p. 299.

8) Walter Benjamin, "The Work of Art in the Age of Mechanical Reproduction," in *Illuminations*, p. 247. A more recent discussion of this idea can be found in Susan Sontag's essay "Fascinating Fascism," *Under the Sign of Saturn*, p. 83, where she notes that the Nazi staging of a 1934 Nuremberg rally was partly determined by a decision to film the event, with "the historic event serving as the set of a film *[Triumph of the Will]*." In her words, "history became theatre."

9) Kenneth Tynan, *Curtains*, p. 47.

10) Manfred Wekwerth, *Notate Uber die Arbeit des Berliner Ensemble 1956 bis 1966*, pp. 53-55.

11) Tynan, p. 47.

12) Wekwerth, *Notate*, pp. 53-55.

13) Jan Kott, "Brecht's *Arturo Ui*," in *Theater Notebook*, p. 109.

14) Keith Hack, "We Have Come to Free You," in *Drama in Calgary*, Vol. II, No. 3, pp. 43-50.

15) Brecht, *The Resistible Rise of Arturo Ui*, trans. Ralph Manheim, in *Collected Plays*, Vol. VI, p. 268.

16) Wole Soyinka's 1984 satire about the African leader Idi Amin also ridicules a dictator's self-image, by having the tyrant pose for a wax museum sculptor and inappropriately offer his unfinished statue to the United Nations. Soyinka's *A Play of Giants* could be regarded as an African variant on *Arturo Ui*. Both works show dictators turning to armed force when their speeches fail to command respect, and in both cases their tyranny veers between the horrific and the preposterous. Amin may be our closest approximation of a contemporary Hitler; he has confessed great admiration for the German dictator.

17) Brecht, *Collected Plays*, Vol. VI, p. 268.

18) Brecht, *Brecht on Theatre*, p. 139.

## Chapter 10

1) Angelo Maria Ripellino, *Maikovsky et le Théâtre Russe d'Avant Garde*, p. 255.

2) Mayakovsky is quoted here by Frantisek Deak in "The AgitProp and Circus Plays of Vladimir Mayakovsky," *The Drama Review*, No. 57, March 1973, p. 52. I am also indebted to Deak's translation of the play *The Championship of the Universal Class Struggle*," and to Victoria Nes Kirby's translation of *Moscow is Burning*, both in the same issue of *TDR*.

3) John Towsen, *Clowns*, p. 322.

4) John Berger and Anna Bostock, "Mayakovsky: Language and Death of a Revolutionary," *Praxis I*, p. 49.

5) Quoted here by Claudine Amiard-Chevrel, "La Cirquisation du Théâtre Chez Maikovski," in *Du Cirque au Théâtre*, pp. 103-119 (My translation). All quotations from the same source.

6) Amiard-Chevrel, p. 117.

7) Ripellino, p. 220 (my translation).

8) Vladimir Mayakovsky, *The Bedbug*, trans. Guy Daniels, p. 195. All quotations taken from this version.

9)  Walter Benjamin, *Understanding Brecht,* p. 96.
10) John McGrath, *A Good Night Out,* pp. 42-43.
11) Brecht, in *Brecht on Theatre,* p. 108.
12) K. Rulicke-Weiler, "Since Then the World Has Hope," in *Brecht As They Knew Him,* p. 199.
13) Quoted by Deak in *The Drama Review,* No. 57, p. 67.
14) Mayakovsky, *The Bath House,* trans. Guy Daniels, p. 232.
15) Marjorie Hoover, *Meyerhold,* p. 22.
16) Quoted by Hoover, p. 62.
17) Edward Braun, *Meyerhold,* p. 150.
18) Braun, p. 15.
19) Mayakovsky, *Mystery-Bouffe,* trans. Guy Daniels, p. 137.
20) Benjamin, p. 89.
21) Carl Weber, Introduction to *Hamletmachine and Other Texts for the Stage,* p. 24.
22) Fo is quoted here by Tony Mitchell in *Theatre Quarterly,* No. 35 (1979), p. 15.

## Chapter 11

1)  Henning Rischbieter, "Peter Weiss 'Wie dem Herrn Mockinpott das Leiden ausgetrieben wird," *Theater Heute,* June 1968, p. 33 (my translation).
2)  Peter Weiss, *How Mr. Mockinpott Was Cured of His Suffering,* trans. Christopher Holme, p. 202.
3)  Translator Holme calls Mockinpott "a modern Job," p. 166.
4)  Weiss, *Marat/Sade,* English version by Geoffrey Skelton, p. 27.
5)  Weiss, interview in the *London Times,* Aug. 19, 1964, p. 5.
6)  A. Alvarez, "Peter Weiss in Conversation with A. Alvarez," *Encore,* No. 56, July/Aug. 1965.
7)  Michael Roloff, Introduction to *The Contemporary German Drama,* p. 16.
8)  June Schlueter, *The Plays and Novels of Peter Handke,* p. 45.
9)  Peter Handke interviewed by Arthur Joseph, "Nauseated by Language," *The Drama Review,* No. 49, Fall 1970, p. 60.
10) Handke, *Kaspar and Other Plays,* trans. Michael Roloff, p. 85.
11) Nicholas Hern, *Peter Handke,* p. 62.
12) Joseph interview, p. 61.
13) Handke, "Brecht, Play, Theatre, Agitation," trans. Nicholas Hern, *Theatre Quarterly,* Oct. 1971, pp. 89-90.
14) Joseph interview, p. 57.
15) Handke, *They Are Dying Out,* trans. Michael Roloff. All dialogue is taken from this translation.
16) Schlueter, p. 116.

## Chapter 12

1)  Michael Kustow, "Introduction to 1789," in *Gambit,* No. 20, p. 6.
2)  Judith Graves Miller, *Revolution and Theater in France Since 1968,* p. 55.
3)  Jack Zipes, "Theatre and Commitment: Théâtre du Soleil's *Mephisto,*" in *Theater,* Spring 1980, p. 62.

4) Emile Copferman, "An Interview with Ariane Mnouchkine," in *Gambit*, No. 20, p. 67.
5) *Ibid.*
6) Zipes, p. 58.
7) Quoted by Zipes, p. 57.
8) *Mephisto* script (unpublished in English) courtesy of Théâtre du Soleil and the Ubu Repertory library. I am also grateful to the Ubu Rep for allowing me to see a videotape of the *Mephisto* production.
9) Andre Gorz, *Farewell to the Working Class*, p. 67.
10) Walter Benjamin, *Illuminations*, p. 255.

## Chapter 13

1) As an aside, it is interesting that two other clowns who performed at the Liberated Theatre with Lotte Goslar appeared in a scene, "Schweyk's Spirit Lives On," with which Brecht was associated in New York. The clowns were George Vaskovec and Jan Werich; the scene was performed on April 3, 1943, as part of a Brecht/Weill evening at Hunter College.
2) James Lyon, *Brecht in America*, p. 196.
3) Brecht, "Short Organon for the Theatre," in *Brecht on Theatre*, p. 195.
4) Brecht, *Brecht on Theatre*, pp. 40-41.
5) *Ibid.*, p. 187.
6) Lyon, p. 196.

Special thanks to Diana Scott for assistance in interviewing Lotte Goslar.

## Chapter 14

1) Siegfried Sassoon, *The War Poems of Siegfried Sassoon*, p. 56.
2) Quoted by Enid Welsford, *The Fool*, p. 312.
3) Howard Goorney, *The Theatre Workshop Story*, pp. 125-26.
4) *Ibid.*, p. 127.
5) David Edgar, "Ten Years of Political Theatre, 1968-78," *Theatre Quarterly*, No. 32, Vol. VIII, 1979, p. 29.
6) Goorney, pp. 127-28.
7) John McGrath, *A Good Night Out*, pp. 46-48.

## Chapter 15

1) Stephen Dixon, interview with Trevor Griffiths, *Guardian*, February 19, 1975, p. 10.
2) The decline of British clowning traditions—particularly music hall comedy—is also explored in John Osborne's *The Entertainer* and Tom Stoppard's *Jumpers*. In these works entertainers (a comedian and a popular singer) suffer losses and setbacks, both personal and professional, which reflect the decline of the British Empire itself. The clowns in these plays do not comment as directly on political events as do others examined in these pages. It could be argued that in portraying radicals and liberals as acrobats in *Jumpers*, Stoppard is commenting on re-

cent British politics, and conservatively suggesting that the ideas of the "radlibs," as he calls them, are as precarious and unstable as their gymnastics. In any case, the political clowning in *Jumpers* is much more airy and fleeting than that in *Comedians*. John Arden and Margaretta D'Arcy also deserve mention for their use of popular entertainment forms (not necessarily clowning, more often ballads) in political drama. Arden and D'Arcy staged a "War Carnival" at New York University in 1967; their carnivalesque protest against the Vietnam war is vividly described by Arden himself in his book *To Present the Pretense*, pp. 51-60.

3) "Grock's Entrée," translated by John Towson, *Mime, Mask and Movement*, Vol. I, No. 1, 1978, pp. 25-40.

4) Adrian Wettach, *Grock, King of the Clowns*, p. 84.

5) Dixon, p. 10.

6) Simon Trussler, ed., *New Theatre Voices of the Seventies*, Interview with Griffiths, p. 132.

7) Trevor Griffiths, *Comedians*. All quotations from the Grove Press edition.

8) Wettach, p. 179.

9) Ronald Hayman, Interview with Griffiths, *London Times*, December 13, 1973.

10) Austin Quigly, "Creativity and Commitment in Trevor Griffiths' *Comedians*," *Modern Drama*, December 1981, pp. 404-23.

11) Dixon, p. 10.


## Chapter 16

1) Richard Sogliozzo, "Dario Fo: Puppets for Proletarian Revolution," *The Drama Review*, Sept. 1972, p. 72.

2) I am indebted to Charles Mann and Dale McAdoo for their as yet unpublished translation of *Throw the Lady Out*, which I quote here. I hope their version will be staged soon. In 1982 Fo wrote for clowns again. *Patapumfete*, a series of revue sketches concerned with drug abuse, video games, violence and factory work, was performed by two circus clowns known jointly as I Colombaioni, who also appeared in *Throw the Lady Out*. I thank Tony Mitchell for this information.

3) Dario Fo, preface to the Gavin Richards adaptation of his *Accidental Death of an Anarchist*, p. iv.

4) Fo, quoted by Laura Ross in "Following Fo in N.Y.C.," *American Theatre*, Jan. 1985, p. 36.

5) Fo, Preface to *L'Opera Sghignazzo (The Sneering Opera)*, trans. Edward Jefferson (unpublished).

6) *Ibid.*

7) Walter Benjamin, *Understanding Brecht*, p. 83.

8) Tony Mitchell and Steve Grant, "An Interview with Dario Fo and Franca Rame" in *Theater*, Summer/Fall 1983, p. 45.

9) Translation by Tony Mitchell. For another version of this passage, see *About Face*, trans. Charles Mann and Dale McAdoo, pp. 41-42.

10) Fo, "Les Intellectuels et La Culture," in *Travail Théâtral*, No. 31, pp. 64-67.

11) Fo, Preface to *Accidental Death*, p. iii.

12) Mikhail Bakhtin, *Rabelais and His World*, p. 255.

13) Fo, *Accidental Death of an Anarchist*, trans. Suzanne Cowan, p. 28.

14) Bakhtin, p. 48.
15) Fo, *We Can't Pay, We Won't Pay!* trans. Lino Pertille, adapt. Robert Walker, p. 34.
16) Brecht, *Brecht on Theatre*, p. 139.

## Chapter 17

1) Augusto Boal, *The Theatre of the Oppressed*, p. 119.
2) Charles B. Driskell, Interview with Boal, in *The Latin American Theater Review*, Fall 1975, pp. 71-78.
3) Joel Schechter, private interview with Boal, New York City, July 1984.
4) *Ibid.*
5) *Ibid.*
6) Paulo Freire, *Pedagogy of the Oppressed*, pp. 32-33, 54.
7) *Ibid.*
8) Schechter interview.
9) Boal, "The Joker System," *The Drama Review*, Vol. XIV, No. 2 (Winter 1970), p. 93.
10) *Ibid.*
11) Brecht, *Brecht on Theatre*, pp. 137, 139.
12) Boal, *The Drama Review*, pp. 93-94.
13) Boal, *The Theatre of the Oppressed*, p. 119.

## Chapter 18

1) Lenny Bruce, *The Essential Lenny Bruce*, ed. John Cohen, p. v.
2) Robert Brustein, "Why American Plays Are Not Literature," in *American Drama and Its Critics*, ed. Alan Downer, p. 254.
3) It could be argued that the situation has changed slightly since the 1980 election. While recent satires have not been particularly topical or aggressive, political satire has surfaced in the playwriting of Philip Bosakowski (*Chopin in Space*); Keith Reddin (*Rum and Coke*); and Richard Nelson (his adaptation of Dario Fo's *Accidental Death of an Anarchist* and his own play *An American Comedy*), Spalding Gray (*Swimming to Cambodia*), Mabou Mines (*Dead End Kids*), and in Paul Zaloom's one-man shows.
4) Richard Gilman, *The Confusion of Realms*, p. 245.
5) *L'Amant Militaire*, adapt. Joan Holden from Goldoni; published in R.G. Davis' *The San Francisco Mime Troupe: The First Ten Years*, p. 177.
6) J.S. Kennard, *Goldoni and the Venice of His Time*, pp. 408, 506.
7) Davis, p. 125.
8) Theodore Shank, "Political Theater as Popular Entertainment," *The Drama Review*, No. 61, March 1974, p. 113.
9) Lee Baxandall, "The San Francisco Mime Troupe Performs Brecht: A Comradely Criticism," *Praxis I*, pp. 118-19.
10) William Kleb, interview with Holden, *Theater*, Spring 1985, p. 60.
11) Beth Bagby, interview with Luis Valdez, *The Drama Review*, No. 36, Summer 1967, p. 77.
12) Theodore Shank, *Alternative American Theatre*, p. 75.

13) Richard Condon, "Cantinflas," *Holiday* magazine, Dec. 1960, pp. 161-64.

14) Beth Day, "Mexico's 'Little Nobody' Who Made Good," *Reader's Digest*, Oct. 1966, pp. 221-22. Other information about Cantinflas is also drawn from this article.

15) Luis Valdez and El Teatro Campesino, *Actos*, pp. 13-14. All quotes taken from this book.

16) Julia Yolanda Broyles, "Brecht: The Intellectual Tramp/ An Interview with Luis Valdez," in *Communications of the International Brecht Society*, April 1973, Vol. XII, No. 2., pp. 33-44.

17) Shank makes a similar point in his book, pp. 89-90, to which I am indebted.

18) Although the *pachuco* in Valdez's play is *not* a clown, the Mexican poet Octavio Paz once described *pachuco* Mexican Americans as "impassive and sinister clowns" whose purpose is to "cause terror instead of laughter." (Paz, *The Labyrinth of Solitude*, p. 8.)

19) R.G. Davis and Betty Diamond, "*Zoot Suit* on the Road," *Theatre Quarterly*, No. 34, 1979, p. 22

20) Luis Valdez, "El Teatro Campesino" in *Aztlan*, ed. Valdez and Stan Steiner, p. 361.

## Chapter 19

1) Peter Schumann is quoted here by Francoise Kourilsky in "Dada and Circus," *The Drama Review*, No. 61, p. 107.

2) Kourilsky, p. 108.

3) Schumann, in a leaflet distributed by The Bread and Puppet Theatre.

4) Kourilsky, p. 105.

5) Edward Hoagland, "Let Them Have Bread and Puppets," *Vanity Fair*, Vol. 16, No. 5, July 1983, pp. 101, 106.

6) Helen Brown and Jane Seitz, interview with Schumann, *The Drama Review*, No. 38, Winter 1968, p. 64.

7) Florence Falk, "Bread and Puppet: Domestic Resurrection Circus," *Performing Arts Journal*, Spring 1971, p. 26.

## Chapter 20

1) Francois Rabelais, *The Histories of Gargantua and Pantagruel*, trans. J.M. Cohen, p. 390.

2) Brecht is quoted here by Martin Esslin in *Brecht: A Choice of Evils*, p. 53.

3) Brecht is quoted here by Walter Benjamin in *Understanding Brecht*, pp. 106-07.

4) Brecht, *The Caucasian Chalk Circle*, trans. Eric Bentley, p. 128.

5) Dario Fo, "Popular Culture" (speech), in *Theater*, Fall 1983, pp. 53-54.

6) Hans Mayer, "Culture, Property, Theater," trans. Jack Zipes, in *Radical Perspectives in the Arts*, ed. Lee Baxandall, p. 319.

7) Quoted by Nicholas Hern, *Peter Handke*, p. 21.

8) Peter Handke, "Brecht, Play, Theatre, Agitation," trans. Nicholas Hern, pp. 89-90.

9) Fritz Teufel, "From A-libi to B-libi," in *Semiotext[e]*, No. 11, p. 144.

10) Ron Sossi and Frank Condon, *The Chicago Conspiracy Trial*, Scene 4.

11) Jerry Rubin, "Inside the Great Pigasus Plot," in *Do It!*, pp. 176-78. Rubin and Hoffman deserve further consideration as political clowns. In 1985 they are per-

forming variations on some of their earlier routines by debating each other at college campuses across the country. The debate is entitled "Yippie Versus Yuppie," with Rubin playing the role of the Young Urban Professional (Yuppie), and advocating that his followers try (as he has) to become successful entrepreneurs in the eighties. Hoffman continues to advocate sixties-style political activism and grassroots organizing. The director (and San Francisco Mime Troupe founder) R.G. Davis recently suggested to me that Hoffman is the American activist/comedian closest in spirit and celebrity to Dario Fo, and that he could be cast in some of the comic roles Fo writes for himself. This casting for buffoonery would be far less presumptuous than an article in *The New York Times* which argued that Abbie Hoffman's theatrical protests made him the Shakespeare of our time.

12) Abbie Hoffman, *Soon to be a Major Motion Picture*, p. 123.
13) Charlene Spretnak, "Green Politics is Not like the New Left of the '60s," *In These Times*, Jan. 16, 1985, p. 11.
14) Brecht, in *Brecht on Theatre*, p. 131.
15) Robert Brustein, *Revolution As Theatre*, title and first chapter.
16) I met a number of Greens in a 1984 visit to Bonn and Frankfurt. The Green delegate who told me this requested anonymity. Transformation of German politics into theatre has been considered earlier in this survey, in discussion of Nazi leaders and Brecht. (See Chapter 3.) In this regard, the Green Party's politics can be seen as a renewal of Brecht's resistance to State leaders' theatre.
17) Rudolph Bahro, *Socialism and Survival*, p. 150.
18) Petra Kelly, *Fighting for Hope*, p. 50.
19) This speech has been published in mimeographed form by the Greens. It is titled "Inaugural Address," and was delivered on Feb. 18, 1983, at the Nuremberg Meistersingerhalle.
20) Jean-Paul Sartre, quoted here by Richard Falk in his essay "Keeping Nuremberg Alive," *Marxism, Democracy and the Rights of Peoples/ Homage to Lelico Basso*, p. 813.
21) Joachim Wernicke, in a letter to me dated Sept. 21, 1984.
22) Philip Agee kindly mailed me a copy of this statement and granted permission for its publication. The number 572 in his speech refers to the 572 new American missiles which NATO defense ministers agreed to install in their countries (United Kingdom, Belgium, Netherlands, Italy, West Germany) in 1979.
23) Abbie Hoffman, "In Search of Philip Agee," *Square Dancing in the Ice Age*, p. 157.
24) *The Program of the Green Party of the Federal Republic of Germany* (pamphlet in English), p. 19.
25) For this information and more I am indebted to John Ely's article, "The Greens: Ecology and the Promise of Radical Democracy" in *Radical America*, Feb. 1983.
26) The students of May '68 also shared Cohn-Bendit's identity by announcing "We are all German Jews." This information comes from Rosette Lamont. I am also grateful to Jack Zipes for advice on this section.
27) Daniel and Gabriel Cohn-Bendit, *Obsolete Communism: The Left-Wing Alternative*, pp. 254-55.
28) One pamphlet published by the Green Party in Frankfurt could have been co-authored by Daniel Cohn-Bendit. His name does not appear in it, but the document's phrasing echoes his own book on May '68. The pamphlet asserts, "The

Greens are organized according to the principles of decentralization and democracy 'from the roots' . . . . We want to achieve this in state parliament by a principle of rotation [of offices]. We shall not accept any political careerists and do not want professional politicians."

29) In his lifetime Vladimir Durov was famous for his gentle, non-coercive animal training methods as well as his clowning.

30) Rudolph Bahro, "Capitalism's Global Crisis," *The New Statesman*, Dec. 17, 1982, p. 27.

31) Rudolph Bahro, *Socialism and Survival*, p. 155.

32) The Green Party continues to develop new programs and new leadership at a fast pace, rendering this chapter slightly out of date even as it appears in print. On June 23, 1985, Rudolph Bahro resigned from the Green Party at its national convention, after complaining that the Greens were becoming a "normal party." It is possible that as their popular support and numbers in parliament increase, the Greens will cease to parody those in power through theatre and satire. In the spring of 1985 the Greens refused to participate in a theatre exercise organized by NATO, which called for representatives of parliament to convene as if they had just survived a nuclear war. The Greens declined to play the roles of nuclear war survivors, preferring to avert the war rather than rehearse for its aftermath.

# Bibliography

Althusser, Louis. *For Marx*. Trans. Ben Brewster. New York: Vintage, 1970.

Alvarez, A. "Peter Weiss in Conversation with A. Alvarez." *Encore*, No. 56 (July-Aug. 1965), pp. 16-22.

Amiard-Chevrel, Claudine (ed). *Du Cirque au Théâtre*. Lausanne: L'Age D'Homme, 1983.

Appaignanesi, Lisa. *Cabaret*. New York: Grove Press, 1985.

Artaud, Antonin. *The Theater and Its Double*. Trans. Mary Caroline Richards. New York: Grove Press, 1958.

Aufderheide, Pat. "Zaloom's Junky Comedy." *In These Times*, June 12, 1985, p. 20.

Bagby, Beth. "Interview with Luis Valdez." *The Drama Review*, Vol. XI, No. 4 (Summer 1967), pp. 70-80.

Bahro, Rudolph. "Capitalism's Global Crisis." *The New Statesman*, December 17, 1985, pp. 26-29.

*Socialism and Survival*. London: Heretic Books, 1982.

Bakhtin, Mikhail. *Rabelais and His World*. Trans. Helene Iswolsky. Cambridge: M.I.T. Press, 1968.

Barthes, Roland. *Critical Essays*. Evanston: Northwestern University Press, 1972.

Baxandall, Lee. "The San Francisco Mime Troupe Perform Brecht." *Praxis*, No. 1 (1975), pp. 116-21.

Beckett, Samuel. *Waiting for Godot*. New York: Grove Press, 1954.

Benjamin, Walter. *Illuminations*. Trans. Harry Zohn. New York: Schocken Books, 1973.

*Understanding Brecht*. Trans. Anna Bostock. London: NLB, 1977.

Bentley, Eric. *The Brecht Commentaries*. New York: Grove Press, 1981.

Berger, John, and Anna Bostock. "Mayakovsky: Language and Death of a Revolutionary." *Praxis*, No. 1 (1975), pp. 48-55.

Boal, Augusto. *The Theatre of the Oppressed*. Trans. Charles A. and Maria-Odilia Leal McBride. New York: Urizen Books, 1979; New York: Theatre Communications Group, 1985.

"The Joker System." *The Drama Review*, Vol. XIV, No. 2 (1970), pp. 91-95.

Braun, Edward. *The Theatre of Meyerhold*. New York: Drama Book Specialists, 1979.

Brecht, Bertolt. *Baal, A Man's a Man* and *The Elephant Calf*. Trans. Eric Bentley. New York: Grove Press/Black Cat, 1964.

*Brecht on Theatre*. Ed. and trans. John Willett. New York: Hill and Wang, 1964.

*Collected Plays*. Volumes I, II, VI, VII. Ed. John Willett and Ralph Manheim. New York: Random House, 1974-77.

*Conversations in Exile*. Adapt. Howard Brenton, 1982 (unpublished).

*Diaries, 1920-1922*. Ed. Herta Ramthun; trans. John Willett, New York: St. Martin's Press, 1979.

*The Jewish Wife and Other Plays*. Trans. Eric Bentley. New York: Grove Press/Black Cat, 1965.

*The Messingkauf Dialogues*. Trans. John Willett. London: Methuen, 1965.

*Poems, 1913-1956*. Ed. John Willett and Ralph Manheim. London: Methuen, 1976.

*Prosa*. Vols. I and II. Frankfurt am Main: Suhrkamp Verlag, 1961.

*Seven Plays*. Trans. and intro. Eric Bentley. New York: Grove Press, 1961.

*The Threepenny Opera*. Trans. Eric Bentley. New York: Grove Press/Black Cat, 1964.

Broyles, Yolanda. "Brecht: The Intellectual Tramp/An Interview with Luis Valdez." *Communications of the International Brecht Society*, Vol. XV, No. 2 (April 1983), pp. 33-44.

Bruce, Lenny. *The Essential Lenny Bruce*. Ed. John Cohen. New York: Ballantine Books, 1967.

Brustein, Robert. *Revolution as Theatre*. New York: Liveright, 1971.

"Why American Plays Are Not Literature." *American Drama and Its Critics*. Ed. Alan Downer. Toronto: University of Toronto Press, 1965, pp. 245-55.

Calandra, Denis. "Valentin and Brecht." *The Drama Review*, No. 61 (March 1974), pp. 86-98.

Case, Sue-Ellen. "Introducing Karl Valentin." *Theater*, Vol. 13, No. 1 (Winter 1981), pp. 6-11.

Chaplin, Charles. *My Autobiography*. New York: Simon and Schuster, 1964.

Cohn, Ruby (ed). *Casebook on Waiting for Godot*. New York: Grove Press, 1967.

Cohn-Bendit, Daniel and Gabriel. *Obsolete Communism: The Left Wing Alternative*. New York: McGraw-Hill, 1968.

Condon, Richard. "Cantinflas." *Holiday*, Dec. 1960, pp. 161-64.

Copferman, Emile. "An Interview with Ariane Mnouchkine." *Gambit*, Vol. 5, No. 20 (1971), pp. 63-74.

Cowan, Suzanne. "Dario Fo, Politics and Satire." *Theater*, Vol. 10, No. 1 (Spring 1979), pp. 7-12.

Davis R.G. *The San Francisco Mime Troupe: The First Ten Years*. San Francisco: Ramparts Press, 1977.

Day, Beth. "Mexico's 'Little Nobody' Who Made Good." *Reader's Digest*, Oct. 1966, pp. 221-22.

Deak, Frantisek. "The Agitprop and Circus Plays of Vladimir Mayakovsky." *The Drama Review*, No. 57 (March 1973), pp. 46-53.

Demetz, Peter (ed). Brecht: *A Collection of Critical Essays*. Englewood Cliffs: Prentice-Hall, 1962.

Dvinsky, Emanuel. *Durov and His Performing Animals*. Moscow: Foreign Languages Publishing House (no date).

Durov, Vladimir. *In a German Prison* (pamphlet). New York Public Library collection. Privately translated excerpts courtesy of Laurence Senelick, 1914.

*My Circus Animals*. Trans. John Cournos. New York: Houghton Mifflin, 1936.

Eagleton, Terry. *Walter Benjamin; or, Toward a Revolutionary Criticism*. London: Verso Editions, 1981.

Ebstein, Jonny. "Le Cirque Dans la Dramaturgie de F. Wedekind: Lulu." *Au Cirque du Théâtre*, ed. Claudine Amiard-Chevrel, pp. 77-87.

Edgar, David. "Ten Years of Political Theatre, 1968-78." *Theatre Quarterly*, Vol. VIII, No. 32, (1979), pp. 25-33.

Ely, John. "The Greens: Ecology and the Promise of Radical Democracy." *Radical America*, Vol. 17, No. 1, (Feb. 1983), pp. 23-34.

Esslin, Martin. *Brecht: A Choice of Evils* (fourth ed.) London: Methuen, 1984.

Ewen, Frederic. *Bertolt Brecht: His Life, His Art, His Times*. New York: Citadel, 1969.

Fabbri, Jacques and André Sallée (eds). *Clowns et Farceurs*. Paris: Bordas, 1982.

Falk, Florence. "Bread and Puppet Theater: Domestic Resurrection Circus." *Performing Arts Journal*, Vol. II, No. 1 (Spring 1971), pp. 19-30.

Falk, Richard. "Keeping Nuremberg Alive." *Marxism, Democracy and the Rights of Peoples/ Homage to Lelico Basso*. Milan, 1979.

Feuchtwanger, Lion. *Success*. Trans. Willa and Ewin Muir. New York: Viking Press, 1930.

Findlater, Richard. *Joe Grimaldi: His Life and Art*. Cambridge: Cambridge University Press, 1978.

Fo, Dario. *About Face*. Trans. Dale McAdoo and Charles Mann. *Theater*, Vol. 14, No. 3 (Fall 1983), pp. 7-42.

*Accidental Death of an Anarchist*. Trans. Suzanne Cowan. *Theater*, Vol. 10, No. 2 (Spring 1979), pp. 13-46.

*Accidental Death of an Anarchist*. Adapt. Gavin Richards. London: Pluto Plays, 1980.

"Dialogue with an Audience." Trans. Tony Mitchell. *Theatre Quarterly*, No. 35 (Autumn 1979), pp. 11-16.

"Les Intellectuels et Le Culture" (speech). *Travail Théâtral*, No. 31, Paris, 1978, pp. 64-67.

*L'Opera Dello Sghignazzo (The Sneering Opera)*, Milan: Edizioni F.R., La Comune, Milan, 1981.

"Popular Culture." Trans. Tony Mitchell. *Theater*, Vol. 14, No. 3 (Fall 1983), pp. 50-54.

*Throw the Lady Out*. Trans. Charles Mann and Dale McAdoo (unpublished).

*We Can't Pay, We Won't Pay!* Trans. Lino Pertilé, adapt. Bill Coevill and Robert Walker. London: Pluto Plays, 1978.

Fo, Dario and Franca Rame. *Female Parts: One Woman Plays.* Adapt. Olwen Wymark. London: Pluto Plays, 1981.

Foucault, Michel. *Madness and Civilization.* New York: Vintage, 1982.

Freire, Paulo. *Pedagogy of the Oppressed.* Trans. Myra Bergman Ramas. New York: Herder and Herder, 1970.

Garson, Barbara. *MacBird.* New York: Grove Press, 1967.

Gilman, Richard. *The Confusion of Realms.* New York: Random House, 1969.

Gittleman, Sol. *Frank Wedekind.* New York: Twayne Publishers, 1969.

"Frank Wedekind and Bertolt Brecht." *Modern Drama,* Vol. 10, No. 4 (1967), pp. 401-09.

Goorney, Howard. *The Theatre Workshop Story.* London: Methuen, 1981.

Gorz, André. *Farewell to the Working Class.* Trans. Michael Sonenscher. Boston: South End Press, 1982.

Griffiths, Trevor. *Comedians.* New York: Grove Press, 1976.

"Joking Apart" (interview by Stephen Dixon). *Manchester Guardian,* Feb. 19, 1975, p. 10.

"Transforming the Husk of Capitalism: An Interview with Trevor Griffiths." *The New Theatre Voices of the Seventies,* ed. Simon Trussler. London: Eyre Methuen, 1981, pp. 121-33.

Die Grünen (The Greens). *The Program of the Green Party of the Federal Republic of Germany* (pamphlet in English). Bonn, 1984.

*Tribunal Against First Strike and Mass Destruction Weapons* (program book in German and English). Bonn, 1983.

Hack, Keith. "We Have Come to Free You." *Drama in Calgary,* Vol. II, No. 3, pp. 53-55.

Handke, Peter. "Brecht, Play, Theatre, Agitation." Trans. Nicholas Hern. *Theatre Quarterly,* Vol. I, No. 4 (Oct. 1971), pp. 89-90.

*Kaspar and Other Plays.* Trans. Michael Roloff. New York: Farrar, Straus and Giroux, 1976.

"Nauseated by Language" (interview by Arthur Joseph). *The Drama Review,* Vol. XV, No. 1 (Fall 1970), pp. 56-61.

*The Ride Across Lake Constance and Other Plays.* Trans. Michael Roloff with Carl Weber. New York: Farrar, Straus and Giroux, 1976.

Hauser, Arnold. *The Social History of Art.* Trans. Stanley Godman. New York: Anchor Doubleday (no date).

Hayman, Ronald. *Brecht.* New York: Oxford University Press, 1983.

Heitner, Robert. *German Tragedy in the Age of Enlightenment.* Berkeley: University of California Press, 1963.

Hern, Nicholas. *Peter Handke.* London: Oswald Wolff, 1971.

Hoagland, Edward, "Let Them Have Bread and Puppets." *Vanity Fair,* Vol 16, No. 5 (July 1983), pp. 101-06.

Hoffman, Abbie. *Soon to Be a Major Motion Picture.* New York: Berkeley Books, 1982.

*Square Dancing in the Ice Age.* Boston: South End Press, 1982.

Hoover, Marjorie. *Meyerhold: The Art of Conscious Theatre.* Massachusetts: University of Massachusetts Press, 1974.

Jenkins, Ron. "Acrobats of the Soul." *American Theatre,* Vol. I, No. 11 (March 1985), pp. 4-10.

Kauffmann, Stanley. *Persons of the Drama.* New York: Harper and Row, 1976.

Kelly, Petra. *Fighting for Hope*. London: Chatto and Windus, 1984.

Kenner, Hugh. *Flaubert, Joyce and Beckett: The Stoic Comedians*. Boston: Beacon Press, 1962.

Kennard, J.S. *Goldoni and the Venice of His Time*. New York: MacMillan, 1920.

Kleb, William. "The San Francisco Mime Troupe a Quarter of a Century Later: An Interview with Joan Holden." *Theater*, Vol. XVI, No. 2 (Spring 1985), pp. 58-61.

Kott, Jan. *Theatre Notebook*. Trans. Boleslaw Taborski. New York: Doubleday, 1968.

Kourilsky, Francoise. "Dada and Circus: The Bread and Puppet Theater." *The Drama Review*, No. 61, (March 1974), pp. 104-09.

Kustow, Michael, "Introduction to *1789*," *Gambit*, Vol. 5, No. 20 (1971), pp. 5-8.

Lessing G.E. *Hamburg Dramaturgy*. Trans. Helen Zimmern. New York: Dover Books, 1962.

Liebknecht, Karl. *Militarism and Anti-Militarism*. Trans. Alexander Simis. New York: Dover Books, 1972.

Loeffler, Peter. *Hanswurst*. Basel: Birkhauser Verlag, 1984.

Lukacs, Georg. *Realism in Our Time*. New York: Harper and Row/Torchbooks, 1971.

Lyon, James. *Brecht in America*. Princeton: Princeton University Press, 1980.

Marx, Karl. *Capital*, Vol. I. Trans. Ben Fowkes. New York: Random House, 1976.

Mayakovsky, Vladimir. *The Complete Plays*. Trans. Guy Daniels. New York: Simon and Schuster, 1968.

Mayer, Hans. *Bertolt Brecht and the Tradition* in *Steppenwolf and Everyman*. Trans. Jack Zipes. New York: Apollo Editions, 1971.

"Brecht oder die plebjische Tradition," *Anmerkungen Zu Brecht*. Frankfurt: Suhrkamp Verlag, 1973.

"Culture, Property, Theatre." Trans. Jack Zipes. *Radical Perspectives in the Arts*. Ed. Lee Baxandall. Baltimore: Penguin, 1973.

"Dogs, Brecht and Beckett." Trans. Jack Zipes. *Essays on Brecht: Theater and Politics*. Ed. Siegfried Mews and Herbert Knust. Chapel Hill: University of North Carolina Press, 1974, pp. 71-78.

McGrath, John. *A Good Night Out: Popular Theatre—Audience, Class and Form*. London: Eyre Methuen, 1981.

Miller, Judith Graves. *Theater and Revolution in France Since 1968*. Lexington, Ky: French Forum, 1977.

Mitchell, Tony. *Dario Fo: People's Court Jester*. London: Methuen, 1985.

"Dario Fo's *Mistero Buffo*." *Theatre Quarterly*, Vol. IX, No. 35, pp. 3-10.

Müller, Heiner. *Hamletmachine and Other Texts for the Stage*. Ed. and trans. Carl Weber. New York: Performing Arts Journal Publications, 1984.

Munk, Erika (Ed). *Brecht*. New York: Bantam Books, 1972.

Parmalee, Patty. *Brecht in America*. Columbus: Ohio State University Press, 1981.

Piscator, Erwin. *The Political Theater*. Trans. Hugh Rorrison. New York: Avon Books, 1978.

Quigly, Austin. "Creativity and Commitment in Trevor Griffiths' *Comedians*." *Modern Drama*, Vol. XXIV No. 4 (Dec. 1981), pp. 404-23.

Rabelais, Francois. *The Histories of Gargantua and Pantagruel*. Trans. J.M. Cohen. New York: Penguin, 1981.

Reagan, Ronald. Letter to Mrs. Emmett Kelly. Sarasota: Ringling Circus Museum Collection, 1979 (unpublished).

Rémy, Tristan. *Les Clowns.* Paris: Bernard Grasset, 1945.

Ripellino, Angelo Maria. *Maikovsky et le Théâtre Russe D'Avant-Garde.* Paris: L'Arche, 1965.

Rischbieter, Henning. "Peter Weiss 'Wie dem herrn Mockinpott das Leiden ausgetrieben wird." *Theater Heute,* June 1968, pp. 32-34.

Roloff, Michael (Ed). *The Contemporary German Drama.* New York: Avon, 1972.

Ross, Laura. "Following Fo In N.Y.C.," *American Theatre,* Vol. I, No. 9 (Jan. 1985), p. 36.

Rubin, Jerry. *Do It!.* New York: Simon and Schuster, 1970.

Sassoon, Siegfried. *The War Poems of Siegfried Sassoon.* London: William Heineman, 1919.

Schechter, Joel. "Beyond Brecht: New Authors, New Spectators." *Brecht Yearbook,* Vol. XI. Ed. John Fuegi, Gisela Bahr, John Willett, 1982. Detroit: Wayne State University Press, pp. 43-53.

"Dario Fo's Obscene Fables." *Theater,* Vol. XIV, No. 2 (Winter 1982), pp. 87-90.

"Karl Valentin (1882-1948)." *Communications from the International Brecht Society,* Vol. 13, No. 1 (Nov. 1983), p. 68.

"Satire Throws U.S. Officials into Terror." *In These Times,* June 18, 1980, p. 23.

"Preface to *About Face.*" *Theater,* Vol. XIV, No. 3 (Fall 1983), p. 6.

"The Un-American Satire of Dario Fo." *Partisan Review,* Vol. LI, No. 1 (1984), pp. 112-19.

Schlueter, June. *The Plays and Novels of Peter Handke.* Pittsburgh: University of Pittsburgh Press, 1981.

Schumann, Peter. "An Interview with Peter Schumann" (by Helen Brown and Jane Seitz). *The Drama Review,* Vol. XII, No. 2 (Winter 1968), pp. 62-73.

*Semiotext[e].* "The German Issue," Volume IV, Number 2 (1982), New York: Hall of Philosophy, Columbia University.

Senelick, Laurence. *A Cavalcade of Clowns.* San Francisco: Bellerophon Books, 1977.

"King of the Jesters, But Not the King's Jester: The Pre-Revolutionary Durovs." *Theater,* Vol. XVI, No. 2 (Spring 1985), pp. 97-103.

Shank, Theodore. *American Alternative Theatre.* New York: Grove Press, 1982.

"Political Theatre: The San Francisco Mime Troupe." *The Drama Review,* Vol. XVII, No. 1 (March 1974), pp. 110-17.

Sogliozzi, Richard. "Dario Fo: Puppets for Proletarian Revolution." *The Drama Review,* Vol. XVI, No. 3 (Sept. 1974), pp. 71-77.

Sontag, Susan. *Under the Sign of Saturn.* New York: Vintage, 1981.

Sossi, Ron and Frank Condon. *The Chicago Conspiracy Trial.* New York: Theatre Communications Group (Plays in Process series), 1979.

Spretnak, Charlene. "Green Politics Is Not Like the New Left of the '60s." *In These Times,* Jan. 16, 1985, p. 11.

Suvin, Darko. "The Mirror and the Dynamo." *Brecht.* Ed. Erika Munk. New York: Bantam Books, 1972, pp. 80-98.

Teufel, Fritz. "Terrorism with a Fun Face." (interview by Sylvere Lotringer). *Semiotext[e],* Vol. IV (1982), pp. 134-49.

Tieck, Ludwig. *Puss-in-Boots.* Trans. Gerald Gillespie. Austin: University of Texas Press, 1974.

Towsen, John. *Clowns.* New York: Hawthorn Books, 1976.

Tynan, Kenneth. *Curtains*. New York: Atheneum Publishers, 1961.

Valdez, Luis and El Teatro Campesino. *Actos*. Fresno: Cucaracha Press, 1971.

"El Teatro Campesino." *Aztalan*. Ed. Luis Valdez and Stan Steiner. New York: Alfred A. Knopf, 1979.

Valentin, Karl. *Der Reparierte Scheinwerfer*. Munich: Deutscher Taschenbuch Verlag, 1976.

Volker, Klaus. *Brecht: A Biography*. Trans. John Nowell. New York: Seabury Press, 1978.

*Brecht Chronicle*. Trans. Fred Wieck. New York: Seabury Press, 1975.

Wedekind, Frank. *Earth Spirit*. In *The Lulu Plays*, trans. Stephen Spender. London: Caldar and Boyars, 1972.

*King Nicola (or, Such Is Life)*. Trans. Francis T. Ziegler. In *Modern Continental Plays*, Ed. Marion Tucker. New York: Harper's, 1929.

*Prosa*. Berlin: Aufbau Verlag, 1969.

Wekwerth, Manfred. "Brecht Today." Trans. Martin Nicholaus. *The Drama Review*, No. 37 (Fall 1967), pp. 118-24.

*Notate Uber die Arbeit des Berliner Ensemble 1956 bis 1966*. Frankfurt: Suhrkamp Verlag, 1967.

Weiss, Peter. *How Mr. Mockinpott Was Cured of His Suffering*. Trans. Christopher Holme. In *The Contemporary German Theater*, Ed. Michael Roloff. New York: Avon Books, 1972.

"Playwright of Many Interests." *London Times*, Aug. 19, 1964, p. 5.

*The Persecution and Assassination of Jean Paul Marat As Performed by the Inmates of the Asylum of Charenton under the Direction of the Marquis de Sade*. Trans. Geoffrey Skelton. New York: Pocket Books, 1966.

Wettach, Adrian. *Grock, King of the Clowns*. Trans. Basil Creighton. London: Methuen, 1957.

"Grock's Entrée." Trans. John Towsen. *Mime, Mask and Movement*, Vol. I, No. 1 (Spring 1978), pp. 25-40.

Welsford, Enid. *The Fool: His Social and Literary History*. Massachusetts: Peter Smith, 1966.

Willett, John. *The Theatre of Bertolt Brecht*. New York: New Directions, 1959.

Witt, Hubert (ed). *Brecht as They Knew Him*. New York: International Publishers, 1974.

Zipes, Jack. "Theater in Paris: Theater and Commitment, Théâtre du Soleil's *Mephisto*." *Theater*, Vol. XI, No. 2 (Spring 1980), pp. 55-61.

# A Chronology of Clowns, Politics and Theatre

| | |
|---|---|
| 1884 | Vladimir Durov begins his career as a clown at the Moscow Zoo. At the age of twenty-one he is advertised as "Durov the Elder," while his brother Anatoly, age twenty, receives star billing as a clown at the Hinné Circus in Moscow. |
| 1888 | Anatoly Durov is expelled from St. Petersburg for an act in which he and his pigs ridicule the city's police chief, Gresser. |
| 1892 | Frank Wedekind sees the clowns Morgenstern and Durov in Paris. Court records indicate that Anatoly Durov briefly stayed in a Berlin prison in the same year. |
| 1894 | Wedekind's play *Earth Spirit* introduces Lulu to the world. |
| 1896 | Alfred Jarry's *Ubu Roi* opens in Paris; members of the audience riot at the first word, "merdre." |
| 1898 | Wedekind is charged with treason for writing a poem ridiculing Kaiser Wilhelm II. |
| 1903 | Adrian Wettach assumes the stage name of Grock, and tours Europe as a clown with his partner Brick. |
| 1906 | Vitaly Lazarenko begins a career as a clown in Russia which will continue for three decades. |

1907    Vladimir Durov and his trained pig ridicule Kaiser Wilhelm II in Berlin, and Karl Liebknecht defends the clown against charges of high treason. Liebknecht himself is charged with high treason for publication of the book *Militarism and Anti-Militarism*. Liebknecht is sentenced to eighteen months in prison. Durov is acquitted.

1908    Karl Valentin begins performing at the Frankfurter Hof Singspielhalle in Munich.

1914    Lazarenko meets Vladimir Mayakovsky at the circus. World War I begins. Vladimir Durov publishes his pamphlet *In a German Prison*, describing meetings with Liebknecht.

1915    Bertolt Brecht, age seventeen and not yet against war, writes a poem, "Der Kaiser," in honor of Kaiser Wilhelm II's first wartime birthday.

1918    Wedekind dies and Brecht publishes a eulogy for him. Brecht also writes his first play, *Baal*.

1919    Marcel Duchamp draws a moustache on the Mona Lisa. Karl Liebknecht and Rosa Luxemburg are assassinated in Berlin; Brecht attends a rally in Munich commemorating the murdered socialists. Mayakovsky's *Mystery Bouffe* is staged by Meyerhold in Moscow to celebrate the Russian Revolution. Brecht sings "The Legend of the Dead Soldier" and "Song of the Red Army Soldier" in an Augsburg tavern. Mayakovsky collaborates with Lazarenko on a circus staging of the poem "The Soviet Alphabet."

1920    Brecht goes to Valentin's Munich cabaret one night and says he "nearly rolled on the floor laughing." Mayakovsky and Lazarenko present *The Championship of the Universal Class Struggle* at the Second State Circus in Moscow. Lazarenko directs the play and performs the role of Uncle Referee.

1922    Brecht and Valentin co-produce a midnight cabaret show, *The Red Raisin*, at the Kammerspiele in Munich, where Brecht's play *Drums in the Night* is also playing.

1923    In Munich, Brecht collaborates on a film, *Mysteries of the Barbershop*, which features Karl Valentin as the barber. Hitler's *putsch* attempt in the same city fails.

1924    Brecht directs *The Life of Edward II* at the Munich Kammerspiele, with advice from Karl Valentin.

1926    Brecht reads *Das Kapital* while writing *A Man's a Man*.

1928    Erwin Piscator stages *The Adventures of the Good Soldier Schweyk* in Berlin, with script collaboration by Brecht. Brecht and Kurt Weill create *The Threepenny Opera* in the same city. Mexican singer Mario Moreno, age seventeen, begins his career as a comedian, and subsequently assumes the name of Cantinflas.

| | |
|---|---|
| 1929 | Meyerhold directs Mayakovsky's *The Bedbug* in Moscow. Brecht's *Baden Learning Play* starts a riot at the Baden Baden Festival. |
| 1930 | Mayakovsky's *The Bathhouse* and *Moscow is Burning* are staged, the latter at the First Moscow Circus. The author commits suicide. |
| 1931 | Charlie Chaplin's *City Lights* is released. |
| 1933 | Hitler becomes Chancellor of Germany. Brecht leaves Germany and remains in exile until 1949. Lotte Goslar also leaves Germany; at age sixteen she joins Erika Mann's Peppermill Revue and tours Europe with the group until 1938. |
| 1934 | Vladimir Durov dies, famous as an animal trainer and clown. A museum which features performing animals is created in his honor. |
| 1939 | Grock meets Hitler. Hitler invades Poland. World War II begins. |
| 1940 | Brecht writes *Puntila*, which won't be performed until 1948. He also writes *Conversations in Exile*. Chaplin creates *The Great Dictator*. |
| 1941 | Brecht writes *Arturo Ui*, which will not be staged in Berlin until 1959. He begins writing *Schweyk in the Second World War*, which will be completed in 1944 and first performed in 1957 in Warsaw. |
| 1944 | Brecht meets both Charlie Chaplin and Groucho Marx on November 7 in Hollywood. They do not collaborate. |
| 1945 | Nuremberg Tribunal for war crimes opens. Hiroshima and Nagasaki are bombed. |
| 1947 | Brecht writes *Circus Scene* for Lotte Goslar, after seeing the carnival scene she choreographed for the Los Angeles production of *Galileo*. After he is questioned by HUAC, Brecht permanently leaves America for Europe. |
| 1948 | Karl Valentin dies. |
| 1953 | Beckett's *Waiting for Godot* opens in Paris, and Brecht plans a counterplay in response. |
| 1953–54 | Dario Fo begins performing cabaret revues in Italy, and marries actress Franca Rame. |
| 1954 | Lotte Goslar founds her Pantomime Circus, which has its debut at the Jacob's Pillow Dance Festival in Massachusetts. Grock retires. |
| 1956 | Bertolt Brecht dies. |
| 1959 | R.G. Davis founds the Mime Studio and Troupe, later known as the San Francisco Mime Troupe. |
| 1962–63 | Peter Schumann founds the Bread and Puppet Theatre in New York City. |

1963    *Oh, What a Lovely War!* is staged by Joan Littlewood in East London. *Ubu Roi* is staged by the San Francisco Mime Troupe.

1964    The Free Speech Movement begins in Berkeley. Peter Weiss's *Marat/Sade* is produced in Berlin.

1965    The Vietnam Day Committee in Berkeley sponsors protests against American war policies; Barbara Garson and the San Francisco Mime Troupe prepare theatre pieces for these protests. Luis Valdez founds El Teatro Campesino in Delano, California.

1967    The San Francisco Mime Troupe stages *L'Amant Militaire*. Bertrand Russell initiates an International War Crimes Tribunal in Stockholm; the panel of judges, which includes Jean-Paul Sartre and Peter Weiss, concludes that the United States is guilty of genocide in Vietnam. *MacBird*, written by Barbara Garson in 1965, opens at the Village Gate in New York.

1968    Peter Handke's *Kaspar* opens in Frankfurt. Peter Weiss's *How Mr. Mockinpott was Cured of His Suffering* opens in Hannover. Ringling Brothers' Clown College opens in Sarasota.

1969    *Les Clowns* is staged by Théâtre du Soleil in Paris. *Mistero Buffo* is performed by Dario Fo. The Conspiracy Trial begins in Chicago.

1970    Dario Fo's *Accidental Death of an Anarchist* opens in Milan. Daniel Berrigan's *The Trial of the Catonsville Nine* is staged at the Mark Taper Forum in Los Angeles.

1972    Lotte Goslar's Pantomime Circus performs Brecht's *Circus Scene* for the first time, at ANTA's Dance Marathon in New York.

1974    Augusto Boal publishes *The Theatre of the Oppressed*. Dario Fo stages *We Can't Pay, We Won't Pay!* Peter Stein directs Peter Handke's *The Unintelligent Are Dying Out* in Berlin.

1975    The first Domestic Resurrection Circus is produced in Glover, Vermont, by the Bread and Puppet Theatre. The Pickle Family Circus is founded in San Francisco by former San Francisco Mime Troupe performers Larry Pisoni and Penny Snider.

1975    Trevor Griffiths' *Comedians* opens at the Nottingham Playhouse. American troops are withdrawn from Vietnam.

1977    The Big Apple Circus is founded in New York by Paul Binder and Michael Christensen, both former members of the San Francisco Mime Troupe.

1978    Luis Valdez's *Zoot Suit* is produced at the Mark Taper Forum in Los Angeles.

1979    The Plutonium Players form in Berkeley. Théâtre du Soleil presents *Mephisto* in Paris. NATO defense ministers agree that 572 new

American missiles will be installed in five NATO countries (United Kingdom, West Germany, Italy, Belgium, the Netherlands).

1981     Heiner Müller's *Heart Play* is first performed in Bochum, West Germany. Dario Fo's *Klaxons, Trumpets and Raspberries* and his musical, *The Sneering Opera*, open in Italy.

1983     The Green Party convenes its Nuremberg Tribunal in February. Later in the year the Greens win enough votes to send twenty-seven delegates to parliament in Bonn.

1984     United States foreign policy is placed on trial in Times Square, New York; the tribunal is sponsored and conducted in part by Artists Call Against Intervention. President Ronald Reagan announces that Russia has been outlawed and the bombing will begin in five minutes; it does not begin, and he is re-elected. Ladies Against Women visit Dallas during the Republican National Convention, and hold a bake sale to help end the federal deficit.

1985     Bill Irwin stages *The Courtroom* in New York, and appears as Galy Gay in a La Jolla Playhouse production of *A Man's a Man*.

# Index